All the best !

Tish Baldrige
(many years later !)
Oct. 26, 1978

Juggling

Juggling

The Art of
Balancing Marriage,
Motherhood, and Career

Letitia Baldrige

The Viking Press
New York

First published in 1976 by The Viking Press, Inc.
625 Madison Avenue, New York, N.Y. 10022

Published simultaneously in Canada
by The Macmillan Company of Canada Limited

LIBRARY OF CONGRESS CATALOGING IN PUBLICATION DATA
Baldrige, Letitia.
Juggling.
1. Baldrige, Letitia. I. Title.
CT275.B316A29   301.41'2'0924   75-41400
ISBN 0-670-41043-8

Printed in U.S.A.

To RH, Clare, and Malcolm—
who collectively complicate my life
but also imbue it with
love, happiness, and fulfillment

Contents

Juggling

1
Introduction

The writing of a book requires an incredibly strong motivation. The work of writing is difficult enough, but finding the time, energy, and self-awareness necessary to do a bookful is an exercise in masochism. One calls down upon oneself a plague of anguish and torment, but, as a woman who happens to live in this particular place at this particular time, my motivation is there. And the anguish and torment are easier to bear than many of the things I manage to undergo every day in my office.

Everyone, no matter how successful, or how pure an intellectual, writes in part for fiscal reasons. There is nothing that binds the seat of the pants to the seat of the chair more effectively than a need for money. But there are other compelling reasons, too, for such an exercise in self-discipline. Writing is deliciously satisfying ego food, for one thing. To see someone at the hairdresser reading your very own book under the dryer, to pass by your very own book residing in the corner window of the bookstore—these are gratifying moments. No, more than that; they are moments of ecstasy. Some writers enjoy the feedback of dispensing valuable information, of holding readers in suspense or making them laugh. There are writers who have suffered, and who must unburden themselves to a large public that longs to suffer right along with them. Other writers simply like to preach. A few know where the real money is, and write about the things that interest people most: health, making money, becoming sexual athletes, and thinking thin.

This book, alas, possesses none of these best-selling attributes. It has a very simple thesis: that a woman gifted with good health and a sense of humor (and this goes for her family, too), cannot only survive our sexual revolution but be very happy in it. She can still even cling to some of the old traditions such as religion, morality, and the bearing of legitimate children.

This will therefore be a positive book, because we should be able to withstand the pressures that sometimes make us feel as though we are being sucked down into quicksand. I myself am a constant complainer, but perhaps we women should do a little less complaining and a little more rejoicing over how far we really have come since the time of our colonial sisters two hundred years ago. We should be glad we were not born in Martha Washington's time, when most women were illiterate, with short life spans, with no voices in any decisions, and with their existences based on being the chattel property of their men. Today's woman's preferred career is still marriage, but her anatomy is no longer her destiny.

Yes, women are not only surviving, they are flourishing, and even in places like New York, where the only news seems to be bad news. One learns to keep on chuckling no matter what, and no matter what can sometimes be pretty bad. If a working mother finds herself with too many balls in the air at once, she can either have a nervous breakdown and withdraw from the world, or she can learn the art of juggling. I prefer the latter.

If I feel sorry for anyone in this era, it's for the men. As long as women keep on going up in their status, it's logical, in the balance of things, that something is going to have to come down. If women have been yanked from their traditional ruts in recent years, then men have been blasted from theirs. The battlecry for everyone right now should simply be: *Cope*. Coping means making every minute count and not wasting time fighting the other sex. Coping for working women means not resenting the fact that there are no moments for oneself any more. Coping means getting on with the task of living while being buffeted from all sides. Coping means knowing what to do and doing it when one is walking into a meeting with one's most important client and the school telephones to say that one's child has been hurt. Coping means arising at five-thirty in the morning to cook a roast beef to leave behind for the family's dinner before taking a plane to give a speech to five hundred women in another city. (One has to stand up on that platform, looking rested, well groomed, and ready to "give"; one does not smell of cooked roast beef but of perfume.)

Coping means holding back one's laments and complaints when one's husband looks depressed and tired. Coping means staying up all night to be able to hand in a writing project the next day so that one can leave the office in midafternoon to watch one's child perform in a school recital. (Fathers are not expected to be present in midafternoon.)

Perhaps women are born with a greater capacity than men to struggle with and juggle all these things successfully. Perhaps we are tougher, and by that I do not mean physical strength. Up to and including my generation, women were taught to be hostesses, chief cooks, and bottle-washers. We still carry out these roles today, but many of us hold demanding jobs as well. I'd like to see a man who can work a ten-hour day after having been up until two o'clock in the morning preparing for tonight's dinner party. I'd like to see him come home at six in the evening, one hour before the guests arrive, with just enough time to reheat everything on the stove, only to find one of the children throwing up from intestinal flu on the living-room carpet. Today's Woman sympathetically embraces the sick child and congratulates him for throwing up front and center, so that at least the spot on the carpet will look symmetrically placed. Today's Woman cleans up the mess, puts the child to bed, and then listens to her husband complain about the smell in the apartment while he dresses for the party.

Coping means keeping one's marriage intact in the wake of the often antimarriage attitude of the women's movement. It's hard for a man to keep his cool when he feels as though the women militants are pointing accusing fingers at his sex and asking, "What did *you* do today toward *her* having an orgasm?" In my view, sexual fulfillment has nothing whatsoever to do with equal jobs, education, and pay.

The antimale feminist has had her say; the antifeminist has had her say. The men have *always* had their say. Now it's time for a family-loving, tradition-respecting, business-oriented feminist to have *her* say.

There has been an invisible rabbit's foot nestling cozily in my pocket ever since I was born the youngest member of a noisy, loving family of giants. My parents saw to it, with no little sacrifice, that I was armed with the best education available at the time, including the Convent of the Sacred Heart in our home town of Omaha; Miss Porter's School at Farmington, Connecticut; Vassar College; and the University of Geneva in Switzerland. My graduate work at the latter was in psychology, but I also studied European men and received rather good marks.

My older brothers, Mac and Bob, are my closest friends and staunchest supporters today. They gave me another kind of education from babyhood, however. They saw to it I learned to be quick on the defense—whether it was a matter of being tripped up on my bicycle, finding insects in my bed, or having the lock picked on my adolescent diary and hearing its contents read aloud to a large group of high-school boys shaking with laughter. By the time I was eighteen I could no longer be surprised, shocked, or embarrassed by anything the male sex could perpetrate. I was also six feet one inch tall, unloved and undanced with to a dismal degree. (Confucius say, I was constantly reminded, that "small man who dance with tall girl get bust in face.") The only thing that pulled me through my adolescence was remembering how Fred Astaire had waltzed me around the floor of the Rainbow Room in New York when I was full-grown at thirteen. I was wearing loafers and bobby socks. We were alone on the floor, in the spotlight, and to me, I was Ginger Rogers incarnate. (He had known my parents in Omaha, and was being nice to "Jean and Mac's big girl.") I learned then and there that a short man can dance beautifully with a tall girl; the only trouble is that none of the boys I knew were aware of that fact. By the time I was twenty, I was proud of being tall. All the years of suffering suddenly paid off, and height has been my greatest asset ever since. I have psyched myself into feeling queenly. I actually do, and stand very straight as a result.

My parents always treated my brain potential in exactly the same way they treated my brothers'. The same amount of money was expended on my education as on theirs. They also expected me, conservatives that they were, to have the physical stamina to fulfill my role as a wife, mother, and hostess at the same time. They thought I could do *anything* I set my mind upon. Our parents talked to the three of us on the same plane about our business goals, our achievement in careers, our responsibilities toward our communities. Whenever anyone asks me, "What can I do to get the proper motivation for a great career?" my reply is, "Get born into the right family."

I graduated from college at nineteen. After graduate school, when I was barely twenty-one, I went to work, magically assisted by a chain reaction of fortuitous circumstances. If I had not broken a leg skiing, I would not have attracted the attention, as well as the sympathy, of the State Department's Office of Foreign Service Personnel. I hobbled there on crutches several times, dramatically dragging my heavy cast, begging to know when one of those much sought-after "Paris openings" in our embassy would develop. I made everyone sign my plaster cast with French sayings. The personnel officer squared with me. In spite of my fluency in French, a Vassar degree, and most of an M.A. from the Institut Jean-Jacques Rousseau, I was no good to the Foreign Service without secretarial skills. If I had suggested I would make a very good candidate for a Foreign Service officer, I would probably have found my name on a "dangerously subversive" list. I saw young men with far less education and no knowledge of the French language being hired quickly. . . . Woman, know thy place.

If I had not finished the disagreeable chore of secretarial school in two months (thanks to private lessons in shorthand and typing and daily practice sessions from eight in the morning until midnight), I would not have been ready to go when Ambassador David Bruce suddenly staffed up for his operation in Paris. If I had not known the French language, Evangeline Bruce, the ambassador's wife, would not have singled me out as her social secretary. If I had not had the David Bruces as my first bosses, I never would have received first-rate training in diplomatic logistics, the science of protocol, and the art of social power play.

When young women ask me how I became the head of my own public-relations firm, they invariably hope the word "typewriter" will never enter the conversation. I am always sorry to disappoint them. Without secretarial skills, I could never have walked through any of those doors. Born female used to mean born to punch a typewriter. But it's not such a bad machine; in fact it is still my favorite tool. Because of it, in those early days, I was always very close to real power. I already knew how the big fish swam by the time I was twenty-two; I knew the habits of the big shots and how they handled the aggressive schools of small fish around them. If you want to know the inside of any organization, become friendly with the executive secretary to Number One.

If I had not been friendly with a prominent member of the ambassador's World War II OSS team, I never would have become his secretary at the CIA in Washington. (Those were the short-lived, dashing days of bravado in the early fifties, when we were fighting the Cold War, and each member of the staff was either a war hero, an intellectual, or an admirer of both, like myself.) I was appointed by my boss, Frank Lindsay, to be our division's first psychological warfare officer. My PW training was perfect groundwork for a public-relations career later. After all, the establishment of attitudes is what public relations and psychological warfare are all about.

Without a hard-learned and bluffable fluency in Italian, together with my experience as a social secretary in Paris, I never would have been hired sight unseen from across the Atlantic by a desperately busy woman, the first ambassador of her sex to be appointed by the United States to a major foreign power. When Clare Luce and her husband Henry (publisher of Time, Inc.) arrived in Rome in 1953, there was no staff member available to help the ambassador with protocol and with the management of the Embassy Residence. Her large staff of servants spoke no English, and at that point the Luces spoke no Italian. No one could communicate, much less answer the telephone. Before the Luces came to Rome, I had applied unsuccessfully for a job with the Time-Life Bureau there. On a Sunday afternoon in April, my job-application file was uncovered in the Bureau, studied by the Luces, and I was hired by telephone.

If, four years later at dinner in New York, Clare Luce had not sat next to Walter Hoving, the new owner of Tiffany's, I never would have been appointed the first woman executive and first public-relations director of that august jeweler's. The training in merchandising and in decorative arts that I received during those four years, which involved working with our country's leading interior designers and taking night courses at the Metropolitan Museum, gave me the background to do much of what I do today.

If I had not known both Jacqueline Bouvier and the Kennedy family for years prior to John Kennedy's nomination as President, I probably never would have been appointed social secretary to the White House—where every bit of my past training, discipline, know-how, and education were put to use. Few people today would argue that the right time to have been in the White House was as a member of John F. Kennedy's team.

Without following the advice of the President's father, Joseph P. Kennedy, I never would have gone to the Kennedy-owned Merchandise Mart in Chicago following my years at the White House. This was where the real guts of the home-furnishings industry were to be found. Without that Chicago experience I never would have met my future husband, who changed the entire course of my life into a new and happy direction.

By the time I reached my thirties, I had dismissed the idea of marriage and motherhood. People were willing to agree with me that I was doing all right on my own. My career, my social life, and the support of a large, close family kept me happy. Whenever I felt a lack of emotional fulfillment in regard to having children, I went to visit my friends' children, and inevitably returned to the solitude of my apartment with a great feeling of relief. Three months from the day I met Robert Hollensteiner at a dinner party in Lake Forest, we were married. This surprised everyone. We proceeded to have two children, one of each sex, both of them born at the end of a full working day. I stopped work only after they were born—for three weeks for the first baby, and two weeks for the second.

Without the suggestion and help of George Struthers, vice-president of Sears in Chicago, I never would have had the courage to go into business for myself and to set up "Letitia Baldrige Enterprises," with Sears and the Merchandise Mart as my first accounts. This was a new, exulting freedom. After years of fronting for others, serving them, telling white lies for them, and protecting them, I could start thinking and acting *for myself*. Starting my own company was the biggest step up I could have taken. The rabbit's foot was still working.

There is no question about the fact that a number of great women I have known throughout my life have influenced me enormously. My mother was a strong, powerful woman. Although her professional life was confined to a one-year stint as the society editor of the *Omaha Bee*, she was the most organized woman I have ever known. In the fulfillment of her female role as it was structured in her day, she was the perfect wife and mother. She also ran several charities, organized USO and Red Cross chapters during World War II, and was always efficiently and spiritually involved in her work. My first job, working for the talented, elegant Evangeline Bruce, made me realize for the first time that women in official life should receive salaries for their jobs, as well as their husbands. The wives have full-time jobs, too. Working for Clare Luce, one of the early feminists of our age, raised my consciousness far beyond what ten years of discussions with a women's-movement group would ever have done. Because of her, I abandoned my plans to remain a secretary, which was, in those days, about as high a position as most women could realistically envision. It is impossible not to reach for higher goals when one's boss is an ambassador to a major foreign power after having been a congressman, best-selling author, prize-winning playwright, war correspondent, famous orator, champion swimmer, and superb Scrabble player. Clare was perfect proof that rhetorical brilliance, the ability to manipulate power, and unending charm are a great combination for either sex. She continues to be a source of advice and motivation for me today. Although in her seventies and supposedly retired from public life, she is recognized and applauded wherever she goes. She continues to make news with her writing, speeches, and television appearances. Men admire her as much as women do, a fact of which I am constantly reminded.

One day I visited her Waldorf Towers apartment suite when she was in New York for a short visit. I found her feeling unwell because of stomach trouble, and called the hotel druggist to have some medicine sent up. The pharmacist politely took down the information I gave him and then did a double take.

"Would that 'Mrs. Luce' possibly be *the* Clare Boothe Luce?" he asked incredulously.

"The same," I replied.

"And *she* has diarrhea?" His voice implied that such a misfortune does not befall a woman of such distinction. "I have something much better than what you asked for," he added in a fatherly tone, "a much better product to relieve her symptoms."

"Send that up, then," I agreed.

"We can't let Mrs. Luce have diarrhea," he said reverently. "She's too great a lady for that."

When one is famous, apparently even one's intestinal tract becomes part of the public domain.

I have admired women who are excellent in different fields. One does not compare what Indira Gandhi does during the day with Billie Jean King's work; however, the same wonderful discipline and sense of purpose make them do well what they do during the day. Elizabeth Arden and Coco Chanel made women beautiful; former Congresswoman Martha Griffiths sponsored the Equal Rights Amendment. Eleanor Roosevelt brought the role of First Lady forward into serious decision-making; Mary Martin translated her talent in singing and dancing into making people happy on many continents. Barbara Walters showed that women make superb conversationalists on television; Sylvia Porter proved that ability in the financial world is not limited to men. Regardless of what these women give to the world, the quality of excellence has touched them all.

Rose Kennedy's profession might be listed simply as "mother," but she is one of the most impressive women I have ever known. She goes on, in seeming perpetuity, like the Crown of England she much admires, ever steadfast in her faith. She can handle any television interviewer, no matter how tough or skilled; they become gelatinous in her dextrous hands. If they ask personal questions about her family, she turns them around into a discussion of her favorite charity. She is beloved by women because no matter how tough things are, Rose Kennedy has had it tougher. Women who have known devastating tragedy, women on their knees in church, women dreaming of glory for their children, women coping with mental retardation in the home—they can all identify with Mama Rose. Even with her flat nasal tones, she is a crowd-swayer. If she were to suffer a breakdown, renounce one of her children, leave the Church, hundreds of thousands of women the world over would feel deceived. Her religious faith is her source of energy. I cherish a letter she wrote me when she heard our daughter was to receive her First Communion. She defined the significance of the occasion far more deftly than any of the school's religion teachers could have done.

There are successful women all around me in my business life; fortunately, they are no longer a rarity. Many of them are happily married mothers, and many of them are happily unmarried women. Marital status has nothing whatsoever to do with their ability to perform on the job and to function as useful people. For every woman who lets her marital troubles show on the job, a failing that men are quick to notice, I can show you three men who do the same. The older generation has a very hard time accepting the fact that a girl who in 1952 aspired to be the number-one debutante can now be aspiring to be the college president, the chief of the medical staff, the chairman of the board.

The material in this book will never make fodder for a television family show, or even a soap opera. It's the story of the daily life of one slightly hysterical working mother, who happens to be the head of her own firm but who also happens to be the family cook. It's the story of someone who is firmly convinced that keeping a sense of humor is the life source that will get us all through what we have to get through. There's another reason for writing this book. Some time ago, a well-known chairman of the board for one of America's largest corporations gave me a half-hour appointment to listen to my carefully prepared, well-articulated public-relations proposal for his company. At the end, his first words were, "Tish, why isn't a nice girl like you home taking care of your husband and children?"

It takes an entire book to answer him. I shudder to think how many more chairmen of the board there are just like him.

2
Our Family:
Four Equals Seven

The Hollensteiner ménage consists of two parents, two children, one Irish-born, English-trained nannie (called "Nannie," appropriately enough), one junkyard cat with the manners of an aristocrat, and a pedigreed Jack Russell terrier with the manners of a mutt. The six-foot four-inch, blond, and (as he constantly reminds me) *handsome* father figure, Robert, will be referred to as "R.H." in this book. Initials are more remote than nicknames, and since he would rather not be included here at all, I shall try to create an ounce of detachment for him. The tall mother figure is me, and next comes understandably tall eleven-year-old Clare, who has lovely blond hair, blue eyes, and a facile tongue, and who performs ardent gymnastics only after a huge supper and only in our small bedroom (much to the distress of my office-tired ears and our bedroom furniture). Next comes an understandably tall Malcolm, a forever noisy lad now eight who looks twelve and who strikingly resembles his father. He is the only little boy I know who at the age of four could assemble on his person—

and wear all day long—cowboy chaps, an authentic Green Beret, football pads under a Black Hawks hockey shirt, and a sheriff's badge, meanwhile carrying a rifle in one hand with a lasso and baseball bat in the other. He is loyal to all his heroes at one and the same time. While Clare is doing her gymnastics in our bedroom, Malcolm is usually swinging a baseball bat, throwing a football, or casting his fishing line at the lampshades. Malcolm does inside the apartment what all little boys are supposed to do out of doors. He is a one-man wrecking crew. Dustin Hoffman, the dog, is in the meantime shedding white fur all over our bedspread, and Pierre, the cat, is doing his best to knock over *cachepots* full of plants on the window sill. Ours is not a calm household when everyone is home. Ours is not a calm household even when one person is home.

The dependable member of the family is Nannie, short, stocky, and very Irish. The day she arrived to care for new-born Clare, she launched a rat-a-tat attack on American morals, manners, eating habits, and badly made children's clothes, and though we have learned to tune out the barrage, we gather it shall continue full force. Nannie is also one of the Pioneers, an Irish organization whose members have sworn never to drink in order to expiate the excesses of many of their fellow countrymen. Every year on Saint Patrick's Day in New York I tell her that the Pioneers might as well give up and disband, but she simply abstains all the more fiercely.

If Robert Hollensteiner and I were to feed our curricula vitae into a computer match-making machine, we would break the machine. By some sheer accident, we both happen to be big, but there the resemblance ends. There is a popular column in a woman's magazine called "Can This Marriage Be Saved?" Our friends would like to begin a new one, entitled "How Did This Marriage Happen?" We move at entirely different speeds. We are exact opposites. He is a night person; I am a morning one. He loves spectator sports; I am uninterested in them. He is totally unsentimental; I am disastrously so. He believes in letting people alone; I become immediately involved with the personal lives even of casual acquaintances. He is chronically late; I am exasperatingly punctual. He is meticulously neat; I am unconsciously untidy. He is shy and silent in large groups; I will be forever aggressive and noisy. He is blessed with a dry, subtle wit; my humor is as obvious as a popcorn popper. Early in our marriage, I tried to make him conform to what I wanted him to be. When he finally said, "Did it ever occur to you that you need changing in my eyes as much as I do in yours?" I stopped trying.

On our first Valentine's Day, which came a few short weeks after our marriage, I gave him eight different Valentines—sending them through the mail to his office, tucking them into his bureau drawers, pasting them on his shaving mirror, and arranging them under his plate at dinner. He gave none to me. The next day I flew to another city to make a speech and was given a party afterward by friends. When I told R.H. later, with tears in my eyes, that my hostess's bedroom had been adorned with twenty-three lovingly written Valentines from her husband, the only answer to emerge from the depths of the sports page was, "That marriage is in trouble." The fact that the couple was divorced three months later did not help my cause at all.

Every morning R.H. jogs around the Central Park reservoir before going to his office. (I took a few jogging steps in place in front of the mirror one day and realized the New York public would never be able to stand the sight of me doing it.) This morning activity testifies to R.H.'s great fortitude, since he is a nonmorning person and incapable of speaking to anyone before ten in the morning. He sallies forth, ghostlike, around seven from the apartment and returns to read the paper on the chaise longue in our bedroom, sweat dripping from every pore. There is simply no other way to describe it: every morning R.H. smells up our bedroom while I get ready to go to the office, and every morning I lodge a formal protest. "Shower first!" I admonish deaf ears. I have tried squirting room freshener at him; he is impervious to all such tactics.

R.H. was raised by Lucille and Norman Hollensteiner in the classic tradition that the woman's responsibility is housework, cooking, and caring for children. I was raised in exactly the same tradition. In fact, my father always explained that he served only two purposes at home: to tend bar and take out the garbage. But, as proud as my mother was of her immaculate house, I loathe anything connected with housework and would much rather be out in the world earning the money to pay for someone else to do it. Though I love my work, I do not love my children or my home any the less for it.

Nor do I work for the pure joy of avoiding housework. The family needs my income. Educating children in private New York schools requires a great deal of money; so do Nannie and her activities; so do the services of a cleaning woman, laundryman, and seamstress.

I am not a home sewer. If I were to be reborn, one of the first changes in my make-up would be that. I would know how to mend, alter, make things for myself and the children. R.H. can even sew on a button much better than I. In fact, during his military service, he had the reputation of being the best sock-darner in his barracks. (He stretched the sock over a light bulb to do his task.)

I had worked all my adult life by the time I met R.H., and there was never any question of my stopping work, even during the last weeks of my pregnancies. (One of the joys of operating one's own business is that one makes one's own personnel policies, which means no forced maternity leaves.) When I was several days past due with Malcolm, I managed to give a speech on market trends at the Merchandise Mart. The speech went perfectly except for an occasional crashing feedback sound when the baby kicked against the microphone stand.

R.H. knew better than to try to deter me from the pursuit of my own career. He understands perfectly when I have to be away. He is supportive of what I am doing, and of all the qualities a husband can have, *this* is the most important in my eyes. When I have a major problem concerning the office, I discuss it with him, and he shares his problems with me. (I have more of them than he does.) But normally we do not discuss our work at night. We have our children and our lives together outside our respective offices to plan and organize. That consumes all the free talking time.

In many ways we are not a typical family, having married in our mid-thirties, but we are really quite normal people. High-powered woman that I seem to be, I realize that the role that R.H. plays in my life is far from a minor one. I could not bear up under the pressure I have without him. To understate it: I need him very, very much. He also makes me laugh. That is a wonderful thing to be able to say about the person who shares one's boudoir.

If you are a young woman contemplating life ahead as a working mother, and if it sounds exhausting—being all things to all people—you have concluded correctly. It is. The way to maintain sanity is to be organized at all times, to understand your responsibilities, to know your priorities, and to realize that you do, after all, have the strength to balance the whole works efficiently. At times you will have to slack off on the office because your children need you; your husband will need you at certain times more than your children and your job do; and when your office hits the fan, the family will have to muddle along without you during the crisis period. It's surprising how well it all works out in the end, and how you can always compensate for neglect to any aspect of your responsibilities. This involves the fine art of juggling; it is not haphazard. To tackle a demanding career and motherhood without careful planning is to invite disaster. I would not be happy without both elements of family and job present in my life, nor could I function as well on a daily basis. There is a way to keep it all going simultaneously, though one must work at it not a little but a *lot* harder. When R.H. was in the hospital in Chicago with a severe hip-joint inflammation, my wifely duty was to be with him. I stayed in his room the entire first day until visiting hours were over at night. Then I went to my office at home to compose and type up a series of press releases that had to be sent out from the office early the next morning. I returned to the hospital and to work the next day after two hours of sleep. One calls upon an extra measure of adrenalin at times like this, but somehow it always seems to come. All that is required for the handling of a simultaneous emergency on the home and office front is the strength of a lioness.

When office problems force me to cancel our social engagements in the evening or on weekends, R.H. understands. There is no discussion about it. Working conditions in the office are unbearable on weekends, because no air is pumped into the building. So when a true crisis occurs, we transport staff, electric typewriters, files, and supplies up to the Hollensteiner dining room on Friday night. The staff then works right through to Sunday night. It takes a tolerant man to put up with this. The family fends for itself, and the children run relays to the corner delicatessen to keep the working troops fed. One weekend my staff inherited by default the gargantuan task of seating and mailing out the tickets for thirty-two hundred people who had accepted Clairol's invitation to the CBS "Women of the Year" telecast, in conjunction with the *Ladies' Home Journal*. The guest list ran the gamut from the families of the camera crew to the mayor and United States senators.

Each telephone call brought a major complaint. Clare and Malcolm, eavesdropping on the frenetic scene, received an education in current events, such as "My God, no, we can't put the ambassador from the United Arab Emirates next to the Israeli ambassador. No, not right in the middle of the fighting at the Golan Heights!"

Over the years I have found it necessary to divide my time, consciously or unconsciously, into an across-the-board set of priorities for the maximum utilization of my energy, talent, and worry hours. I suppose that if one were to diagram it (public-relations people are always diagramming proposals and plans), it would look like this:

I Time Must Be Found for Family

1. Husband: Time for loving, having fun with, feeding, sympathizing *with*, and gaining sympathy *from*.
2. Children: Ditto. Must add time for guidance, direction, chastisement, and encouragement. Also chores such as chauffeuring children's friends home by bus, staying up nights to cope with fever, coughing, and upchucking. (These medical duties are shared with Nannie.)
3. Animals: Time for supervising their care, feeding, vet visits, and proper share of dog walking and mess-cleaning-up.

II Time Must Be Found for Running the Home

1. The Nitty Gritty
    a. Marketing (an unbelievably bad scene in New York) and cooking.
    b. Supervision of house-cleaning help, including oneself.
    c. Acting as household treasurer, including coping with pay envelopes, payment of bills, social security, unemployment insurance, medical insurance, etc.
    d. Maintenance, which means coping with household

repairs, plant watering, dry cleaning, laundry, sewing to be sent out, and silver polishing; also "thinking ahead" on such matters as window-washing (inevitably performed the day before it rains) and moth-proofing closets.

e. Arranging of get-aways and summer vacations. (They may be get-aways for the family, but they are a large chore for me.)

2. Creativity

a. Decoration of the apartment, an ongoing job in bits and pieces since it entails everything from buying a major piece of furniture to arranging a vase of flowers.

b. Invention and organization of parties big and small.

III Running the Office

1. Assignment of work to staff, and keeping up the morale of same.

2. Supervision of all work that goes out of the office.

3. Search for new business; maintenance of satisfied relationships with present clients.

4. Presence at endless but usually ineffective committee meetings of professional organizations. (Exceptions to this are the Fashion Group and the National Home Fashions League, which are effective.)

5. Development of firm's image through publicity, proper graphics, interior design of the office, etc.

6. Review of material in order to keep informed, which includes sixty-five magazines monthly, seven daily news and trade papers. (This material, taken home in a briefcase each night, inevitably conflicts with children's homework problems.)

IV Time for the Community

1. Participation in the affairs of our children's schools and in my own alma mater's.

2. Assistance in fund-raising projects for above.
3. Free PR assistance to city institutions, including museums, beautification projects, drug-addiction centers, and the like.
4. Volunteer work for political candidates, particularly women.

V Time for Self (always last, but never least)

1. Maintenance of status quo (improvement of status quo is only for women with lots of free time).
    a. Regular hair appointments; good beauty habits for skin.
    b. Regular doctor and dentist visits—to keep machine well-oiled and in good working order.
2. Embellishment
    a. Keeping in fashion in clothes and accessories (important to clients, unnoticed by one's husband).
    b. Floor exercises, beauty masks, eye packs.
    c. Investigation of latest trends in make-up.
3. Tension relievers
    a. Neck and back exercises.
    b. Use of vibrator and wet hot pad on neck and shoulders.
    c. Weekly massage from "Miraculous Max," a medical masseur who goes after and conquers those tension knots in the neck.
4. Mind improvement: Something of a joke since the children were born, but a very important priority that will resume when children are older and less demanding. Then spare time for reading, attending lectures, opera, ballet, and concerts will resume.

One day I spoke at a career seminar to high-school students at the Convent of the Sacred Heart on Ninety-first Street in New York City. A sixth-grader happened to hear part of it, quite by accident, and after it was over she shyly took my arm, indicating that she wanted to ask me a question.

"What is it, dear?" I asked.

"Tell me, Mrs. Hollensteiner, why is it so important, as you just said, for a woman to work, when our greatest woman, the Mother of God, the Virgin Mary, didn't work?"

Some questions simply have to go unanswered, but I jumped right into it.

"She certainly did work," I replied.

"She didn't get a salary, did she?"

I had an appointment to keep. I would let Sister Joan Kirby, the head of the school, answer that one.

If a working mother in the over-thirty generation who is not financially desperate does not have guilt feelings toward her children, then her nonworking friends will soon give them to her. Those who criticize us for leaving our children during the day in someone else's care are not as outspoken as they used to be, but they still let us have it behind our backs. Sometimes their hostility shines boldly forth, particularly, I've noticed, during the evening hours. There's nothing some women resent more than listening to men talk to other women about their jobs.

Many women are appalled that I took only three weeks off from work to produce Clare and only two to produce Malcolm. They realize, of course, that I didn't even allow myself time to suffer post-partum blues. Nannie had entered our lives when the first was born, and that meant I could return to work at once. The energy flowed back immediately. It had to. (My first night home from the hospital I cooked dinner, as usual; I kept muttering about my mother's description of being kept in bed like an invalid for four weeks after each birth.)

Hostile remarks made to those of us who leave our children during the day are sincere enough. "How *can* you let another woman raise your children?" is the usual remark. I always answer, "I don't." I don't criticize women who choose to stay home with their children—there is both merit and a great deal of beauty in this kind of relationship between mother and child. But I won't accept being called a bad mother because I choose to do differently. If I were home all day, playing an active role in the children's lives, day in and day out, I would release all my pent-up frustrations on them. The children sense this. We even talk about it. I have them also convinced that when the red trouble flag is out, I'll be there. There is no hiding of the emotions in our relationships. When they are being insufferable, I scream at them, and they scream back when they are angry at me. None of us needs a psychiatrist to tell us that screaming and yelling are an effective release.

R.H. takes his role of father more seriously than most. Perhaps he instinctively senses there is a greater burden on his shoulders with a wife who has to travel on business as much as I do. We do not discuss it. He simply comes home a little bit earlier on the nights I am away, and his paternal patience is endless. He plays Monopoly with Malcolm for hours on end, even when his young son continuously beats him at his own game, real estate. We stagger almost all of our business trips so that one of us is always home, and our weekends are invariably a group activity. All invitations for "adults only" weekends or vacations are automatically declined, except on rare occasions. What we lose out on in our social lives is more than compensated for by a reduction of guilt feelings toward our children.

Occasionally I long for the children to be older, more independent, less demanding of us. The minute we return from our offices, they are on us, with us every second. They follow me into our bedroom and do their television-watching, and fighting, always at a high pitch, right under my nose. My friends keep telling me that these precious years of childhood will be gone all too quickly. When our

TV set is knocked off its stand by two rough-housing, shouting children (and such a scene always seems to take place at the end of a particularly grueling day), my mind jumps gratefully to those years ahead. After each weekend of togetherness, I am always eager to return to the organized chaos of my office. (It's the Thank-God-It's-Monday syndrome.) It is often easier to face pressing executive problems than to cope with my own patience at home when its battery needs recharging.

When Clare was born, I was working out of our Chicago apartment and continued to do so for a while. I made room in my large office for her crib, Nannie's bed, and the necessary paraphernalia, including a "Nannie's chair." This last item is the traditional English piece of furniture which permits a nannie to feed, change, and pot the baby, all on her ample lap. The chair must be armless, comfortable, and impervious to spit-ups, spilled milk formula, boiled egg, and spilled prune goo. No one else is allowed to sit in this chair. (No one else ever *wants* to sit in this chair.)

The office-nursery worked very well. In the middle of the room I had built a rather wildly colored room divider made from Sears's plywood stacking units, which we had painted in alternating blue, red, green, yellow, and orange colors. One of our friends brought Clare a baby present after he had viewed the nursery in advance. His present: a pair of sunglasses. Clare spent the first two years of her life with the contrasting auditory stimuli of music boxes, the soft humming and clicking of the electric typewriter, the constant sounds of business calls, the clack of the stapler, and the rhythmic noise of file drawers being opened and closed. When she began to crawl, she headed right for those bright blue file cabinets, and when she learned to walk, she did it by pulling herself up on the drawers. My typewriter, forbidden territory, was always a source of suppressed desire, because if touched it made magic sounds and movements.

Now that the children are older, we always schedule a

"trip to Mommie's office" on school holidays. The children love coming to the brightly colored place that is so much a part of their mother's life. The staff lets them peek in their drawers; there is the endless electrical equipment to play with, and the ringing telephone lights which give the signal to pick up the telephone and say, "Good morning, Letitia Baldrige Enterprises." For Clare, the contents of the file drawers become more interesting each year. For Malcolm, there is no interest. I would have to sneak in some files saying "Chicago Black Hawks" or "Chicago Cubs" before he would desire to explore. Each trip is climaxed by lunch in some "elegant" surroundings, such as a nearby cafeteria or the local Burger King.

The one thing the children do not tolerate is my spending part of "their time" when I'm home at night on the telephone, whether it is for business or social reasons. We have always made them feel that the minute we walk in that door, R.H. and I are their property until they go to bed. They are usually doing their own thing, such as watching TV, but they do it with us, and we are available to chat (particularly during commercials). We may well be buried in newspapers, but we all manage to communicate through the barrage of noise.

Once, when Malcolm was turning three, he became increasingly furious as I carried on a lengthy conversation with the West Coast on business. He kept tugging at the receiver, trying to cut us off. When, in total exasperation, I swatted him on the rear, he went into our bathroom and closed the door. I began to hear strange noises coming from behind the door, and in near panic I told the man on the other end of the line, "Hold on! I must see what has happened to my son." In a matter of seconds I was back. "Terribly sorry," I said, "but we'll just have to continue this later tonight. Malcolm has been trying to flush my brand new sable hat down the toilet. He has not as yet succeeded." (Although sables are used to rain on their coats, the silk linings of fur hats are not.)

Malcolm always knows how to hit where it hurts when he gets mad at his mother. One morning I was to put in a good twenty minutes appearing on television on a program about decorating. As I left for the studio, I told Malcolm I hoped he and Nannie would be watching me. That evening, Malcolm, then five, was miffed about something as he went to bed, and turned on me with blazing eyes. "Your old TV show this morning was yucky, Mommie, *yucky!*" He had paid me the consummate insult in his own vernacular. It was the first time he had mentioned the show, but at least it proved he was watching me.

The very first thing that has to be settled in a working mother's life—far more important than how her husband feels about her being away—is the care of the children. For a woman who has to travel as part of her job, finding a good solution to the problem is essential. A mother who worries during the entire time she is away because she lacks confidence in the baby-sitter does an injustice to herself, her husband, and her job, to say nothing of her children. Peace of mind is a precious commodity, and the woman who travels must have faith in the home substitute. A haphazard succession of baby-sitters who may be unfamiliar to the children can so unsettle those children that every trip for the mother becomes an emotional crisis for everyone. A friend of mine who works for a large retail chain and is away two days a week used to "settle for anyone," as she put it, to stay with her children. During that first year, the personalities of both children changed and they both failed in their schoolwork. Their mother eventually realized she had been giving them short shrift. Instead of abandoning her excellent job, and consequently a good deal of her happiness, she looked long and hard until she found a live-in baby-sitter, an older woman who treats the children as lovingly as a grandmother would. The children are now doing excellent work in school and have returned to their happy, normal selves.

I began to organize the nurse situation when I was three months' pregnant with our first-born. It was the first planning project made for the new member of our household. My job involved a lot of traveling and I knew I would need to have someone who was totally responsible to care for the baby. We advertised for a live-in nurse-housekeeper in the Chicago newspapers. There were no answers whatsoever to my ads, except for several who said they couldn't live in. It was then, at Helene Cummings's suggestion, that I advertised in a little London publication read by all the nannies. I received replies from nannies all over the British Empire (for good reason, as the magazine had mistakenly published our salary offer in pounds sterling instead of dollars.)

Mary Eileen Pakenham came to us from Ireland when our first-born was ten days old. She had stipulated that she would *not* cook for us or do housework, and that she had to be allowed to get to Mass on time. She has been a necessary luxury to me now for eleven years. Beyond her salary, there are the bills of her doctors and dentists, her medicine, uniforms, food, health insurance, social security, unemployment insurance, trips back to Ireland every other year, and bonuses—not to mention the varied activities she organizes for the children, each of which requires a formidable outlay of cash. Even a one-day excursion to Staten Island somehow becomes a costly trip. Nannie could write her own book on what to do with children in New York City, but it would certainly not be based on budget considerations. Nothing but the best is right for her charges. If in celebration I buy two precious steaks for R.H. and myself and hamburger for the children, and do not put name labels on the packages in the refrigerator, R.H. and I will end up dining on hamburger.

Many people would not be able to put up with a nannie who tells them what they should do about their offspring and who treats all parents as if they were potentially naughty children. No woman who stays home all day could stand it. But Nannie is my own solution to the problem, and I have learned to live with the minus part of the deal in order to have the plus part. Because I am a working mother who travels, my husband and I justify the sacrifice of a certain amount of privacy to have someone living in for the sake of our children. I need a housekeeper, one who will market and cook, but the budget allows either for Nannie or for a housekeeper who will go home at night. Obviously, it's Nannie who wins.

For a working mother who does not travel, daily help is usually the best solution. The working mother whose own mother or mother-in-law can come to stay when she has to be away is the most fortunate of all. Each woman must find her own answer. An encouraging factor is that the solution is always there, if enough effort is expended. Some women find their help by using employment agencies, or by placing an effective want ad in the newspaper. Ads placed in small neighborhood papers in large cities often bring good results, as do bulletin board notices in club houses, grocery stores, and other neighborhood shops. Some women have found the right person by asking their pastor, minister, or rabbi. One friend of mine needed a woman to take her children to school, pick them up afterward, and supervise their homework until 5 p.m. She found that person quite coincidentally by talking it over with her shoe repairman, whose aunt started working for her the following Monday and has been with the same family for five years now.

There are many middle-aged and older people in good health who would make marvelous companions for children during the day and carry out the relatively light duties involved in taking them to and from school, preparing their lunches, checking on their homework, and over-seeing their play activities until a parent returns from work. The employment of older people with time on their hands is a natural in child caring, since these men and women are often lonely or bored, in need of income, and longing to share their experiences in life with someone younger. Until the Utopian day comes when there will be excellent day care centers in all communities for children of all ages, the utilization of older people is the answer (and it will be the answer for the staffing of a part of those day care centers, too). A seventy-year-old woman I know has been caring for the children of an executive secretary for five years and tells me that she "grows younger by two years for each child's birthday." As soon as she became in-volved in this job, she woke up to her own creative abili-ties with children and realized that she was needed and loved. Her life began all over again when she responded to a notice posted in the local senior citizens' center.

Another encouraging development is that young women have been increasingly successful in solving the sitter problem through joint action, by forming informal day care centers in their own neighborhoods. I know an artist who takes care of two other women's small children as well as her own toddler during the day. She keeps them busy painting on a canvas-covered floor in her studio and takes them out to the park with their own sketch pads to imitate her when they are not playing games. The artist receives a small amount of money for this; her lunches are paid for; and she also gets free care of her own child any evening or weekend she and her husband want to get away.

Whatever the solution, I have never yet found a woman who was honestly committed to working outside the home who could not find suitable care for her children if she looked hard enough. Like anything else that is important, proper child care requires advance planning.

Something that worries many a working mother is how

to take time off from work when the children need her. Most of us agree that we do not leave for the office when the sitter does not show until alternate emergency arrangements can be made. Sitters get sick, too. Time off is also needed when a child has an operation or is seriously ill, when he or she graduates, performs the lead in the class play, or plays a piano solo in a concert. Some of these absences can be worked out ahead of time with one's employer, and the probability of planned emergency absences should be discussed frankly and openly before the woman begins her job. A woman can deduct emergency situations from her annual leave or she can make up for lost time by coming in early, staying late, working through her lunch hour and not charging overtime—and by working harder and better than her colleagues. When our civilization advances to the point where there is true equality between the sexes, husbands and wives will alternate in taking emergency leaves to care for the children. Until that day, the mother has the responsibility. If her spirit and her enthusiasm for the job are positive, any sensible employer will settle for those emergency absences without feeling the company has been cheated. If the working mother is an executive, the problem of making up the extra time is not as difficult. It's the clock-puncher who must anticipate the short emergency absences and handle them efficiently.

Because my solution to child care, Nannie, is such a dominating factor in our household, I would like to give her some further description. In her late fifties, she has a powerful pair of legs made muscular from years of heavy, well-built English buggy ("pram") pushing. When we lived in Chicago, she was known as "The Pram Queen," and when we moved to New York she was called the "Buggy Pusher," with no compliments intended, by the neighborhood toughs. We had to import a Sol Whitby pram from

London, or she would have returned to England. This vehicle was oiled and cleaned on a maintenance program that would have made the most conscientious chauffeur with a Rolls Royce look delinquent in his duties. The pram could not be kept downstairs with everyone else's assorted strollers, buggies, and bicycles. No, our pram had to be kept in the middle of the front hall, where it sat like a charished antique, and guests were forced to flatten themselves against the wall to get past it. I learned early in my relationship with Nannie that I could not win on certain points. To her, the pram came second to her charges, and R.H. and I simply had to wait until Malcolm had outgrown it before the front hall became a free access area.

Nannie and I maintain a guarded truce, with minor skirmishes occurring, much like the Afghanistan-Pakistan border situation. Every time there is a battle scene, R.H. absents himself. I admire the way he can always disappear as if by magic at such moments. Clare's and Malcolm's friends respect her just as I do. She stands for no nonsense, but she loves to tell them all jolly tales of her charges in English castles, in French châteaux, and aboard the yachts of the Golden Greeks in the Aegean. She very definitely descended in social status by coming to work for us. It was the first time, in fact, that she had to subsist without a "nursery maid" working for her. Her duties concern mainly the children—their food, clothes, and rooms. Her greatest joy is when I'm away on business, leaving her as captain of the ship. She would have, in fact, made a great marine. The children's clothes are always clean; their shoes are always polished. When they grow up they will, I hope, be well groomed and meticulous about their appearances.

When the children invite friends to a meal, it is often a "party," with a place card and favor at each place. Although Nannie is not famous for her gourmet cuisine, her egg-salad sandwiches are legendary. The children believe what she has told them—that she received the recipe from a leprechaun. There is always background music for these parties: records that reflect the wide range of Nannie's musical tastes, from Irish jigs to "Chitty Chitty Bang-Bang" and "Frère Jacques."

Whenever we move our apartment or I move my office (which happens more often than my nerves can stand), Nannie traditionally makes a large platter of her egg-salad sandwiches for the movers, and we buy them beer. I overheard a six-foot four-inch brawny moving man on the telephone, talking to his wife at lunchtime. "Jesus, guess what I'm eating, a bunch of little white egg-salad sandwiches, with the crusts off!" He consumed five of them.

I have always tried to maintain the semblance of an interior-design scheme in the nursery quarters. In fact, I have designed several attractive and functional nurseries for my clients. But no matter how many times we have moved into newly furbished apartments, and no matter how many admonitions Nannie has received, the area always looks like the inside of an abandoned tenement within three weeks. Squiggles made by the children are pasted on coordinating lamp-shades; paint is chipped off the corners of newly painted furniture, as if a truck had just driven through the rooms. The bulletin boards I hang everywhere are not enough; the walls are festooned with children's art, posters, signs, and a multitude of holy cards. Everything is fastened to the walls in crazy patterns of tape and when the tape is removed, so is the paint.

"Nannie's Bag" is another legend in our household. The worn navy canvas tote always accompanies her wherever she goes with the children, and it serves equally well for car trips and forays into Central Park. It contains fresh water in a plastic bottle, cups, tissues, insect repellent and suntan lotion in summer, Band-Aids and disinfectant, children's aspirin, motion-sickness pills, a small tin of biscuits, and a smaller tin of peppermints. Like the Coast Guard, she is *semper paratus*. R.H. and I no longer make fun of Nannie's Bag; we have made use of it on too many occasions ourselves.

Nothing involving children is a crisis for Nannie. Indeed, she seems to thrive on situations that would drive me crazy. One Sunday afternoon, as we were driving back to New York from a country weekend, Nannie sat between two little boys in the back seat, calmly in charge. Five-year-old Malcolm was on one side of her throwing up into one of the plastic boxes from her tote bag; his four-year-old friend Oliver was on the other side, throwing up into another of the plastic boxes. R.H. drove grimly ahead, ready to be sick himself any minute. I just sat in the front seat looking out the window thanking God for Nannie, but realizing after all that this is what I am paying her for. Her only comment during this scene was a request. "Mrs. Hollensteiner, will you or Mr. Hollensteiner please bring back with you a couple of those airsick bags they place in the seat pocket in front of you on airplanes? They are much easier to pack than plastic boxes for times such as these."

When one of the children is ill, be it a cold, an ear ache, a broken arm, or pinkeye, I manage to exaggerate the child's discomfort far beyond reality. My imagination can take a normal illness and turn it into something with which not even Marcus Welby could contend. Everyone usually tells me to go back to my office. When four-year-old Clare had to go to the hospital to have her tonsils and adenoids removed, I accompanied her in spite of Nannie's protestations. Nannie argued that since she was experienced at this sort of thing, she should care for Clare and sleep over with her in the hospital room. I would have none of it. *I* was her mother and the duty to my child must be fulfilled. Off we went in a taxi, with my reading to her aloud from a cheerful little book about how exciting the hospital experience would be, how her throat would hurt "a little" after the operation, but how there would be ice cream and ginger ale and lots of presents.

I have never been so upset by any twenty-four hours in my life. Clare had actually looked forward to her first hospital stay, but after the operation, she suffered a great deal for several hours, as would any child with a small throat from which swollen tonsils and adenoids had been pulled. I was miserable with empathy. When she gagged, I gagged. The only thing I couldn't do was spit up blood when she did. When we were allowed to go home, Clare was put to bed and became immediately her old self. I was put to bed by the pediatrician, in far worse shape than the real patient, with a "sympathetic temperature, dizziness, nausea, and a terrible case of nerves." If Malcolm has to have his tonsils removed, Nannie will go with him. There will be no argument.

When a child calls one of our children, or when a parent calls to arrange for a party, Nannie reaches the heights of bristling efficiency. She keeps their social engagements documented in two carefully maintained spots—a book and a wall calendar. Nothing is ever forgotten. The children are brought to and from each place at the exact hour. Birthday presents are wrapped well beforehand. Everything is managed to perfection. But if the telephone should ring for R.H. or me, it might just as well go unanswered. The message is rarely relayed at all, and when it is, the name is usually illegible or the telephone number is missing.

I have no worries about the religious education of our children. Nannie is devout and her idea of unmitigated joy would be to go to Mass twice a day. On her day off, she spends her time with nun friends. Given the number of times that Nannie dragged Malcolm to morning Mass (his kindergarten and nursery-school classes were in the afternoon), I was convinced she had designs on turning him into a priest. When he was five I overheard his reply to someone who asked him the traditional question of what he wanted to be when he grew up. "I'm going to give my life to Gawd," replied Malcolm in his then Dublin accent, "and to the Black Hawks." (Maybe he can become the Chicago hockey team's first chaplain-defenseman.)

When a religious event such as a First Communion occurs, Nannie is always seated front and center, her face wreathed in beatific smiles. It does not matter where R.H. and I are sitting; on religious occasions, Clare and Malcolm are *her* children. All her money goes to the Church; she will obviously enjoy a high place in heaven one day. Because a person's saint's day is much more important to her than a birthday, we always have big celebrations for the children's Feast days of Saint Clare and Saint Malcolm, including a present, a cake, and a party. The neighborhood kids are jealous that those "Hollensteiner kids" have two birthdays apiece every year.

Nannie's office hours in Central Park are famous. She readily dispenses advice when young mothers, noticing her white uniform and maturity, seek her out. She also gives advice when it is not solicited, and has been known to criticize the fact that a child has been kept too long in diapers so that it is "affecting his walking." She even frightened one young father on a Saturday into rushing to a store to buy training pants, a term that had never entered his vocabulary until that day. If she feels that a mother is feeding her child an improper lunch from a nutritional point of view, she says so. She has also witnessed any number of playground accidents and has sagely informed mothers when their children's injuries merit a visit "right away" to the nearby hospital emergency clinic. Without frightening the mother, Nannie clearly determines the difference between a bump on the head and something much more serious. (With me, every child's head bump is a concussion or a skull fracture; therefore, people learn not to ask my opinion.)

She often vocalizes her distrust of the long-haired generation—"those rude hippies"—who do not have proper Central Park manners. As far as Nannie is concerned, people who don't know how to behave in a place primarily designed for children and old people should be expelled from the area. Four-year-old Malcolm demonstrated his indoctrination one day while walking up Park Avenue with me. A very distinguished patriarchal gentleman in a long black cassock and tall black-velvet hat emerged from the Russian Orthodox Church residence. A commanding, dignified figure, he was probably the archbishop. Malcolm took one look at the long beard and shouted, "Dirty hippie!" It took me five minutes of monologue to express my apologies to the gentleman, who kept smiling at me benignly. I finally realized he did not understand one word of English. We were saved. But I quickly reindoctrinated Malcolm about hippies.

There have been many such times when Nannie's and my opinions have clashed head on. I can never inspire her to capitulate, to change any of her attitudes. My only retaliation is to get the children alone and work on their basic sense of logic. Walking to school one morning, when Clare was six, she and I talked long and seriously about the problems of drug addiction. Both children have seen junkies; they have seen people on highs and on lows in the streets of our neighborhood. We had a methadone clinic next door to our old apartment, and that in itself was an education. As Clare and I walked along this bright, sunny morning, I impressed on her how important it was never to experiment with any kind of drugs. She nodded wisely and suddenly began to talk on another subject, how she, Nannie, and Malcolm had watched a pro abortion parade the afternoon before. I chuckled, knowing she did not understand anything about the subject. The parade had taken place at the height of the dispute over the pending New York State abortion law. "Nannie got very mad at the ladies parading," Clare said, and went on to say that women who had abortions were naughty, because they were killing the little babies inside them. With obvious displeasure, I checked Clare at once, explaining that there were definitely two sides to this question, that I did not agree with Nannie, and that she must forget about the entire subject until we had more time to discuss it. If I had said, "We'll discuss it when you are older," she would not have left me off the hook.

We reached the door of the convent school. "I'll make you happy when I grow up, Mommie," she said, with shining sparkly eyes ready to please me in every way. "When I'm a big girl, I *won't* ever take drugs, and I *will* have an abortion!"

The doors closed behind her before I had time to reply. I didn't know whether to laugh or cry, but decided on the former.

R.H. and I successfully fought having pets for several years. We had both been raised with dogs, but not in New York apartments. I have always disliked cats (and the feeling is mutual); besides, the dodging of dog-do while walking on the sidewalks on Manhattan's upper East Side had convinced us that we would not add to the city's pollution.

But then a cat and a little dog came into our lives, a week apart. We saw a real longing develop in Clare to express her deep affection for animals. We also noticed Malcolm becoming a little afraid of dogs, any dog. It was a double signal to us. We must get them pets. We answered an ad in a local Connecticut paper one weekend, and drove to fetch a six-week-old kitten, one member of an entire litter to be given away. The address was quite literally a junkyard for old cars on the outskirts of town. Clare picked up a scrawny little animal from one of the several litters of cats and stray dogs that were running around. She took this nondescript glob of gray into her hands and said lovingly, "Why, Pierre, you have a new home now." Why the name Pierre came to her, no one knows, least of all Clare, but he has grown into a princely, haughty creature who now hisses only when confronting the large porcelain snow leopard in the den. He obviously feels vastly superior to that proud animal. R.H., who never suffered an antipathy toward cats, takes Pierre for what he is. I have practiced tolerance and have learned to agree with Clare about "how beautiful he is" because of the strength of her love for him. So Pierre has become a member of the family, even if I would like to train him away from his unerring sense of taste. When he jumps on a window sill, mantle, or library shelf, he invariably heads for the antique porcelains. A very selective cat, he chooses only our finest things.

Dustin Hoffman was given to us by my brother Mac and his wife, Midge. Jack Russell terriers are an English breed with an exceptionally sensitive nose, traditionally trained for hunting. The Mac Baldriges bought him as a tiny puppy, thinking he would be very useful in a year's time hunting the woodchucks that gouge ugly holes in their land. He should have become useful. Instead, he grew up loving every human and animal being. He would never go after a woodchuck, except to nuzzle it. All he wanted to do was jump on laps, cuddle, and be caressed. He couldn't even be a watchdog, because he frankly refuses to bark, except on the rarest of occasions, and we have never figured out what the stimuli have been. There he was, brown and white and very, very small, in contrast to a group of very big, shaggy dogs on the Baldrige property. He was therefore banished from the farm into the arms of the Hollensteiners. The transition from country dog to city lap dog took Dustin about twenty minutes. Silly-looking, a lover of all mankind, Dustin is now rather a celebrity in the far corners of our neighborhood.

Nannie worries about our animals almost as much as the

children. Her special love is Dustin, who sleeps in her room at night and accompanies her on all her rounds. We keep telling Nannie that Dustin's love for her is predicated on the fact that she is home all day with him, but this is just to soothe our own egos. One particularly hot summer day Nannie related how she had run out of water in Central Park, and how, coming home, Dustin had almost collapsed from the heat. He needed water badly.

"What did you do?" I asked, not a little worried. Dustin's needs are very important to me, too.

"I did what I should have in an emergency," she said perfunctorily. "We were right in front of church, so I went in and let him drink from the holy-water fount."

I tried not to laugh in her face. The sight of religious Nannie, holding little Dustin up to the holy-water basin in the back of the church, was almost too much. "But Nannie," I protested, not so much from the sacrilege of the holy-water fount but because of the age and dirtiness of the water, "what about all those germs?"

"God would *never* let anyone become ill from holy water," she retorted in a huff. And she's probably right.

Dustin and Pierre engage in daily wrestling matches that are far funnier and more engaging than any professional match ever staged for the public. When Pierre gets fed up with his adversary, he performs a series of fast flying jumps over the dog's back that remind one of the leaping acrobats depicted on Mycenean art objects. These feats signal the end of the feigned combat, and each returns to his lair—Pierre to the pink-gingham confines of Clare's room, and Dustin to his much-washed mat on Nannie's wicker bedroom chair.

I frankly do not need the added responsibility of these pets. In the final analysis, it is I who have to worry about their welfare, the stocking of their food, arranging the constant trips to the vet. Nannie does her share of animal-escorting to the vet's and helping Clare cope with kitty litter.

When it's pouring rain at six-thirty in the morning and I have a client presentation to make in a couple of hours, though, it is still "Mommie" who is saddled with getting Dustin out in that rainstorm in the midst of her schedule. R.H. handles the late-night detail of Dustin's walk, but if he is away on a business trip, I change from my nightgown into a one-piece woolly zip-up spacesuit. This rather strange attire, topped by a coat, keeps me warm and decent on the street, although I would be mortified if I ever ended up in a police station dressed in this manner. The security guard on our block told me that my wardrobe is always noticed by the midnight shift, especially if I am walking Dustin after a formal party and am dressed in my flowing black-velvet cape. Dustin's daytime trips are handled by Nannie. If she is going somewhere where dogs might not be welcome, she stashes him away in a shopping bag. If Pierre is the property of Clare, then Dustin is the *Jedermann* of dogs. He belongs to Everyman, including each of us, the doorman, the postman, and the street cleaner. He is too small to pollute New York's air to any degree, but his heart is big enough to take care of us all.

3
The Chosen Profession: Public Relations

There are two inevitable questions: just what is public relations anyway, and how does a woman start her own business? The latter part of the question is easier to answer than the former. A married woman needs one account (signed on the dotted line, not just promised), a small office space, a telephone, a typewriter, a lawyer who "will wait until things are better to get paid," someone to set up the accounting books, and a healthy relationship—otherwise referred to as credit—with a nearby office-supply store. An unmarried woman needs all the aforementioned, plus a lover or a close friend to whom she can complain at night and on weekends. I have one colleague, unmarried, who has neither. She complains lengthily each night into her bedside tape recorder. It fascinates her to listen to the playback, she says, because she feels such instant sympathy for anyone with *all* those troubles.

It was inevitable that my own business would be public relations. Women have always been able to make their way in this field without flinging themselves against a barricade of male objections. Public relations is a creative field, but it is also relatively new. It is also totally misunderstood by most, so perhaps this is another reason why the male sex has allowed us to make our stumbling way along in it.

One has to have certain talents in order to excel in the field. One must be able to write, spell, and punctuate. (The latter two qualities seem to have slipped by many recent college graduates.) One must be able to react creatively to anything, from a great work of art to a great hot dog, and one must be able to "take the rap" with regularity, from one's own errors to those of everyone on the client's own staff. The chin must become abrasion-proof.

Women have been "allowed" for years to be creative in fields such as writing, fashion, interior design, advertising, and public relations without impinging upon masculine prerogatives. But when I was a little girl, there were really three careers that were freely open to women: nursing, teaching, and secretarial work. (I am omitting prostitution from the discussion for good and sufficient reason, and if I ever had designs on becoming an airline hostess, such dreams were dispelled quite thoroughly when I passed six feet in height.)

By climbing the career ladder in a female profession, the secretarial one, I was a cop-out from the point of view of today's militant feminists, who react to the typewriter as they do to a bad case of leprosy. I'm very proud of my secretarial jobs, however. I was close to Real Power all the time (which is a lot more than I can say for the struggling, ambitious, opportunistic young men who were earning much more than me, but whose jobs were one-tenth as interesting as mine). Being close to Real Power is what it's all about, although my years for the Bruces in Paris and the Luces in Rome could not come close to the glory of it all in the White House. Of course, if I were twenty today, I'd head straight for graduate school in business or in engineering. Along the way, I'd learn something about the carpentry, plumbing, and electrical trades, with a view to leading a less frustrated life on the home front. But no matter what my career aspirations would be, I would learn how to type well; this would hold true even if I aspired to the Presidency of the United States.

I was never much of a fighter against the male sex. My big brothers Mac and Bob saw to that. I was inevitably overpowered by their physical strength, though they always attributed their victories to cerebral superiority. Our childhood rows were nothing, of course, compared to what goes on in the adult work world. As I look back on my life now, I realize I let a lot of men walk over me on the job. I had been trained to take it on the chin, then to forget it. Now I take it in the shins, and swear revenge—thanks to some elementary consciousness-raising.

When I graduated from college, my mother's plans to have me marry immediately and to produce four children in rapid succession were soon thwarted. Still, if one had to work, the secretarial field, particularly a job in an elegant foreign embassy, was all right for a *"jeune fille de bonne famille."* The transition to an executive capacity in public relations from diplomatic life was a logical one. I had been doing public relations all my life anyway. Having inherited my father's congressman personality, I was constantly running for class president or head of school. I politicked quite naturally all my young life, and later on, it came naturally in my jobs. As social secretary to the American ambassador in Paris, my job was almost entirely a public-relations function. I gave speeches in French to groups throughout France on American policy, because very few Americans at the embassy were bi-lingual. I had to soothe the hurt feelings of everyone from American tourists to French Foreign Office officials who felt they should have been invited by the Bruces to dinner. I learned to feed newsy tidbits to journalists who were doing stories on the Bruces and the embassy. Even my seating plans for official dinners were important from a PR point of view. I would be lobbying, for example, for an increase in the House Appropriations budget for the Foreign Service by seating at dinner an irascible member of the House committee between a brilliant American Foreign Service wife and the prettiest girl in Paris. When the congressman turned to his right, a peppy Gallic breeze would increase his sex hormones. When he turned to his left—and at official dinners one *has* to turn to the left—he received a lot of straightforward, important information on Foreign Service budgeting he could never have obtained or would never have listened to otherwise. It was an advantage to learn early in my business life how important these nuances are in the diplomatic and official world. It is the same in the business world.

During my two-year stint at the CIA in Washington as the psychological warfare officer for the Eastern European Division, I learned about the principles of creative persuasion, image-building, and image-breaking. There's a direct relationship between psychological warfare and public relations in business, the major difference being, thank God, that the latter is more welfare than warfare. In the former, one tries to sway an entire populace into thinking a certain way and into acting in a certain manner, through the stimulation of their patriotic emotions. In public relations, one tries to give good information to a specific group, to make a concept or an idea attractive to them, and to stimulate them to act positively—whether it be to buy something, attend something, support something or someone, or just plain like something or someone. I learned another thing at the CIA—how to secure all combination lock safes properly in the office before leaving for the day. Because a Marine safe-checker found one of my six office safes open one night, I had to spend the next two weeks accompanying the Marine security guards on their rounds after office hours, checking every safe in four temporary buildings near the Lincoln Memorial.

My next boss, Clare Luce, was a master of public relations. A writer herself, and married to one of the world's most famous journalists, she knew the importance of each and every editor who wrote about her. She had me write them warm, newsy letters from Rome about her ambassadorial activities, and the news in them was always printed. She had a good personal relationship with at least a hundred of these editors, and many top columnists and editorial writers were her personal friends. The press conferences in Rome were always handled the way every reporter wants them to be. The ambassador was prepared and organized; the conference was short, concise, and informative.

The jump from government life in Rome to the job of public relations director at Tiffany's was a big one. I was the first person to hold the job, their first woman executive. My better judgment told me to tread lightly but my creative urges made me behave like an innocent, enthusiastic, wiggling puppy dog. Whenever I had a small success, a failure was always so close on my heels that there never seemed to be time to enjoy it. There was much to learn and my ignorance couldn't help but show. My first responsibility was to engender publicity on Tiffany's products, which were pretty pleasant to contemplate: all those girl's best friends, as well as rubies, sapphires, and emeralds, not to mention fine gold and silver objects, sparkling crystal, and beautiful porcelains. This was quite a switch from worrying about ambassadors, embassy security matters, protocol, and the Cold War.

It was indeed an education, those years at Tiffany's. I had a diamond necklace sewn onto a velvet-and-lace garter, photographed it on a perfect leg, and proudly watched the photograph appear in every newspaper in America. (I could never do anything so sexist again, but consciousnesses were pretty low in those days, mine included.) I brought back the vogue of wearing jeweled chokers when my series of photographs went out over the wires, and costume-jewelry manufacturers ripped us off all over the place. . . . I learned how to photograph jewels on dogs, cats, and baby lambs, and had to cope both with animals falling asleep under the warm lights and with models sneezing from fur allergies. . . . I even managed to set fire to the hair of one of New York's top beauties. We were photographing her close up, wearing a huge diamond necklace that looked like a Christmas wreath. When I pushed a big lighted candle too close to her carefully coifed head, the inevitable occurred. . . . I immersed four jeweled flexible fish in the bottom of a tropical fish tank during a color photography session of "jewels of the sea," only to learn the jeweled fish contained very delicate (but now ruined) cigarette lighters. . . . We took millions of dollars' worth of jewels out to rehearsals and to the live telecast of an hour-long spectacular. Tiffany's paid handsomely for insurance and armed guards each time. The star of the show looked magnificent in our sparklers. The only trouble was that when the credits were flashed on everyone's TV screen at the end of the show, a rival jeweler was named instead of Tiffany's. . . . I watched in horror again when a whole bagful of loose Tiffany diamonds was dropped as a joke on the studio floor during a live Jack Paar "Tonight" show on TV. The armed guard's badly shaking hand holding a loaded gun was photographed in closeup by the cameramen while people grappled laughingly on the floor for the diamonds. Thank God the camera stayed away from my own contorted face.

No, Walter Hoving and Tiffany's will never forget me. . . . I was the one who set up in the stationery department an exhibition of letters from famous people of history to other famous people. (They were passionate love letters, far better than the crude porno sold on Forty-second

Street.) I was the one who asked Helen Boehm to bring in her husband's live exotic birds to flutter in a six-foot-high Victorian bird cage next to the shelves of the Boehm porcelain bird sculptures. Some of the tropical birds escaped onto Fifty-seventh Street while they were being brought into the store, which set off a widely publicized bird hunt for the poor little creatures. The police were only too glad to be able to help out Tiffany's in something other than a jewel robbery. While NBC/TV News was filming the bird exhibit, two more tiny birds squeezed through the narrow bars of the cage to their freedom. They flew around in madness all over the china and glass floor, dive-bombing into priceless plates, figurines, and crystal objects. We captured them when darkness came by drawing them to a flashlight, the last beam of light left on the floor. . . . I was the one who finally talked Walter Hoving into letting me accessorize a fashion show of furs and designers' gowns at Bonwit Teller's. We nearly lost a $12,500 diamond clip on that expedition. My assistant and I, after searching the store for a frantic hour, finally found the diamonds residing like a pile of rhinestones on a fifteen-dollar black-velvet beret in the hat bar. . . . I was the one who wanted to put some pizzazz into the inauguration of a new bridal-silver flatware pattern with heart-shaped handles. A pushover for romance, I had rented from an animal talent agency a pair of white "love doves" called Bill and Coo to make a centerpiece in living color in a pink, flower-festooned cage. The setting literally dripped with sentimentality. The birds were delighted to be making the grade socially at Tiffany's and proceeded to lay a pair of lovely pink eggs, which matched our color scheme perfectly. This was Tiffany's first recorded birth, and to lend it distinction, the Bronx Zoo's chief birdkeeper came to advise us, surveyed the scene, and told us not to disturb their nest in the cage, which the birds had made with a Tiffany box and some white excelsior from the shipping department which they shredded into the tiniest of pieces with their beaks.

Making something commonplace into something quite special or amusing by a simple change of phrase or visual context is an important tool of the public-relations craft. Why *not* refer to plain yellow-bordered dinner plates as "honey and mimosa accented"? Why not in a press release refer to candlesticks as "the silver, stately fluted Greek columns guarding the centerpiece"? Why not refer in a photo caption to a diamond and platinum pin as a "sun-slashed waterfall of shimmering droplets"? Such statements are not deceitful tricks. They are not sins against consumerism. It is all mere romanticizing, and we can all use a little more romance in our lives. (One of the interesting twists of fate is that Duane Garrison, my secretary, returned to Tiffany in 1973 as director of public relations.)

When the John F. Kennedy administration began, I joined the White House team as the social secretary and head of the First Lady's secretariat. I had known both Kennedys for many years, and I had had more experience than perhaps anyone else around in the "art" of social secretarying. The science of public relations suddenly became more important than it will ever be again, at least for me. It was fascinating to watch the press do our jobs for us. They wanted to build up this extraordinary young man and this beautiful, bright young woman into the king and queen of the world. The press didn't just cover the Kennedys; it rhapsodized over them. This was pre-Watergate, of course, and in those days the term "the President's public relations" did not have the connotation it has today.

One thing every White House staffer does is worry twenty-four hours a day. One worries about the "Chief" and the "First Lady," working to see that they continue to be loved and that the pressure and criticism will not get to them. One worries that the Presidential family is doing too much; one worries that it is not doing enough. One worries about oneself, about how good and necessary a job one is doing for the team. One's lips are zippered at cocktail parties and dinners for fear of being misquoted and misconstrued on the front page of the *Post* the next morning. But mistakes are made nonetheless. A typical headline I caused was "Jackie's New Aide Says Kennedys Will Jazz Up the White House; Fine Arts Commission Says No They Won't." Another was "White House Social Secretary Steals French Ambassador's Chef," an event that developed into an international incident. I was the victim of my own overenthusiasm on the White House "jazz up" charge. I was totally innocent of the "chef snatch" charge.

One of my responsibilities was to establish policy for Jacqueline Kennedy's public relations—what community projects she would visit, what charities she would lend her name to, which groups would receive her written message, which official invitations she would accept. It was a rocky road, fraught with danger. Behind all her glamorous appearances, which inevitably made front-page headlines, was acute heartburn for us. There I was with my staff, suffering every minute, being pressured from all sides to have Jackie do this, have Jackie do that. The President's staff thought they owned her and could use her for their own ends, but she showed them. Jacqueline Kennedy Onassis has always owned herself.

Our first Sunday in the White House, I organized my first large party and made trouble for the President with the entire Baptist community. I unknowingly broke precedence twice by having liquor flow from *bars*, heretofore a White House no-no, and by having the party on a Sunday. In the days when avowed Communists were *personae non gratae* in any official American household, I let one slip through the guest list at an important luncheon. When I magnanimously gave away all of Mrs. Kennedy's flowers in Mexico City to the poor and the sick, I did not notice that one of the containers, which held an arrangement of orchids, was actually a twenty-four-carat-gold museum piece. When I didn't have enough rehearsal time to check on our stage lights for the performance of *Brigadoon* before the King of Morocco, a trooper light blew every fuse in the east part of the White House and plunged us all into darkness. The Secret Servicemen dashed to the doors with guns drawn and there was a ghastly quiet. The President finally said in an embarrassed stage whisper to the confused King, "It's all part of the show, Your Majesty." It was a long two and a half minutes until those fuses were fixed.

I once spent an entire month getting Mrs. Kennedy's state gifts ready for her trip to India. I ordered sixty handsome dark-blue leather frames, embossed with the Presidential Seal stamped in gold at the top. I had ordered five different sizes of photographs of the Kennedys in order to acknowledge the different degrees of importance of the Indian officials. The embassy in New Delhi informed me just before Mrs. Kennedy's arrival that not one of the frames could be given away. They were made of blue cowhide, an affront to the Hindus, to whom the cow is a sacred animal.

I worried about everything at the White House, night and day. The long reach of the White House telephone operators followed me everywhere, especially home at night. I worried about the Bay of Pigs on a national level; I worried about the Kennedy and Auchincloss relations who felt they were being slighted on a personal level. I worried about how we were handling the important groups of women received at the White House; I worried about all the groups of women who were not being received at the White House. I developed a repertory of white lies that stretched from Washington around the world and back again in order to say no graciously and imaginatively. It was impossible to be a perfectionist. My staff and I greeted the day of the dinner for the president of Pakistan at Mount Vernon (an historic "first") with the absolute certainty that we had thought of everything during those weeks of constant labor. But the Army bug-sprayers had to be called back to wage war on the mosquitoes again; the chef complained that his portable heating equipment didn't work properly; the National Symphony Orchestra began rehearsing their program at four in the afternoon only to discover that they could not perform without an acoustical shell. So we had one built, between four and seven o'clock, when the guests arrived.

I learned something invaluable during those wonderful, history-making days. It is the knowledge that one must toss off today's crisis with a shrug; it is just not very important. Tomorrow's will be far worse.

It was a logical transition for me to go from the White House to the Kennedy family's huge property in Chicago, the Merchandise Mart. Joseph Kennedy had told me before he had his stroke that I needed some real business experience in the home-furnishings industry and that the Mart was the place to get it. It is impossible to work in that four million square feet of space, predominately devoted to showrooms of home furnishings, and not be influenced by the whole field of interior design. My job was to help promote the big wholesale selling markets that took place several times a year. Buyers would come from everywhere, from big stores and small stores alike. I had worked with leading interior designers at Tiffany's and again at the White House during Mrs. Kennedy's refurbishment of the mansion. I had also taken courses in interior design at the Metropolitan Museum, and I believed that my taste was pretty impeccable. So I swung in and out of the Mart showrooms, exclaiming over the pieces that pleased me, only to have the managers of the showrooms laugh uproariously. If I enthusiastically loved a design, it inevitably turned out to be a bomb, something they couldn't sell at all. One of the leading furniture manufacturers went so far as to offer me a monthly retainer if I would analyze all his designs in the drawing stages. The ones I liked best would be the ones he would not cut at the factory. I declined his offer, but managed to absorb the fact that my taste was not everyone else's. It gave me an inferiority complex, but for only a short time.

It was George Struthers, a vice-president of Sears, Roebuck in Chicago, who gave me the courage to go into business for myself. He gave me the push that I needed and he also gave the account that I needed to start with—Sears. I rented a little office on the fifteenth floor of the Mart, in the middle of the giftware showrooms, hired an extraordinarily hard-working secretary-assistant, Angela Gillespie, and we were in business. I sent out a postcard announcing my new business to everyone I knew. Most of the replies were initially polite, but the last sentence would invariably read, "But, Tish, aren't you doing something rather risky? Isn't this a bad time to be in business for yourself?" The answer, of course, is that any time is a bad time to be in business for yourself. It is far easier to have a "Big Daddy," to belong to a corporation that takes care of your medical benefits, gives you profit sharing, and helps pay for your funeral. Many were the times I couldn't pay Angela, and there were even times I had to borrow money from her during the same week I couldn't pay her.

We hustled. And the business came, in bits and pieces. We handled the opening of the Elizabeth Arden Salon on Michigan Avenue, and then were retained on a monthly basis to help it along. Walter Hoving let us help open the Chicago Tiffany branch, and also kept us on retainer. We began working with banks and managed to present a major self-betterment program for the women employees of the Northern Trust, the First National Bank of Chicago, and the First Federal Savings. We structured the Burlington

House Awards program and launched a whole new dimension for Burlington Industries. And, in the middle of everything, I got married, much to everyone's total surprise. Along with everyone else in the world, R.H. did not understand public relations as a business, but he supported whatever it was I was doing because whatever it was it made me happy.

Then, in 1969, R.H., our two children, Nannie, and I did what everyone said we could not possibly do. We moved to New York from Chicago over a weekend without even taking one day off. R.H. was to enter a real-estate consulting firm in the Pan Am Building, and I was to become Burlington Industries' first director of consumer affairs. Burlington had been wooing me for over a year to become their first top-level woman executive in the corporation (the largest textile company in the world). I had enjoyed my work on the Burlington House Awards with President Ely Callaway and Executive Vice-President Ray Kassar. I was confident I could do the job, but there was R.H. to think of. Then the time became ripe for him to make a change, too, in his real-estate business. Because of the Burlington offer to me, he looked for a new position in New York as well as in Chicago, and New York provided the better move for him, too. We left Chicago with great reluctance as far as our life styles were concerned. We knew we could not live as well in expensive Manhattan as we had in Chicago, but the gamble was on the future.

On a Friday in September in Chicago, R.H. and I both worked at our old jobs until six o'clock. We packed up the family and left the next morning by plane, taking with us basic clothes and Nannie's infernal, bulky gear for the children. Clare was four, Malcolm was twenty months old, and their parents were feeling very old indeed. On the following Monday morning we started our new jobs, and Clare went to her first day of formal schooling at the Convent of the Sacred Heart on Ninety-first Street. She had not even been to nursery school before. I accompanied her, and left her off at kindergarten with tears in my eyes. Obviously, she was about to undergo terrible emotional strain, starting school for the first time in a strange new city. But she chuckled at my tears and literally skipped away to join all the new friends awaiting her. Except for Clare, however, this rapid jump-shift to New York was a traumatic experience for the family. R.H. and I remained in a state of shock for some time; Nannie couldn't stop grumbling; and baby Malcolm surveyed his new surroundings and immediately dissolved into tears.

The Big City had changed a lot (and not all for the better) since I had left it nine years earlier. But I had changed, too. I was coming back to New York a married woman, with two children and a host of responsibilities I could never have imagined in those carefree single days. The New York press corps had changed; many newspapers and magazines were dead; new ones had been born. The fashion industry on Seventh Avenue had changed, and I had to learn everything and everyone all over again. My job as director of consumer affairs kept me busy, but not so much so that I could not study the city and swim my way back into the mainstream again. By 1971 it was time to be on my own again, with my own public-relations firm. My feelings of independence, of chafing against the corporate structure, of wanting to prove what I could really do, were too strong. Happily, Burlington gave me the job of continuing to run the Burlington House Awards for American homes, a program I had started in 1968, and I was ready to start anew.

It is very hard to work for a corporation after one has tasted the delicious independence of being in business for oneself. In spite of the responsibility and administrative headaches of coping with accounting, billing, and taxes, of meeting the payroll, of paying the rent, and of wrestling with the always existing possibility of failure, I had enjoyed being my own boss far too much. At Burlington I missed that extra measure of creativity required of oneself when faced with "the buck stopping here." At Burlington I had also resented not being taken seriously in the corporate hierarchy, proven by such actions as excluding me from management meetings, where executives, all male, including many ranking under me, made policy. They were not yet ready for women. I could not crack through the wall of resentment and suspicion.

Madeline Zuckerman, my Jane-of-all-trades secretary, and I watched with no small emotion as the sign-painter lettered in red the words "Letitia Baldrige Enterprises, Inc." on the glass door in our new Sixth Avenue offices. We hired a famous lawyer to incorporate us in the state of New York. His clients, except for us, were all big-time and big-monied. Thank heavens he was of the act-now-pay-later school. We hired an accountant to set up our books and to come in once a month to take care of insurance, Social Security, unemployment tax, corporate rent tax, and a variety of nagging, annoying matters I neither understand nor have any desire to understand.

On piles of boxes Madeline and I sat with dirt-smudged faces and bloodshot eyes on that historic January day, thinking about the future. Our only accounts were Burlington Industries and a home-furnishings project for Sears. Not bad, but not enough to compensate for the high overhead. Our first batch of mail was a pile of bills for office furniture, movers, and telephone installers. Our bank balance was low and the nation's economy was not in good shape, but we had an office, two telephone lines, a lawyer, an accountant, and a charge account at the office stationery store. Our hopes were high. We were in business, precariously financed but nevertheless *free*.

It's ironic that the profession most in need of good public relations today is the public-relations business itself. No one outside the field really understands it, and thanks to Watergate and Presidential public relations in the early seventies, it has become synonymous with deceit and dirty tricks. The term "public relations" has been so maligned, in fact, that many companies have changed the name to "corporate communications" or "marketing communications." Our little company, however, will stick with the name. We will continue to call ourselves what we are, public-relations consultants. The word "consultant" sounds rather impressive to some, if not also rather vague. In actual fact, "consultant" as we use it means that we are saddled with all the dirty work on a project, including a great deal of work that should be our client's responsibility.

It is true, sadly enough, that certain con men cover up their activities with the title "public relations" to give their operations some class. They remind me of a Broadway massage parlor, staffed by prostitutes, calling itself a "physical-fitness salon." Cheap press-agent tactics do not help the profession, either. They feed items about their clients to columnists in the hopes that something like the following will result: "Actress _____'s cleavage finally escaped from her low-cut dress, just as the patrons ringside at Morocco hoped that it would. The flustered star tucked everything back into place, recovering her composure enough to tell ringsiders she hoped they wouldn't forget to go see her new film, _____."

A lot of people think that public-relations professionals spend all their time lunching in expensive restaurants, discussing confidential matters. I would certainly like to find a client who would pay for those expensive lunches with me. I consider myself lucky to be offered a cup of coffee in their offices.

One of the most lucrative areas of specialization in this field is that of financial public relations. These specialists (and they are almost always men) spend a lot of time with security analysts; they write speeches, prepare annual reports, and feed story ideas to the editors of financial publications, as well as to the financial editors of the daily newspapers. Their efforts are intended to create a better image for the company they represent or to assist in raising the value of the stock, though there are many other possible affirmative side effects.

When we had been in business about a year, a good friend of mine, Bill Salomon, the head of prestigious Salomon Brothers, felt that we should try for a financial account. He recommended us to a very conservative blue-chip investment-banking house, which was about to hire its first PR firm. One of the partners made an appointment to see me, and I rushed to prepare myself for the interview. After three days of research at the New York Public Library, I found out that this company's name had hardly even been mentioned in the press at all. An economics student from New York University, who was also working in the library, heard me muttering and complaining in my corner of the big table. In a fit of compassion he decided to lend me a hand. After a thorough search of the microfilm files, he came up with two small mentions of the Wall Street firm.

"Man," he whispered, looking at me rather sceptically, "they really *do* need some PR help. But—er—excuse me, are *you* really trying to land the account?" He had obviously not heard of the Emancipation of Women.

Finally the day came when the financial wizards made their visit to our office. We embarked on a crash cleanup, putting everything to rights and misplacing half our files in the process. We hid all our women's magazines, which we study carefully each month, and littered the area with issues of *Forbes, The Wall Street Journal, Fortune, Barron's, Money, Dun's Review,* and financial publications we had never even heard of, borrowing them from offices all over the building. I doubt that the president of the New York Stock Exchange could boast the library of publications we had ready and waiting that day.

A managing partner of the firm and an earnest young Harvard Business School graduate arrived punctually for our morning meeting. The moment they crossed our threshold, I knew that all was lost. They took one look at our bright red, yellow, orange, green, and blue environment full of bold graphics, and they winced perceptibly. They took in our giant floor-to-ceiling three-paneled screen, covered with a print of large, prancing leopards, and they shuddered. They sat down by my desk briefly, showing discomfort in every movement. They could hardly wait to flee and return to the brown leather, mahogany-paneled confines of their own conservative world. This had only been a token visit, anyway. We were, after all, women. But we could have done a good job for them. Given a little time to learn their business and their lingo, we could have given them a whole fresh new look.

I often see that company's name in print now; the male PR firm they hired is doing a good job for them. But we will let our women's magazines stay where they are in the future. We will be us. We will manage to have *The Wall Street Journal, Fortune,* and many of the other financial publications tucked in there every month, but we will still be us. Love us for our sense of fashion, our interior-design and product knowledge, and our understanding of the consumer. Love us for ourselves.

Industrial PR professionals are yet another breed of cat. They try to spread information about their company's new products to the trade. They work on plant labor relations and relations within the community where the plants are based. Many of these departments write and publish "house organs," newspapers or journals that are an effective means of improving communication between management and employees. Many also write their companies' annual reports.

In spite of the diversity of responsibility, everyone in

the field works to improve his company's or his client's image, and this can entail anything from arranging to have the boss invited to speak at an important gathering which the press will cover to promoting a plan that will reduce the pollution of the town's rivers from the plant's waste-disposal system. A public-relations person may handle a company's prompt donation of food and supplies to a disaster-struck area, or arrange to have the town's high-school choir sent abroad on a summer European tour.

Fashion publicists feed photographs and story ideas on the designers' latest collections to newspapers, magazines, and television. (I managed to place a rather impossible collection of furniture in a wire-service photograph by photographing a model wearing a famous designer's dress next to the table and chairs.) Home-furnishings specialists take photographs of room settings that use the client's furniture, rugs, draperies, lamps, or whatever, but they are also intended to teach decorating tricks to the consumer. Food specialists and home economists employed by the food industry relay recipes, menus, and nutrition information to women's editors. Some publicists scratch pretty hard to get their client's product a free play in the press, and sometimes they incur the wrath of feminists by their sexist approach. A publicist for a lawn-mower company will take a picture of the new model power mower with a voluptuous bikini-clad girl in the driver's seat. He sends it into the business editor of the local newspaper, who includes it in tomorrow morning's paper because the cheesecake appeals to him. (What he's forgetting, of course, is that nowadays women read the financial page, too, and that a lot of them are disgusted to find that the major feature of the lawn mower is the size of the chest of the girl astride it.)

Generally speaking, photographs and releases will be published if they are timely, lively, and accurate, and if they are educational, newsworthy, or full of human interest. A photograph must be well made and tell its story clearly without confusing the reader. I was asked once by a Chicago toy company to publicize a new set of children's alphabetical blocks. My "clever" idea was to put the blocks in the form of a giant scrabble game and photograph them. The women's editor sent back the picture by return mail with a note saying, "Tish, I asked every editor on this newspaper, including the sports editor and the obit writer, if they knew what the hell this picture was all about. . . . Negative."

It took many years of experience for me to learn that if one has a very unexciting product—such as a set of colored table linens—one can get them into the paper by taking a picture of them with something else that is more photogenic. No editor will use a photograph of a pile of place mats and napkins, but when I set a Fourth of July party table with those linens, utilizing a centerpiece of popcorn balls decorated with tiny paper American flags, the editor ran the picture on half the page because she liked the corny centerpiece idea. She also gave my popcorn-balls recipe to her readers and credited the store carrying the linens and the manufacturer.

I also had to learn that in order to do a proper Fourth of July picture and get it to the papers on time, I had to plan it far ahead, in the dead of winter. The mass mailing of a picture story to newspapers all over the country takes time—time to get the photographs retouched, duplicates made, prints captioned, and press releases assembled; time to type up all the labels with editors' names and addresses, to stuff each envelope with a stiffener to protect the photograph, to stamp, seal, and mail them. An editor needs the picture and the story about six weeks ahead of the holiday in order to work it in with her other commitments. So we do our Christmas photography in July and "think Easter" at Thanksgiving. I jot personal notes on the releases to editor friends all over the country, and those notes guarantee that they will at least read the release. They may still file it in the wastebasket, but at least they will have read it.

Advertising agencies don't have to guess or hope their material will be published because they pay for its placement and they know exactly when and how their client's message will be presented to the public. But public-relations people do not pay editors to have their material used, and in fact, we can't even send Christmas presents to editor friends, for fear of having the newspaper management consider it bribery. We must use our own creativity to make our stories desirable to the editor, and once the story is handed over to the newspaper or magazine, we start to pray.

Everyone has unmentionably bad luck at times. The worst luck of all is having one's story used without a credit line being given to one's client. One has taken all that time, labored long and hard over the story—and there it is, in living color, without so much as a mention of the product that inspired it all and paid for it all. I will never forget working over a hundred hours on a table-setting story for a breakfast-cereals company. I hired designers to design a series of stunning breakfast settings. The photographs were published all over the country without one single mention of the oatmeal and dry cereals produced by my client.

In actual fact, there is precious little space given over to free publicity in newspapers, what with the newsprint shortage, and all public-relations firms are in competition for that same little space, and for those precious slots on television shows. At Christmastime, editors are literally deluged with press releases on every company's "Christmas Gift Ideas," but the release that contains something a little unusual or informative (such as "Make it now in June for his Christmas" or "Give a Christmas party for less than $25") has a better chance of being used than a release that promotes only the product.

There is just one thing certain in public relations: the only successful practitioners are those who have complete integrity in their work. The successful ones are truthful. They may tell a story with imagination, but they never lie about the product, company, or person they represent. Overexaggeration and untruths can spell disaster for everyone concerned. One loses the good contacts with the press that one has spent years building up. When credibility is gone, it's gone for good in our business. Good public relations in our era of consumerism means truthful information that is given quickly, accurately, and maybe even with a little pizzazz.

Ours is a pressured business, requiring a strong constitution and a set of adrenal glands in good working order. I wrote a twenty-minute film script in two days and an hour-long decorating lecture in three hours, simply because there was no other choice. Adrenalin must have been the answer.

The disappointments are always with us in our profession, too. For example, we designed a fancy audio-visual show for Elizabeth Arden's Fifth Avenue window, only to discover it was all for naught. There was much too much sunlight showing in or reflected back into the windows for anyone to be able to see the slide show properly.

Months of work have gone similarly down the drain because of a newspaper strike occurring just when the scheduled event, the fruit of our labor, takes place. A news blackout means no crowds, no press, just failure in all of its starkness.

To have the client forced into a cancellation of a carefully constructed project is just as heartbreaking. We worked for months on the opening of Carborundum's new Museum of Ceramics. I made a couple of trips to Niagara Falls in winter snowstorms while Bob Quayle and I formulated plans for the greatest bang-up opening ever with the "beautiful people" in attendance. I evolved a plan of inviting as honored guests, and as our drawing card, the ambassadors from every country where Carborundum had a plant. This meant that every major country in the world would be represented. We invited them, with their families, to experience a real American tourist dream for two days. A charter plane was to pick them up in Washington and whisk them to Niagara Falls. Baby-sitters were arranged to take care of ambassadorial small fry in the evening. Young guides were chosen to take the teen-agers in hand at nighttime. The ambassadors and their wives, in the meantime, were to be wined and dined in royal fashion at dinner on tables spread with specially designed linens; lilies-of-the-valley in clay pots; the most elegant of silver, porcelain, and crystal. Mrs. Kasavubu, an architectural designer, was to stretch hundreds of yards of white nylon fabric in sweeping curves all over the ceiling and walls of the unfinished concrete section of the new Carborundum building, where the dinner was to be held. She even devised an ingenious "fruit being consumed" effect. A colored slide of a bowl of fruit would be projected on a large portion of a wall during the dinner. The slide would change once every fifteen minutes or so, unnoticeably. Gradually, during the course of the meal, the bowl of fruit would be eaten away, until finally, after the demitasse hour, there would be a projection on the wall of only the remaining pits, stones, and cores of the fruit—a subtle reminder that the evening was over, and that it was time to go home.

I persuaded an old friend, Acting Chief of Protocol Joe Smoak, to lend us his official support and that of the State Department. He was going to bring his wife and daughter along. The ambassadors were enchanted to be able to see "something so typically American as Niagara Falls." The press was excited, too. They were coming en masse—

society, fashion editors, travel editors, art editors. We scheduled a trip to Fort Niagara for everyone so as to include a little Indian-wars history for our diplomats. Bob Quayle arranged for the traditional trip around the Falls on the *Maid of the Mist* boat. We signed up photographers to take pictures of each family by the Falls, which we would then transmit to all of their countries' local newspapers through our United States Information Service. Tourism in Niagara Falls would be aided. Attendance at the museum would be aided. Good will for the Carborundum plants abroad would be aided. We would photograph each ambassador standing by his country's porcelain objects on loan to the Museum of Ceramics, to help the cause of culture and international relations along. It was all too beautiful. It was the perfect public-relations event. I was very proud that my ideas had come to fruition because of past government experience and contacts in Washington. Only Letitia Baldrige Enterprises could have put it all together.

It was cancelled a couple of weeks before it was to have taken place. The museum was simply not ready to open, and Carborumdum did not want to have a public-relations backfire. Several weeks later, when the museum was in perfect operating condition, all of our ambassadorial invitees had already returned to their home countries for summer vacations.

The museum received excellent notices from the art editors, and Niagara Falls is a very interesting place to visit. But just think of all that lovely fruit that was to be eaten away, bit by bit, projected on the wall during dinner. A pity.

Giant public-relations firms tend to attract giant corporations as their clients. Their size and their well-established reputations make them "safe" to deal with, since a corporation has an understandable (although chicken-hearted) feeling that if they are going to undertake so misunderstood a service as public relations, they might as well associate themselves with a large, prestigious firm. They feel they can thus more easily defend their actions before the stockholders if someone complains about expenses. All of this means that the man or woman who heads up a small firm like mine has to hustle twice as hard to land the accounts. I would become extremely depressed if I were to count up the number of times I've had an idea and have sent proposals to companies making everything from soap to beer. The recipient always refuses to consider the project, though one has the feeling the proposal is never discarded but simply turned over to someone in the company with a scribbled suggestion, "Why don't we try something along these lines some day?" By the time they've "tried" it, of course, the originator of the idea has been long forgotten. In fact, the stupidest thing a public-relations firm can do is to give away its secrets and ideas, but we do it all the time. We become enthusiastic about an idea, and it simply has to be communicated, even when no one asks us to. We are constantly jumping on "targets of opportunity," as they are called, and just as constantly, failure meets our efforts. It's like coming down from a high jump on the trampoline and missing it.

When Bobby Fischer and the Russian chess master Boris Spassky were making great news with their chess competition in 1973, we contacted the United States Chess Federation, gained their support, and drew up a proposal for the biggest international chess tournament ever staged —to be held at the Waldorf Astoria with closed-circuit television. The sponsor was to be either a cookie manufacturer or a soft-drink company. The bisquit company was to package cookies shaped like chessmen and include a cardboard chessboard on the sides of the cookie box. The soft-drink company, were it to be the sponsor, was to package the chessboard in the bottom of the eight-pack. The chess figures would be stamped on bottle caps. History has been spared such a promotion. There were no takers.

Undaunted by defeat, when Olga Korbut, the Russian gymnast, became the darling of the world during the Munich Olympics in 1974, we rushed to several big food companies with a forty-page plan utilizing Olga's personal appearances in the United States for the sponsor, and then establishing a series of street demonstrations of young, trained gymnasts, who would work with the kids in the ghettos and crowded urban areas in summer. They would hand out nutrition and exercise brochures, utilizing the food companies' products.

Although we never found a corporate listener for any of these projects, we continue to work them up, as they are excellent brain gymnastics in themselves. They also make good training in moving fast in relation to world events. The giant public-relations firms with rosters of large corporate clients are the ones who are called in by a large company to come up with an idea to help that company's image on a national basis. They are therefore assigned the task. We come up with the idea and then search for the sponsor, which doesn't work. By remaining small, we are thus penalized, but we frankly cherish our independence. Every time I feel depressed about this situation, I call up a friend in one of the superagencies and make a lunch date. That lunch conversation is the only therapy I need to remind myself of *our* advantages.

For every major disappointment, there always comes along something to compensate for it. In January 1974 Phyllis Flood of the Push-Pin Graphics Studio recommended our firm to Roger Horchow, the head of a luxury mail-order company in Texas. Roger wanted to change the name of the company from The Kenton Collection to The Horchow Collection, and along with it, he wanted increased sales.

I met him for lunch at twelve-thirty in the Oak Room of the Plaza Hotel to present my ideas, and by two-thirty our "Letter of Agreement" had been drafted in my office. The speed with which Roger Horchow moved that day was typical of the speed with which he always moves, and one of the reasons he has become such a fantastic success.

His big Dallas operation is very relaxed. Everyone works in blue jeans; the staff and their children often pose as the models in the catalogue pictures. Caroline Horchow often works with her husband but is home when the children return from school. Endless carloads of merchandise keep arriving from all over the world, delivering one-of-a-kind objects along with the eight-thousand-of-a-kind objects. Roger Horchow seems to have a kind of computer in his head telling him to order so many sets of silver coffee spoons from Egypt for hostesses and so many Hero Helmets for little boys' Christmases. In one London neighborhood he might buy a Coromandel screen to sell for $60,000 and five thousand boxes of English soaps to sell for $4.50 each. The public relations for such a merchant can entail anything from getting a story on him in *Fortune* magazine to placing his merchandise in the shopping columns of *Seventeen, Playboy,* or *Vogue.*

Sometimes it takes literally years to land a client. It took me three years of letter-writing and telephoning to Norbert Considine, vice-president of Blue Bell, Inc., to convince him we could be of good use to his giant apparel firm. Finally, he called me in.

The project he wanted to discuss was blue jeans, a garment I have resisted wearing since I saw the backside of myself in the mirror on graduation day from college. These weren't ordinary blue jeans, however. Their fabric was 100 per cent cotton denim treated with liquid ammonia to make them wrinkle-proof and less than 1 per cent shrinkable. I went to work for the Sedgefield division of the company the next day. It is easier to be an advertising agency for a new product than it is to be the public-relations agency. An advertiser concentrates on the product, but we have to concentrate on promoting all around it, disguising it in "editorial information."

Therefore, the basis of my promotion campaign was to feature a group of five specially trained, attractive "Miss Sedgefield" spokeswomen, who would visit major cities, appear on local TV and radio talk shows, and make department-store appearances to talk to the customers about "Sedgefield Do-Nothing Jeans and Jackets."

We soon discovered we had taken on a job big enough to keep a very large agency in a swivel for a year. Four of us did it by working seven-day weeks for a few months. We did all our photography on weekends, because we couldn't afford to be away from a battery of telephones during the week while the Miss Sedgefields' schedules were being arranged across the country. We spent a day in Connecticut, photographing twenty-eight talented, attractive kids, ages eight to seventeen, performing fantastic gymnastics at the West Hartford Gym Club—tumbling, somersaulting, balancing on the beam, working out on the rings, jumping on the trampoline—all wearing jeans and T-shirts.

We photographed fashion models wearing the jeans with different tops and accessories. Our apartment was used as a background, and even the dog got into the act. One photo of a model kissing an appreciative doggy—Dustin— made the newspapers solely, we're convinced, because of Dustin's appeal. In another sequence, a young couple was cooking spaghetti in our kitchen. Thinking ahead of our family menu-wise, I had the models actually cook a pound of spaghetti for me while Bernard Vidal clicked his lens. That spaghetti, which was tested and tasted with giant wooden spoons in the final picture, was the same that fed the Hollensteiners at a large family meal that evening. I don't believe in wasting food—or time for that matter. (I reheated the pasta *al dente* in a double boiler with defrosted frozen sauce thrown in for good measure.)

At the height of the action on the Sedgefield project the telephones were ringing off their hooks as we talked to a hundred stores each week. The floors of our offices looked like a set of confused litter, but, in actuality, it was our complicated system for assembling five hundred press lists of three different sets of material, with personal notes written on two hundred of them. In the midst of this morass of captioned photographs, releases, brochures, and mailing materials, we were also training the Miss Sedgefields for their city tours. An important client walked in unannounced and saw me in the middle of the room, clutching a broom enthusiastically by the handle, giving forth with an oration. I did not see him, and he retreated with relief. He laughingly reported to me later that he first thought I was a member of a witch's coven, since he saw me with a broom, surrounded by five young women seated in a perfect circle and listening attentively.

A large PR agency would have its own fancy screening room, with audio-visual equipment, projectors, microphones, podiums, and the like. Our small agency cannot afford such luxuries. We just know what to do in front of a TV camera. (David must take a shot at Goliath every once in a while.)

I now wear jeans again on weekends. I keep threatening R.H. that I will have entwining hearts sewn on the side seams of both our jeans to make them "His and Hers." His answer is that if I begin practicing at home what I preach in my office during the day, I can start looking for another "Him."

We are often called upon to do one-shot short-term projects, which inevitably require as much time and effort as the larger continuing jobs. Each one, however, takes us into yet a new group of press people, and we acquire a new set of knowledge about our fair city. We have handled painters and sculptors, benefits, politicians, and designers of every kind. Handling the press for a benefit like the dinner at the Pierre when the first MacDowell Colony Medal for the Dance was awarded to Martha Graham was doubly satisfying. We got a lot of publicity, and having been a MacDowell Fellow myself, in that magnificent four-hundred-acre wooded retreat in New Hampshire, was one of the greatest things that ever happened to me. The Mac-Dowell Colony is a nonprofit haven for people representing all the arts—sculpture, music, painting, writing, film, printmaking, and the like. One is given a small, secluded cabin in the woods where catching one's muse is easy. I can write more in that private, undisturbed world in two weeks than I can in snatching writing weekends at home during a three-year period. Lunch is dropped at the doorstep of one's cabin at noontime, beautifully packed in a wicker basket. At home, on weekends, I am cooking it for everyone else. At the MacDowell Colony, if a Fellow can't pay anything for his room and board, he doesn't. He shares the privacy and the stimulation of the Leonard Bernsteins, Aaron Coplands, Russell Lyneses, and other geniuses of our world who are Fellows in Residence, too.

Handling benefits for no money at all is fiscally dangerous for my business, but it has its compensations. When the late ambassador to England Lewis Douglas, a longtime friend of my family's, called to say, "We are counting on you, dear Tish, to do the publicity for the *Young Winston* movie première and a supper for the benefit of my Winston Churchill Foundation," there was no way in which I could refuse him. When he was ambassador, he had arranged to have me presented to the Queen at court, along with his daughter Sharman. While we were working on the benefit, my office had to refuse a three-months' project that would have brought us eight thousand dollars. That hurt.

We were glad that the Winston Churchill Foundation made a lot of money that night, though the only thing we really got out of it was the correct way to organize a receiving line that includes Their Royal Highnesses the Duke and Duchess of Kent. However, one never knows when Mayor Beame's office might call me up and want to know just that. The real reason I took on that task, of course, was a sense of appreciation for the greatness of a man like Lew Douglas, one of the eminent statesmen of our time.

We are constantly working without compensation on endless benefits for my old schools and for my children's schools. But all working mothers do this. The nonworking mothers organize the benefits; their working colleagues supply the frosting for the cake. Suzanne Flynn, beauty editor of *Seventeen,* goes after the beauty industry for donations to the Convent of the Sacred Heart Auction; Erica Wilson donates canvases and needlework lessons to her children's Spence School fund-raisers; Gloria Vanderbilt Cooper donates collages and textiles she has designed to Dalton School benefits.

We are certainly overbenefited in my office—maybe it makes us all feel good inside, but if it continues, we will eventually have to work on the toughest benefit of all, one for Letitia Baldrige Enterprises, Inc.

One day, New York University came to us to ask for assistance with the dedication of its new library which Elmer Holmes Bobst, the octogenarian "vitamin king," had given to the university. The Philip Johnson–designed red-sandstone building, the largest open-stack library in the world, sprang up like a giant on a corner of historic Washington Square. It had been a core of controversy since it had been announced. Some people thought it was wasteful; others argued it was not in keeping with the architectural harmony of Washington Square. Some said it was too modern; others that it was too classical. The building was ready to be dedicated in December 1972, and Julie Eisenhower was to come from Washington to read the President's speech. The university retained us to help get national coverage of the event. Their public-relations department was easy to work with and we divided our responsibilities in a clear-cut manner. They were to handle the local and educational press; we were to handle special magazine coverage, social press, special out-of-town stories (such as in Philadelphia, where Elmer Bobst had once been a pharmaceutical clerk), and protocol details. When I met the advance team for Julie Eisenhower from the White House in order to go over each step of her program and her movements, I sat back in my chair and felt a touch of irony, remembering all the times I had done just this very thing, in all corners of the world, for Jacqueline Kennedy.

Thousands of people, distinguished guests and students alike, filled the great hall of the library, and the ceremonies were very impressive. To help liven up the reception after the dedication, I had ordered a large cake from a pastry chef which was to be a replica of the library. The cake arrived an hour before Julie Eisenhower and Elmer Bobst were to cut into it and, to my horror, I saw that the dark-red-stone library had become the color of pink toothpaste. The cake seemed to be made of cardboard, with the windows outlined in pencil. It looked terrible—so I raced through the crowds to find Philip Johnson and soothe his anger in advance.

"Don't hate me," I pleaded.

"Your press release says the cake is the exact facsimile of the building's exterior," he said smiling.

"You will throw up when you see it," I replied.

He laughed, for which I was grateful, and assured me it would be all right, though the color did drain from his face during the cake-cutting.

Fortunately, it looked fine on television. And one of the camera crew did say to me, "I'm glad you had that cake. It gave us some action, which is pretty hard to come by at ceremonies like these. But no one will have to eat the awful-looking thing, will they?"

I believe that the diversity of what we do every day is the key to the high level of enthusiasm around the office.

In the same afternoon we can all be working on a newspaper story of Enzo's coiffures for the holiday season, planning a Philippines food story (promoting the Manila Hotel) with a magazine, arranging for Roger Horchow to be interviewed by *Women's Wear Daily,* and making arrangements for a press party to launch a new line of fabrics for Inger McCabe Elliott's China Seas company. At times like these, we press the button to summon our free-lance talent pool, which includes Evelyn Clark, Mary Eager, and Ruth Ann McKeown—all experts in their fields. As business comes in, we adapt and expand. When Jane Stark moved to Spain, we lost a vice-president but gained a European representative. Madeline Zuckerman, who had begun as my secretary and had worked her way up to vice-president and office manager, suddenly had to move to California with her husband, because of his job change. It was a day of mourning for all of us, and it pointed up quite dramatically the dilemma of husband and wife with separate careers. The strongest kind of friendships result from working together ten hours a day. The office is after all a large part of our lives, and we seem to share all our personal problems along with our business ones. A courageous man and a travel expert, Steve Lamb, finally joined us, and was immediately christened our "lamb in the den of lionesses." He could write his own book now, I guess, about women executives. When Rosemary Sheehan came over from Burlington, and Pat Beard from Wamsutta, to join me as associates, the team grew stronger yet. These two were well-known and respected experts in the fields of fashion and home furnishings.

A small firm such as ours is buffeted by the problems of the economy far more than the big firms are. We have lived "close to the vest" when there were no fat profits at the end of the year to fall back on. When a large account moves away from us, we do not survive just by firing members of the staff, as large advertising agencies are forced to do. Our entire staff is so small and so involved in the handling of all our accounts that everyone is indispensable. Therefore, we all take a salary cut until the account is replaced and work extra time looking for new business. Somehow, we always manage to survive, because we have *the will* to survive. In the day and age when small businesses seem to be failing right and left, the determined ones do manage to hang on. Another account is always around the corner.

The woman who heads her own business and who has a family is fortunate in many ways. I have loving ears to receive my messages of complaint and I get advice from two different generations. R.H. and the children, whether they like it or not, hear all my problems articulated in full. I never underplay it; I always overdramatize it. R.H. then supplies some comforting words, and the children add solace with their "It will all be better, Mommie," much as they would pat and comfort a sick dog. And that is all I need.

Clare is a potential businesswoman. There is no way she can grow up in our household without being influenced toward a working career. One day she sat down at her bedroom desk, pushed aside her French homework, and wrote me a memo. She was seven at the time.

"Dear Mommie,
    I think you need more clients. I will give you a list of the ones you need: Ivory Snow, Woolite, Lux, Miss Clairol, Prell, VO$_5$ Hair Spray, and Topps Chewing Gum.

                                             Love,
                                             Clare."

One can tell she is a very clean person. One can also tell the power of TV commercials, since we have only three of those products in our home.

Perhaps Clare was prophetic, because Bruce Gelb, the head of Clairol, retained us the next year to help with the national CBS telecast, "Women of the Year," sponsored by Clairol. The awards part of the operation was handled by the *Ladies' Home Journal,* and the ceremony was to be broadcast live from Avery Fisher Hall in Lincoln Center, which holds well over three thousand people. Another PR firm was to handle the TV critics and the TV pages in the newspapers, but our job was to fill the hall and to attract good national coverage and to worry about all the rest of the press. Clairol went along with our plan for inviting TV hostesses from around the country to attend as honored guests. We would also arrange for each of them to tape themselves separately with some of the "Women of the Year" honorees, which they could then show on their own home stations when they returned. We also invited some of the top newswomen in the country to attend as honored guests. They, of course, would cover the proceedings, too. The "Woman of the Year" the TV women most wanted to talk to was, of course, Barbara Walters. She represented the epitome of everything they wished to become. When she came to the Plaza Gold and White Suite for the press conference, she had appeared on the "Today Show" for two hours, had then taped two "Not for Women Only" shows, and was about to face our half-hour press conference, followed by four additional taped interviews in our makeshift television studio upstairs. After that, she would have to go into rehearsal at Avery Fisher Hall for several hours to prepare for the evening's live telecast.

She is a trooper. She kept her cool, was polite to everyone, answered the same questions graciously. At the end of that April day, she had been "on camera" a total of seven hours, in five different costume changes.

Another trooper is Billie Jean King, who also patiently

answered identical questions time and time again. I had always considered her to be rather abrupt, a tomboy, lacking in graciousness. Quite the contrary. Her sense of humor is delightful. She is exceedingly pretty, with a delicate pink-and-white complexion, shining eyes, lustrous hair, and she wore a pale pink angora sweater and skirt that made her look like everyone's favorite college girl dressed up for a Saturday date.

Our firm had labored under severe handicaps in getting the final guest list compiled, approved, and typed up on invitation envelopes. We researched every VIP in New York, from ballet stars to labor-union bosses. We knew we had stiff competition for that April evening; Frank Sinatra was giving his first concert at Carnegie Hall the same hour. The final count of invitations in the mail was five thousand, addressed to every state in the union. To add to the confusion, there was a dinner beforehand for certain people, so two types of invitations had to be issued.

I wrote up a fifteen-page master battle plan for the day, beginning with the first press conference at nine in the morning, and ending up at midnight when we hoped to clear out the last guest from the post-telecast reception in Avery Fisher Hall. I wrote detailed instructions to our "Clairol helpers" and to the Avery Fisher Hall ushers, detailing what to do and whom to find in case of a fist fight, a loud drunk, a fainting, or an accident of some kind. With that many people, anything could happen.

We had been in daily contact with the mayor's office (His Honor was co-host of the event). The Diplomatic Corps called constantly. A sample call was from an African embassy: "And just why are women being honored and not men?" We even had to handle telephone calls from the "Women of the Year" who lived out of town and who needed hair appointments. My staff's nerves were raw and none of us could sleep at night from exhaustion. We passed the Vitamin C bottle from desk to desk; everyone was sternly warned she could not possibly become ill until after the telecast.

The Clairol staff and the management of Avery Fisher Hall were magnificent in the handling of the hordes of people that evening. We had a good walkie-talkie system in operation between floors of the huge theater. Several groups of women whose requests for tickets had not been honored because they did not meet the ticket deadline came anyway. They were all dressed up, and had taken great pains to look well. We asked them to wait in the corners of the lobby until the very last minute, when the telecast was about to begin. Then, with the help of the walkie-talkie, we sent them to be seated in the "no-show" seats.

The big hall was filled. Our firm had gotten top newspapers from all over the country to be here tonight for this telecast. We had first-rate television coverage guaranteed, with our women hostesses all able to return home on the morrow with good tapes in their suitcases. I slunk down into a seat in the rear, behind large camera equipment. I could not even see the stage. For one hour that was fine. I slept—the first deep sleep I had had in several weeks. It was just fine.

Handling a public relations project of some importance in a foreign country is a challenge of the highest order, but when that country is English-speaking as the Philippines are, everything is much easier.

Benigno Toda, Jr., the multi-lingual international financier who is president of Philippine Airlines, hired our company to do the public relations for a hotel in Manila— the landmark Manila Hotel, which had been the center of the city's social life since the early 1900s. It had fallen into disrepair and was now to be restored to its original historic state, as well to be greatly enlarged. Among the others whom management consultants Harris, Kerr, Chervenak & Co. put together for "Beni" Toda as the hotel team, were design award–winning Leandro Locsin (the Filipino architect who won acclaim for such buildings as the Cultural Center in Manila); Dale Keller and wife Patricia (famous hotel interior specialists who work as a team all over the world); George Lang, the international food expert; and Earl Blackwell, party-giver extraordinaire, who was signed on to organize the international jet set for the Manila Hotel opening.

A business trip to the Philippines is like winning the charity raffle grand prize of an "all-expenses-paid, two-weeks luxury vacation." One minute I am tramping around in the wet cement, wearing my yellow hard hat at the construction site, and the next I am checking the tourists' tours and restaurants or picking out *ternos* for our American press parties (*ternos* are the graceful national party dresses, with butterfly sleeves and low, scooped necklines, like those always worn by President Marcos' wife). The hours pass in a fast tempo of smiles and new sensations to enjoy. Since the American participation in the Pacific in World War II is graphically memorialized in the Philippines by the big guns left behind at Corregidor and by the bodies left behind in the enormous American Military Cemetery, I find myself fighting back the tears in such places, without success.

There are many things I like about this country, including the handsome people, the fruits, baskets, seashells and the "jeepneys." Jeepneys are a very amusing and colorful mode of transport in Manila. The Filipino government bought thousands of surplus jeeps from the U.S. military at the end of the war, and converted them into passenger-carrying vehicles by installing two benches on the sides in back. Now the vehicles are manufactured locally. Meant to hold about eight people, they usually hold about twelve, causing an unraveling of bodies at jeepney stops not unlike that of the circus clowns who emerge en masse from a very small car. The entire surface of a jeepney is painted with bright, multicolored designs; a conspicuously large radiator ornament, often a shiny silver horse, glitters in the sunshine. (The designer of the Rolls Royce would roll over in his grave.) Jeepneys jiggle with colored fringe, tinkle with bells, and bear such signs as "Jose's Delight" and "Jaime's Sweetie-Pie." Even the windshield is often bordered with hand-painted designs. The vehicles go racing by, each one looking like a jazz finale in a Fourth of July fireworks display. My ambition is to be the first to drive one up Park Avenue.

I cope with my jet lag problems in flying out to the Philippines from New York by stopping off in Honolulu for twenty-four hours, both going and coming, at Clare Luce's beautiful home. I know I am always welcome in the guestroom, provided that the constant stream of Clare's other jet lag–coping guests like Henry Kissinger and the Bill Buckleys, aren't already ensconced.

Once in the Philippines, if I'm lucky, I can spend my weekends on Beni Toda's private tropical island northwest of Manila, on the China Sea. One flies to "Ermana Mayor" in one of Beni's private planes over two more reminders of World War II: Subic Bay and Clark Air Force Base. One is met at the airstrip by a smiling islander in a jeep and taken up to the main house. All of the rooms in the big house open out to the sea on one side or to a velvety green golf course on the other. The stunning floors are made of shiny bamboo rods, placed in a kind of herringbone pattern. The walls and ceilings are made of natural woven straw mats, held in place by squares of narrow wooden slats. All of the furniture is made of natural materials from the country— rattan, cane, wicker, and bamboo. All of the decorative accessories come from Mother Nature, too—ashtrays and boxes of local woods, giant clam shells sitting on driftwood bases that are used as planters, mother-of-pearl serving bowls, and things made of tortoise shell. Baskets are utilized for everything—from tiny ones to store saccharine at the breakfast table to giant ones swung on trees with ropes, holding fresh towels for beach use. The big house and the guesthouse are cooled by old-fashioned three-blade electric ceiling fans, just like in a Humphrey Bogart movie. The shell-laden white beaches surrounding the island melt into a blue-green water that is absolutely remarkable in color. The beach house, boat house and islanders' homes are made of thatched grass and matting, again with bamboo floors. I visited some of the islanders in their little houses on stilts (each family has a member working for Beni). Their houses are much cleaner than mine, but then again, so is their air.

At times my conscience hurts me on these weekends. I am not working or caring for my family. I am simply playing. So I begin to "work" a little, by industriously teaching other guests how to play the game my friend Roger Tuckerman invented, called "Counterstrike." I talk another porcelain bird enthusiast into purchasing an Edward Marshall Boehm bird to add to his collection; then I pass out several copies of Roger Horchow's Christmas catalogue, much to the amazement and pleasure of the guests from Hong Kong ("the shopping center of the world"), who have never seen a luxury mail-order operation before.

Every night we watch a movie, sitting with our drinks, slouched in comfortable easy chairs on the porch. The huge screen is out on the lawn. Some drive-in movie! And when I walk to the other side of the house, I can look out at the sea, with the tiny lights of the fishermen's boats from Santa Cruz rimming the dark horizon. I hear the gentle murmurs of the palm trees that sound like a rustling of silken skirts. That's when I wonder why in hell Robert Hollensteiner is never with me at a moment like this.

4
The Home

If there is one area where I constantly drown myself in self-pity, it's in running the home. My idea of paradise is to live in a house decorated by me but maintained by a push-button army that operates in my absence—washing, fixing, running all errands, cooking, and cleaning up according to my written orders. I would still want to call the shots on what is to be done, but I would like not to have to execute *any* of it or be present while it is being done.

My biggest *bête noire* is marketing. Marketing in New York is the most masochistic activity one can undertake. Because of the lack of city space, aisles in the markets are hardly wide enough for one market cart if a single object from that cart protrudes from the side by an inch. Head-on collisions are commonplace, accompanied by all manner of spoken and unspoken expletives, masked by an occasional "sorry." The checkout lines are always long and exhausting, because I can go only in the evenings around six or on Saturdays. I vent my wrath to anyone within earshot on having to spend so much money in such discomfort at the end of such a day. My neighbors agree enthusiastically, are too bored to react, or simply look terrified, as though they felt that at any minute I was going to start throwing Molotov cocktails. Sometimes I get my trade-paper reading done while standing in line, but those calm and useful minutes are few.

One night I was particularly pressed to get home. The supermarket was crowded, and I was exceptionally short of patience. The place was jammed with working people, but there were also many older, retired persons and some nonworking young mothers hanging on to tired children. The traffic jam at the checkout counters grew worse, and after I had waited twenty minutes without reaching the finish line, I delivered an impromptu speech—loud and clear—which carried to all five checkout lines.

"It's plain to see," I proclaimed in my most arrogant Roman proconsul manner, "that many of the people here tonight do *not* go to work and do *not* have to be shopping in the middle of the evening rush hour. I think it would be a lot nicer for EVERYONE if those who could did their shopping during the day when there is hardly anyone here."

An old woman in front of me turned around and answered sharply. "You've made your statement," she said, "so now I'll make mine. I happen to live in a walkup—the kind I'm sure *you*'ll never have to see in your whole life. I don't see no one all day. I'm lonely. If I choose to come here when there are people, people who have been doing things, then that's my business. No one like you is going to tell me not to come. I have just as much right to listen to some normal conversation as *you* do."

"I'm sorry," I said softly. And I was. I have not made any speeches lately at the supermarket, but have learned to take out my frustrations by stamping on empty milk cartons instead.

At times I long for the good old days in New York when

I was single and when my total grocery bill came to roughly seven dollars a week (mostly breakfast items). Now, because of a large household full of constantly hungry people coming and going, my food bill is astronomical. Gone are the days when I could call up the chic little high-priced corner grocery and have everything delivered within ten minutes to my door. In those days I used to treat myself to an occasional tin of *pâté de foie gras* or a tiny jar of Romanoff caviar with imported crackers. Now it's breakfast cereal and frozen spinach all the way. The champagne, a bottle of which was always kept on ice in the refrigerator, has been replaced by dozens of soda bottles lugged home from the supermarket and ruthlessly consumed almost before they can get to the shelves. Every time my unmarried friends complain about their lonely state in life, I gently remind them about their lovely life styles. As we talk, they are usually comfortably seated in their apartments, feet up, waiting for their delivery boys to bring them something like frozen lobster bisque laced with sherry for their supper. I am usually standing at the kitchen telephone, having just walked in the door, laden with endless bags of groceries, surveying a bulging briefcase that is ready to pop open because I had added a dozen eggs to its contents at the supermarket.

When we drive up to my father's house in Connecticut, I will stop the car at a discount supermarket halfway to our destination. There the market is wide-aisled, clean, and full of sunny-faced people. I fill the station wagon with staples for New York and food for our weekend, while the others gorge themselves at the next-door pizza parlor. No one would think of helping me, but I do not feel a martyr racing around these roomy aisles.

We also purchase half a steer from a meat wholesaler when we can, and keep the pieces in the freezer. This can be helpful relief to our food budget, but can also be the cause of hypertension when we have long summer power failures and the freezer begins to defrost.

My weeknight cooking involves little for R.H. and me. We eat broiled meat or chicken every night, a frozen vegetable, and a salad. The washing and preparing of the salad ingredients and the nightly pan cleanups are crosses I bear, though with little patience. We eat dinner almost every night at our dining-room table, with a magnificent view of the park and reservoir right out our window. But when I am inordinately tired, I prepare trays which we use in the library. R.H. always sits in his black-leather wing chair, and I slump down in my red Danish chair and hassock, assuming a near-prone position while eating. The Romans ate that way for banquets; for me it's the end of a very bad day.

All of the advice to young wives about greeting one's husband in the evening bathed, rested, and clothed in perfumed loveliness goes by the board in the Hollensteiner household. There are two briefcases in the front hall every night, his and hers, and it's a toss-up to see who's more exhausted. R.H. remains his usual natty, meticulously groomed self at dinner every night, with shirt and tie in place. But the minute I walk in the door I change into one of my many caftans or peignoirs—call them what you will. They are perfect coverups, comfortable, loose, and flowing, a fashion that I can't manage during the day. I comb my hair and add some lipstick, which is about as close as I can get to "perfumed loveliness." During our relaxed predinner cocktail hour, I manage to open and sort some twenty pieces of daily mail, pile up the various newspapers we both have to read, keep an eye on dinner, set the table, check on Clare's math and Malcolm's writing, pay bills, make out pay envelopes for the household, act interested in what everyone has done that day, and maybe have a drink. (The latter I manage to lose constantly, never remembering where I laid it down during the last interruption.) It is not expected that anyone will ever ask me what

I've done that day. If it is something positively momentous, I manage to slip it in when no one is listening.

I respect, indeed insist on, a clean house, but my attitude toward housecleaning is such that I give it credit for having motivated me into a career outside the house. Juana Vega comes three half-days a week to clean, since we have a large apartment and New York is a dirty city. There are two distinct disadvantages in the relationship between Juana and me: we never see each other and we cannot communicate in any known language. She arrives an hour after I have left for the office, and leaves long before I come home. Juana is from Colombia and speaks a Spanish dialect that is totally unfamiliar to me. She can handle "yes" and "no" in English, and that's about it. When I leave her notes, they can only be written in my fractured college Spanish. My main sources of communication with Juana are two Spanish-speaking people in my office building, whom I call in when an emergency arises. They translate Juana's messages and write out complicated memos in Spanish for me to give her. I feel sheepish when I call upon these two highly paid executives to cope with my vacuum-cleaner problems, but otherwise I am at a complete loss. Once a client was going over his promotional budget in my office when a call from Juana was put through on my telephone. I tried to understand her, but there was no way. Things grew so frustrating my client could stand it no longer. He reached for the telephone and in perfect Spanish spoke to her calmly and announced to me that the only thing that was wrong was that a toilet had overflowed and a pipe had burst simultaneously. After we had coped with the Hollensteiner plumbing crisis together, we returned to his budget problems.

One Friday night I walked in the door, exhausted from a trip to Chicago, and found a note from Juana on the kitchen table. She had asked someone to write it for her in English.

"Mrs. Holstiner. I you salute. I you thank everyting. You been good. But I call you Monday telephone explain. Juana"

It was obvious to everyone. Juana was not coming back. Tired though I was, I knew I must spring into action at once to find a new cleaning woman. A working mother does not waste any time in solving her domestic crises. I called friends and friends of friends for suggestions. I telephoned in a want ad for the Monday newspaper and I made a list of the largest employment agencies to call as soon as their offices opened Monday morning. I have very little time in the office to spend on this kind of thing, so the research had to be done on the weekend.

I also complained about our emergency to the doorman, and happily he came up with a solution at once—a "nice girl named Claire." With great difficulty I reached her on the telephone at her home Saturday night, and on Sunday she came in from Long Island to be interviewed. I spent over an hour with her, showing her what to do. The deal was made. I would not even have to go for one day without help, nor would I have to waste any office time coping with the problem. *Deo gratias.*

Monday morning Nannie called me at the office: "Mrs. Hollensteiner, there are two here now, Juana *and* Claire. Shall I tell each one to clean half the apartment, or what?"

I subsequently found out that Juana had had no intention of leaving me. She had written the note to prepare me for the fact that she wanted to buy our unused television set in the back room.

Our household is not pacific. I often have the feeling that Juana and Nannie, for example, don't get along, but when Nannie went on her day off and left us with her substitute, an English governess, we really had trouble. It was deep in December and it had occurred to me that morning that I had nothing to give R.H. for Christmas. With a ten-minute break between appointments and a firm belief that one should start out with the best and work down every inch of the way from there, I ran over to Tiffany's. It was great to be back in my old store, and it took me five minutes, as usual, to reach the front elevators, as I greeted all my old friends behind the sales counters. Then I made a mistake. I decided to give my office a quick call before looking at anything. My secretary answered with a note of drama in her voice, "We didn't know where you were. Call home at once!" My heart sank. It was Nannie's day off. Something had happened to the children. I was frightened, and my hand shook as I dialed the house. Juana answered, hysterical. I understood not one word, and the more I said *"lentamente"* (a perfectly good word, but Italian), the faster she spoke. I kept trying to interrupt with the words *"Los ninos! Los ninos!"* hoping she would tell me what had happened to the children. I repeatedly asked for the governess. A fresh wave of Hispanic hysteria greeted each request. There was now a line behind me of five people trying to get to the one and only telephone in working order on the first floor. I dashed into the service manager's office. "Is there anyone around who speaks Spanish?" A woman with an umpromising Irish name got up from her desk. "I do. Can I help?" I grabbed her by the arm, led her to the telephone booth, and thrust the receiver at her. "Please," I urged, "try to get the gist of what she is saying!"

The line of people was growing more restive every minute. My rescuer listened politely a long time, muttering *"Si"* every so often. I inserted my third dime. I was told that the governess had insulted Juana and that Juana would not stand for it. It was a long story. Accusation upon accusation was hurled from both sides as the governess took over the telephone and relayed her side of it. I tried to calm them both down (we were on the fifth dime now) and then I asked my rescuer to tell Juana that I would iron out this whole thing next week, but that she should go home now and forget about it. The people in the line had been listening intently. I heard one say to her companion, "I wouldn't have help if I couldn't handle them any better than that." Another said, "I think she's doing the wrong thing. If it were me, I'd have it out with both of them right now. I'd clear the air."

The entire scene would have worked beautifully for a television comedy. I thanked the Tiffany executive; I thanked the queue of people who had become so involved in my domestic difficulties. I looked at the big clock. Not only was there no time to go shopping, but I was now ten minutes late for my next appointment.

R.H. was the person who really got the short end of the whole long story. My frantic attempts to shop for him that Christmas resulted in a lovely red sweater from Abercrombie's, just like the one I had given him the Christmas before. And I had just read an article in a Minnesota paper referring to me as a "superwoman," too.

Next to serious illness, the worst thing in life is moving. Physically, one goes into a steep decline, but there is neither time nor money for hospitalization. Mentally one usually takes that final step across the delicate balance line between normality and neurosis. If there was ever a need for a fifty-fifty responsibility between man and wife on a project, this is it. During the entire moving-decorating period, a strain is put on the marriage that most marital experts would consider insurmountable. One's children, of course, make their own contribution by being unhappy and uncooperative, but through it all the working mother has to continue being all things to all people, and to a few more besides, including the movers, the painters, carpenters, electricians, plumbers, telephone man, building superintendent, and exterminators. In New York, the number of no-shows for firm appointments equals the number who keep their promises. It just makes it twice as hard to operate when one has a job.

We have moved too often. Each move grows more calamitous. Because we are consumers, like everyone else, there is always much more to move every time. The children never collect small things like marbles, only bulky things, such as camping equipment, soccer balls, flippers, and punching bags. The only person who could come into our household and move us efficiently and well would be the man who masterminds the national tours of the Ringling Brothers' Circus.

For a whole month prior to Moving Day, I packed all weekend and came home from the office every night to work from eight until midnight. There is sorting, wrapping, and storage to organize. I fasten a note with a safety pin or with tape to each piece of furniture to be picked up by the movers. I also make a master-plan drawing for the movers, showing them exactly where all the big pieces are to go and explaining what my coding system means. "N-MB" means "North Wall, Master Bedroom," for example, which doesn't seem too difficult to figure out. R.H. shows only a passing interest in all this frenzied activity. When I attempt to chide him into action, he says, "It's too early." (He keeps up this same line of thought until the actual morning of The Move.) Every single item in the mountain of unused, unloved, unneeded items that I have collected from our closets and donated to a thrift shop suddenly becomes "the only thing I ever cared about." Several times I start to pack up the liquor and wines to go to the new apartment, but each time R.H. stops me. Finally he becomes irritated. "*I'll* take care of the liquor!" His tone is irate.

"All right," I answered sarcastically the last time. "*You* take care of the liquor. They will be the only boxes you will have packed other than your clothes during this entire move."

On that occasion for seven consecutive mornings at

seven-thirty in the morning I met a different painting contractor to survey the new apartment and give us an estimate on special colors I wanted in most of the rooms. The difference between the high and low figures was over nine thousand dollars. During the following week at seven-thirty I met the plumber, electrician, window-shade man, and kitchen-appliances representative, respectively. I would arrive at my office practically mud-caked (the result of three years of dust in an unlived-in apartment and my own perspiration) and entirely confused. At night, when I tried to elicit sympathy from R.H., he would listen while reading his sports page and murmur sympathetically in all the wrong places.

For two weekends before the actual move I pushed a grocery cart back and forth between apartments, averaging eight round trips a day. The cart was packed with silver, china, lamps, cleaning materials, and art objects. It was always a very heavy load and I must have looked ridiculous. When I asked R.H. if he would help I knew I did look ridiculous. He simply asked me to be sure no one knew the name Hollensteiner was attached to the operation, and then he left for the day. My arms would hurt from the strain as I pushed the cart five blocks to the new apartment; everyone along my route watched with great amusement, and my dry cleaner was sure I was organizing the biggest Tag Day sale in the city (*and* the least organized!). One early Saturday morning I tried to clutch a heavy porcelain figurine of a snow leopard with one arm and push a full load in the cart with the other. The leopard grew heavier with each step, and my arm ached unbearably. I stepped into the delicatessen and asked if they would mind keeping my figurine until my next trip over. Having watched with sympathy my grocery-cart maneuverings for the past two weekends, they took the prone porcelain animal immediately into their crowded little store. I forgot all about it until late that night. I rushed from the new apartment to the delicatessen, only to find the leopard behind the counter, a proud centerpiece for their cold-food display. The animal reclined gracefully amid the bologna, salami, cole slaw, and smoked salmon, with a carved radish rose in its paws. It was a beautiful setting; it could happen only in New York.

On Moving Day itself R.H. actually pulled himself together. All day long he made runs with his brand new station wagon from one apartment house to the other. On the first run, when he was inside the building for a total of eight minutes, someone stole the spare tire from the new car. This, too, could happen only in New York.

Moving can inspire true acts of friendship. R.H. and I will never ever forget the thoughtfulness of Mrs. Najeeb Halaby, who lived in our new building. We had been on our feet for thirteen hours without stopping the night of the move when we discovered we had had nothing to eat or drink all day. We had plied the moving men with beers as the day wore on, and they had had a lunch break. We dared not stop, to keep ahead of the vans. Then the doorbell rang, and through the door stepped Doris Halaby with a large wicker hamper in her hand. She brought it out to the kitchen, set it on top of a big crate, and opened it for us. Then smiling again and patting us both on our backs, she left just as quietly and as quickly as she had come in, a veritable angel of mercy. I now know how people who were freezing to death in the Alpine passes in the olden days felt when the Saint Bernard appeared with the brandy flask around his neck. Inside the hamper was a silver martini shaker, full of the coldest, driest, best martinis with which our tongues had ever come in contact. There were pieces of foil-wrapped chicken, large linen napkins, elegant plates and flatware, small breads in a basket, a small porcelain tub of butter, a tin of pâté, and a large piece of French Brie cheese. There was a bottle of wine, too, with sterling julep cups to accompany the bottle. I almost wept from gratitude, but R.H. was jumping into the contents of the basket with such animal swiftness that I forgot my tears and rushed to defend my share.

The day after the move, the superintendent of our old building called me at the office.

"Mrs. Hollensteiner," he said, "you have removed everything except for one thing. I was just wondering what you wanted to do about it."

"What did we leave behind, Mr. Konrad?"

"A whole lower cabinet of bottles of liquor and wine. Surely, you don't want to leave them behind?"

I am resolved that the next move I make will be to the cemetery. My advice to a working mother who has to move her family without time off from the office is to be ready with psychotherapy and a marriage counselor.

The minute classes are dismissed on a day early in June, all the children's friends take off for their New Hampshire barns, Swiss chalets, or Cape Cod salt boxes until Labor Day. For the Hollensteiner kids, it means off to Central Park as usual, except for four weeks in July. There are lots of cheery young faces around the city, but all the "rich kids" have vanished; if any are left, they disappear on weekends. I enjoy Central Park at this time. We play games with children we've never met and make some new friends.

Summer vacations manage to keep alive a lot of high-powered people who never let down the rest of the year. The ones I can't understand are those who move their city habits, friends, and entertaining to a vacation spot where they operate exactly as they have done all year. They socialize with the same people, buy the same clothes, beach hats, and sun glasses in order to be "in," serve the same new fads in cocktails, keep count of all the parties, and become very offended if they're not invited to all the "right" ones. My idea of a summer vacation is forgetting one's wardrobe completely, except for washing out one's underwear at night, and dispensing with an engagement book.

In July we go away for four weeks (three weeks for R.H. and me, but an extra one for the children) either to the island of Nantucket or to Martha's Vineyard. R.H. and I love islands because no matter how crowded they are with beings, human and otherwise, they invite a decrease in pressures. (Forget about the island of Manhattan for a minute.) The fact that an island is surrounded by water somehow makes it harder to call the office or even a friend. Maybe it's because the telephones on Nantucket and Martha's Vineyard are constantly out of order. I cherish the silence of this infernal instrument upon which my entire job depends daily at the office.

An island makes us drop out of the mainstream. The only papers we see are the *Martha's Vineyard Gazette* or the *Nantucket Inquirer-Mirror*. The news they contain—about who has just reopened his house for the season, or the sighting of a new bird near Vineyard Haven by the Worcester Bird Watchers' Club, or the fact that a major crime was perpetrated "last night on Baxter Road, when three bicycles were stolen from three different yards"—is mind-relaxing.

R.H. and I stagger our one week of work off-island, so that one of us is always around our rented house to supervise things. When I am away for my week, R.H. miraculously takes over the marketing and cooking chores. His culinary knowledge is limited to the preparation of breakfast and the art of charcoal broiling. The children look forward to Daddy's charcoal-broiled peanut butter sandwiches, for instance. If he has promised to cook something on the grill, he follows through, regardless of the weather. I have seen him more than once, in hurricane weather, out in the sopping garden in his bare feet, wearing foul-weather gear, standing guard over his cuisine with the protection of a huge umbrella emblazoned with "Chicago Bears" in white letters.

Celebrities abound on these islands, but they melt into the scenery like everybody else. Scotty Reston becomes incensed about political issues at a party, then goes out to take a bicycle ride. Walter Cronkite forgets to watch the news on television because his boat isn't working properly and needs attention. Mary Martin spins tales about her life in South America and then jumps up with her needlework to drive herself home. Whether we are fighting over a jigsaw puzzle in a rose-covered cottage in Siasconset, or fighting over binoculars on our front porch during a sail race by the Edgartown lighthouse, we are happy people. There is no time to grow bored or fidgety.

A lot of my New York responsibilities remain, unfortunately. I fight the supermarket aisles six times a week, since there always seem to be at least ten people to feed in our house. But the aisles are wider in Nantucket and Edgartown than they are at Eighty-ninth and Lexington. I am a constant chauffeur for Nannie and the children. I am continually preparing beach picnics or cooking dinners for unknown numbers of houseguests and drop-ins. I am always searching for college girls who will clean house or baby-sit or tutor a child. There is always the lawn to care for, guests to take to the airport, and then to bring back to the house "because the airport is fogged in and the planes aren't leaving today." There is always the fish market to hit at just the right moment when the day's supply of steamers and swordfish arrives.

Along with all the sheet-changing and KP duties, there is inevitably a major work project to hound me—a book to finish, a proposal to write for a client, a speech to work on, or an article for a magazine. The electric typewriter is always there, a symbol of my mental servitude. When everyone goes off to the beach, picnic lunch included, my worktime begins.

This is not a vacation for me. (*My* idea of a real vacation is a family hotel in the Austrian Tyrol, where all one has to do to summon breakfast is to open the green shutters, lean over the geranium-filled flower boxes, and yodel below to the street. With the cost of international air fare rising constantly, however, the chance of that kind of family vacation is remote indeed.) Nevertheless, I feel a great personal satisfaction in knowing that everything is in good order even if I am standing in line to weigh my lettuce and bananas while R.H. lies asleep in the sun and the children are building sand tunnels with Nannie at the beach.

We all remember different things that happen on our island vacation. R.H. and I remember the children's small achievements far better than they do. The thing they always remember first is the freedom to play out-of-doors unsupervised. The chance to ride around on a bicycle, to run from one yard to another (movements that noncity kids take for granted) is very precious to our children, for they are not allowed to walk more than two blocks unaccompanied in New York.

Occasionally I jot down memories and feelings, which I like to reread on snowy days, to remind me of other times.

Edgartown—July 1972

It's wonderful to see independence blossoming, competition thriving in fairly small persons. Clare just swam in her first race at Chappaquiddick and came in second. Malcolm just had his first race, too, and won first prize, a blue ribbon [which he was to carry around in his hand for three weeks, disintegrating it daily]. We had a great celebration in honor of their success, which was only slightly tarnished by the fact that Malcolm revealed later that he had had one foot on the sandy floor of the ocean during the entire race. "That's all right, Malcolm," his father proudly proclaimed, "at least you *walked* faster than the other kids."

At age four Malcolm has shown us strong mercantile ambitions this summer. He saw some children selling McGovern buttons at a roadstand and was suddenly overtaken with a desire to go into business for himself. He had me set up a card table, chair, and waste basket on the sidewalk, and conned me into making up a lot of pink lemonade; he also supervised my purchase of paper cups, plates, and an assortment of cookies. After a brief fiduciary discussion, we made some signs to put on the table, stating that the pink lemonade would cost ten cents a cup, that the cookies were two for a nickel, and that all proceeds would go to New York's Lighthouse for the Blind. I gave him a cigar box to use as a cash register and told him to tell his customers that they should make their own change from it on the honor system. I hoped for his sake that the traffic would be brisk and honest, and went off to do errands for a while.

An hour later I found the lemonade all gone and Malcolm happily playing with his money. There was $8.93 in the cigar box, which seemed like a lot to me for such a short time. Twenty-five cups had been used and discarded, which, at ten cents a cup, should come to $2.50. Four dozen cookies at five cents a pair should make $1.20. Where did he get almost nine dollars? He couldn't explain the miracle. We dismantled the pink-lemonade stand, since there was nothing more to sell, and on the back of the "10¢ A Cup" sign was scrawled "25¢ A Cup." A teenager had come along, Malcolm said, and done that. Depending on how Malcolm felt at the moment, he would turn the sign to the prospective customer to read either "10¢" or "25¢" a cup. He never would have received a commendation from the Better Business Bureau, but when Nannie, Malcolm, and Clare marched into the Lighthouse for the Blind one morning in New York several weeks later to present his hard-earned contribution, he was treated with the same respect shown to heads of major charitable foundations. [They didn't have to know he was one of Edgartown's leading con artists.]

Siasconset—July 1974

What I love most about this island is the way the roses grow in July over the houses. They climb up the gray-shingled walls and then wander up and over the roofs like curious children. This color palette of pale and deeper pinks against the mottled, sea-washed grays cannot be found elsewhere. It is magic. The shingled houses of Martha's Vineyard and Nantucket have always fascinated me. The older the house, the darker the shingles, the more velvety their textures. After one year, new khaki-colored shingles change to a shade of toast, then to caramel, finally becoming a pearl-gray in adolescence. The sweep of the salted wind will weather it gradually to more beautiful, deeper shades of gray.

I arise every morning at six, make breakfast, organize the household, shop, and then eagerly await everyone's departure for the beach. When they finally go, I can sit in the sun room with my typewriter and try not to be distracted by the constant sound of the wind blowing the privet hedges that surround our house like a fertile moat of privacy. There is always the continuous—and welcome— sound of a tap dance as the flag ropes beat against the white iron flag pole in the wind. When they are gone, I do my setting-up exercises, too. Lying down on the grass is a comfortable experience after thumping on the hard wood floors of our apartment. The only disadvantages are squashing occasional bugs with one's back or being attacked by a squadron of aggressive mosquitoes.

We have a college-girl baby-sitter with us this month while Nannie is home in Ireland. I find myself feeding not only our houseguests but also Rena's college friends and sister, not to mention our college-girl house cleaner and Clare's math tutor. There is also the usual contingent of boy friends in attendance who help themselves to R.H.'s liquor supply. Our food bills have shot up two hundred per cent, but I know that it will be all too short a time before Malcolm and Clare reach an age when they can have summer jobs, too.

We have rented the Breckers' house on the bluff again, overlooking the sea, in Siasconset, a village eight miles from the town of Nantucket. It was a poor fishing settlement in the eighteenth century, when the "swells" of the island lived in the town of Nantucket, catching whales and building those beautiful Georgian and Greek Revival houses. The captains would bring the whales to England and return with red bricks, architectural plans, and beautiful furnishings. But Siasconset is more charming, with its climbing roses, magnificent hydrangeas, and narrow streets through which children on bicycles can pass.

Renting a house from a friend is far more difficult than from a stranger. The Breckers' house is so perfectly equipped, so magnificently organized, it makes me feel very humble indeed. I have to keep a list in a diary to remind myself of things that have to get fixed:

"Four new glass bobèches arrived unbroken today from New York to replace the ones that Malcolm broke with his bow and arrow. I will put them away; even if the kids don't break these, the wind would surely do the job when the dining-room door is left open.

"The combination light-horn for Caroline Brecker's bike arrived yesterday to replace the light Malcolm broke while riding her bike. The horn part broke this morning.

"Clare reports that she has just demolished Joan Brecker's bike basket in a road-bump accident. She asked for three band-aids from me for cuts on her leg and also to soften me up before she told me about the damage. A new basket will cost seven dollars in town. However, Clare is okay. A visit to the emergency clinic would have cost more.

"The boys mowing the lawn ran the electric mower

under the new badminton net without even noticing it, making a huge hole. I will report to the Breckers' that we'll get it fixed, but this is *one* time it's not our fault.

"Rena, the baby-sitter, had a flat tire on the Breckers' jeep. I will get it fixed.

"Malcolm just put his fist through the back screen door. I will get it fixed."

I've been wondering if we should put Clare and Malcolm up for adoption. But they just came in, with piles of sea shells they collected, looking like angels. I think I'll keep them. Clare announced this morning that she is not going to be a vet when she grows up. She has now decided to run for Congress, since it would be a cinch to "do better than the ones in there now." At nine, she is enough of a feminist to defend steadfastly every woman member of Congress. Malcolm, at six, is showing signs of wanting to understand adult conversation. He is growing up.

We must soon go home. Tomorrow is my last morning to watch the sun rise over the pond that separates our gray-clapboard house from the sea . . . my last morning to smell the many little creatures who are disturbed at each low tide in their rich beds of wet sand . . . the last time to arrange a feast in the pond for our adopted family of ducks and to watch the pair of sparrow hawks who patrol our grounds . . . the last chance to laugh at the spindly-legged sandpipers picking their way along the sand beds as delicately as toe dancers. The sea gulls have just finished their morning racket along the front of our house, sounding like angry politicians. The next birds we will see will be New York's pigeons and sparrows—poor, greedy, dull-looking creatures. If I were not a career woman I could spend the entire summer here, not just three weeks. But, as I close my briefcase and pack the car for the airport, I suddenly become city-oriented again. I begin to look forward to city clothes, to having my hair look nice instead of like a mangled broom. It will be a pleasure to walk briskly along New York's pavements again, deeply engrossed in finding a solution for a client's problem.

Maybe only three weeks isn't so bad after all.

5
The Design's the Thing

One great thing about the women's equality movement is that men too are becoming liberated in many ways. They have become much more creative in their dress; they are showing their culinary strengths in the home; they have even brought their needlework out from hiding. Best of all, they are free to admit that they are interested in the decoration of their homes. They are no longer accused of being sissies if they assist in or even lead in the decisions about what their homes will look like inside.

The more unsafe our cities become, the more home-oriented we all seem to get. Home is no longer just a place to hang one's hat. It represents freedom from noise and dirt pollution, safety from street crimes and traffic. It symbolizes protection and security, but it also means a chance to express oneself, to show some individuality, artistic talent, or just a plain good eye for design and proportion.

The more expensive home furnishings become, and the less money we all have, the more careful we are about purchasing any "big-ticket items." One must choose wisely and well. Using the services of a professional interior designer can be an economical safeguard against disastrous buys and mistakes, and in large stores designers don't charge anything if you purchase furnishings in their departments. A mistake made in buying a dress is irritating, but a mistake in ordering draperies for the whole house is a calamity. People who live together should choose important pieces of furniture and items such as carpeting and fabrics together. When there is a clash of tastes, a truce must be declared. The best resolution is a "you do this room and I'll do that room" decision. Since I am an avid interior designer of sorts, R.H. left the design of our latest Manhattan apartment to me, with a single exception, the den. I purchased only two new pieces of furniture for this move—a chair with matching hassock—but I gave the entire environment a completely different look from what it had had before, a rather dark and stodgy place, by using color lavishly throughout. R.H. insisted, however, well ahead of time, that the den was his own turf, and that I must leave the planning of this room to him. I did so, except for installing some off-white window shades trimmed in blue; putting an *étagère* of alternating red and white fiber glass shelves in the corner to hold clusters of growing plants; painting the walls a shiny dark blue with contrasting white woodwork and ceiling; slip-covering our old sofa with a blue-and-white cotton fabric; and inserting my fire-engine-red Fritz Hansen egg-shaped chair and hassock into the room.

R.H. laid his faded, worn, dark blue Oriental rug down in the den (the one item he had brought into our marriage as his "dowry") and carried in his old black-leather wing chair. He also hammered the nails into the walls where I had marked with a pencil that our red, white, and blue pictures should be hung. These small acts accomplished, he lit a cigar, settled back into his chair, and surveyed the scene with satisfaction. "The rest of the house may be your work, Tish," he said with a superior air, "but *I* designed this room. And it's by far the best-looking room in the apartment."

Our apartment is, as you can tell, lovingly furnished in what can only be called an "eclectic style." If one has an impossible assortment of styles, colors, hand-me-downs, and possessions acquired while living abroad, none of which really goes with anything else, then one can slap the term "eclectic" on the whole mix and feel chic. In any event our apartment looks inviting and is comfortable, with lots of color and warm, unpretentious fabrics. I like to mix contemporary and traditional styles in every kind of decorating, whether one is talking about fabrics, rugs, furniture, lamps, or just plain picture frames. Like people at a cocktail party, the younger and older generations of possessions should mix well and enhance each other. I have an old armchair, for example, which has become such a beloved part of the living room it can't be thrown away. Everyone likes to sit in it, so I just keep recovering it, and people seem to head for it unconsciously when they sit down.

The best part of our apartment is the view. R.H. and I have to keep remembering it every time our monthly maintenance charge statement comes from the building. To show off that view, I have abandoned draperies and use only window shades with special trims throughout the apartment. The shades are always up except during the hot-summer-sun hours, so we have maximum light in our apartment, a lot of fresh air coming in open windows, and even more than our just share of city dirt pouring in as a result. Most of the window sills are abloom with untalked-to plants in porcelain *cachepots*, through which Pierre the cat cuts a maze with his famous, rapid Mexican hat dance. When he missteps, the resulting mess of dirt and broken bits on the floor does not exactly add to the décor.

My jobs are carefully documented in favorite treasures

scattered all over the house. An antique demitasse collection, gathered during repeated combings of the Flea Market and the Left Bank *antiquaires* in my Paris years, sits in the dining-room corner cabinet, well protected from man and beast. An engraved silver bowl, also in the dining room, is a remarkable gift of friendship from the women of the White House Press Corps, who sent it to me as a wedding present. It is inscribed, "To Tish, from your admiring White House News Women, December 27, 1963." We had gone through a lot of hard times together, sometimes at each other's throats, so to speak, when they accused me of withholding information on Mrs. Kennedy. The silver bowl is a testimonial that they, like me, remember only the good times.

Anonymous but attractive modern Italian paintings which I picked up during my embassy days in Rome dot the walls everywhere. I paid for them when all my withheld withholding tax for my first eighteen months in Italy was returned to me in one lump sum. A fat gilt wood cupid swings from the top of the doorway into the living room. He came from the choir of a seventeenth-century church outside Rome, and was given to me by the American embassy staff when I returned to America.

The living room is filled with memories, too. A vermeil basket sits on the glass-and-chrome coffee table, a wedding present from a very recent widow at the time, Jacqueline Kennedy. A collection of Chinese export porcelain resides on the demilune, a half-moon-shaped sideboard that was designed for use in the dining room. (Ours, of course, is in the living room, just as the hall table is in the dining room.) Every piece of this porcelain was a wedding present—many from friends of my Kennedy years and some from friends of my distant past. All of the pieces of the collection are now held together courtesy of Elmer's Glue, because I had insisted on packing them all by myself during one of our Chicago moves, only to watch the packers place a large crate on top of my flimsy box, resulting in the breakage of every piece. If we had taken them to an expert to repair, it would have cost a fortune, but R.H. did a perfectly good glueing job, so long as no one inspects them too closely.

If our apartment is full of porcelain, broken or otherwise, it's just because I happen to be very fond of it. A collection of small Boehm porcelain birds graces our living-room mantelpiece, each one with a name or occasion handpainted on the bottom. The birth of each child, our wedding day, and other major events have always been highlighted by these gifts from the late sculptor Edward Marshall Boehm and his dynamic wife and successor, Helen. I had worked with them at the very beginning of their career, when Tiffany's sold their first birds in the 1950s, and they never forgot my enthusiasm for their porcelain or the escaped-birds incident that my enthusiasm caused. A giant panda cub joined the birds on the mantel a month after Helen's return from the People's Republic of China, a trip that inspired the production of this much-loved Chinese animal in porcelain. The children will probably finish off the Boehm pieces, too, in time, during a group tag game or with the swing of a baseball bat; if they don't, Pierre will probably do the job in one of his famous flying leaps. Motherhood teaches one to be relaxed about material possessions.

One entire section of the wall shelves is devoted to books autographed by their prestigious authors, again a refrain of crossed paths near the seat of power. (Our books reside in the living room, not in the library, again a note of independence.) These are the only books never lent under any circumstances. I'll never forget how I felt when I came across one of my previously published books lying in a desolate stack of publications in a junk shop. The book had been autographed by me with great sentimentality to one of my best friends. She could have at least removed the written dedication page before banishing it to such an undistinguished exile. I, of course, purchased the book back from the shop for twenty cents; and the shop's proprietor, quite impressed to meet a genuine author, then tried to buy it back from me for fifty cents.

On another table in the living room are two silver boxes. One comes from the Lyndon Johnsons and is engraved with the Presidential Seal, their names, our initials, and the date of the wedding. Next to it is a little box engraved "To Tish—with Our Love" from the boys of the Georgetown University theater group who worked all our stage lights as volunteers for the White House State Dinner performances in the East Room. Every time I look at these objects, there's the pleasantest kind of flashback. On a pale blue damask-covered table sits one single pale pink porcelain rose—a gift to me from an Italian suitor many years ago. He had sent it to me with a card saying, "I can't afford to send you a fresh rose every day of your life, as I would like to. This will have to do." I thought at the time that this was the most romantic thing anyone could ever have sent to anyone. R.H. does not seem to mind the existence of this rose in our living room, but I suspect he thinks the whole gesture was pretty corny. I still think it's pretty romantic.

I took the rose to California once as a prop for an appearance on Dinah Shore's show in a Valentine Day's segment since we were going to discuss objects of sentimentality. The pink rose, of course, broke into a million pieces in my suitcase before reaching Los Angeles. By the greatest of coincidences, while I was getting into a taxi to go to the TV studio, I saw one just like it in a Tiffany branch store window in the Beverly Wilshire Hotel, where I had been staying. I ran in, bought it, used it for the show, and carefully "returned" it to its blue damask table in New York.

In the front hallway on a large Sears, Roebuck table (it goes well with my Italian antiques) is a crowded grouping of silver frames, containing precious family pictures, but also very special historic ones, from my point of view. One photo shows Jacqueline and John Kennedy with French Minister of Culture André Malraux and his wife. The Presidential Seal is engraved at the top of the frame and the Kennedys' signatures and a message to me are engraved at the bottom. Only Jackie and I can appreciate the full significance of the Malraux photograph, because behind the First Lady's serene countenance there lay a backbreaking three months of minute detail and planning. She cared more about the Malraux visit than about any other during the Kennedy years. Her love of France and its culture seemed to obsess her with a desire for its perfection. Next to this photo is a handsome family portrait of my first bosses, the David Bruces, at the embassy in Paris, complete with young David, Nick, Sash, "the Boys," the spaniels. Next to that is a colored photograph of a blond, smiling Clare Luce seated at her desk with a rose in one hand. It is inscribed, "Dear Tish, from the Boss." There are a photograph of the Lyndon Johnson family at the ranch in happy days and one of the Nixons at the White House on Tricia Nixon's wedding day. I hope our children will some day cherish these signed photographs of three Presidents—one martyred, one dead and misunderstood during his Presidency, and one deposed in what is undoubtedly the most tragic development of American history since the Civil War.

The wall of our apartment's long hallway is lined with twenty-five framed photos of White House personalities, evoking memories each time I pass by, plus a great feeling of pride to have been part of that moment of history. There is even a remembrance of the White House in the kitchen, where a large signed photo of René Verdon, the White House chef whom I hired, hangs over the kitchen sink. He is shown standing next to John Kennedy, and I remember the day it was taken. René and I had been experimenting with the punch to be served at the big congressional reception. The President complained that he wasn't going to have any "rotgut" served in his house to his congressional colleagues, and he would therefore personally pass on the punch. He joined us in the kitchen and after several tries and remakes, the right recipe was finally concocted. . . . Above the doorway into the kitchen is a purple-and-orange Madonna and Child, "Our Lady of the Kitchen," one of Clare Luce's first attempts at painting. It's not bad. A lovely engraving of the White House, signed by both President and Mrs. Johnson and dated with Clare's birth, hangs by her bed. In Lady Bird's handwriting the message says, "To Clare, whose mother can spin many happy tales of this house."

I realize how fortunate I am to have these, and many more items that are very special, placed around our home. I am sentimental about each and every one of them, and R.H. now shares my own feelings about them, if you forget the pink porcelain rose.

Through these years of working in the interior-design field, I have become convinced that one's favorite treasures are the touchstone of every attractive interior. Everyone has objects that are meaningful in some way. They don't have to bear the Presidential Seal or come from a Renaissance Italian church. A memory, a personal feeling, a remembrance of how it was collected or given, the evocation of something amusing or sad in one's life—these are the things that mean so much to a room, that bring it to life. A home without some personal clutter is a pretty lifeless place. In all my years of working in Europe, I lived in rented, furnished apartments, each one great in its own way, but always decorated according to someone else's taste. In Paris I had a three-step rise across the entire width of my skylit living room, leading up to a stage (which had been used for piano concerts by the former owner of the house). My friends were constantly falling off the stage at cocktail parties, however, which forced me to carry some expensive liability insurance. In Rome I had an illuminated wall niche over the living-room sofa that gave off a beautiful light and provided an extremely romantic atmosphere. In fact, speaking as a designer, I could recommend this as the lighting scheme for the living room of anyone who lives alone. The only trouble is that the success of such a plan requires the presence of the opposite sex, a service professional designers do not provide.

It was only in New York, while working at Tiffany's, that I encountered the logistical nightmare of furnishing my own apartment. My first was an L-shaped efficiency—a terrible comedown from the Roman apartment with all of its terraces, pots of geraniums, and real serenading guitarists under the balcony. The only positive thing I can say for that modern, low-ceilinged place is that the plumbing worked. (I heard everyone else's in the building working, too.) After years of living abroad in spaciousness, which was all too necessary for my tall frame, I was suddenly stricken with claustrophobia in my own country. One problem was solved by hiding my bed, bureau, telephone, and night table in the angle of the L, squeezed behind a floor-to-ceiling three-paneled screen (upon which was painted a replica of the jacket design of my first book). In those days, I was always late and when a young man arrived to take me out to dinner, I would throw underwear and other personal items on the bed behind the screen. There was never really enough room to be neat and tidy. Each time the bed was thus littered, it was inevitable that the young man had to use the telephone, so I was almost always caught. The logical solution would have been to throw the last-minute mess *under* the bed, but I knew I would probably never remember the next day that it was there. Every time I see photographs of a one-room apartment, I scan them eagerly to see what I missed doing in my own room plan. Plenty. Every inch of space has to be utilized to its maximum, but you have to live in a place before making it really fit your life style properly. It's like buying a dress that needs alterations. That dress will be uncomfortable and wrong for you unless you have the alterations done.

Screens are one of the greatest decorating tools in existence. I have formed a large, efficient storage area and closet in my office by using a large fabric-paneled screen across a room's corner. I have hidden the bar paraphernalia in our front hall with a screen, as well as shut off from view the children's toy area and disguised ugly architectural elements and radiators with screens. One clever friend who lives in a one-room studio keeps changing the sliding fabric panels on her backdrop screen so that the screen always matches the printed tablecloth she uses for dinner parties. That's called making an effort.

Living as I had in the luxurious atmosphere of embassies with large-scaled rooms, oversized antiques, fancy moldings and paneling everywhere, I had no opportunity to pick up practical decorating details. Nevertheless, I did learn balance and scale by being around beautiful things and by haunting museums, touring historic houses open to the public, studying decorating magazines, and perusing picture books. Even a pause to figure out why a department-store-decorator's room setting pleased my eye was a good lesson in taste. Recognizing integrity in design is, after all, a question of self-education. Taste is not inherited; it is learned.

Working in Tiffany's with America's leading interior designers on table settings and dining-room vignettes was like learning about a fascinating new science. Whether it was a "Breakfast for Two in a Single Bed" theme or "Dinner in a Swan Boat" (which doesn't happen all that often in the average person's life), I was so inspired by the designers' efforts with the tabletop that I wrote a book on table settings. I began studying design at night school, egged on by my boss's encouragement and payment of one-half of the tuition. Then, during my days in Washington, everything I had gleaned in the field of design helped me with the early organizing efforts of Mrs. Kennedy's Fine Arts Committee for the White House. The great task of turning an undistinguished mansion into a restored home of early-nineteenth-century museum quality was to be one of the major achievements of Jacqueline Kennedy's tenure as First Lady.

When I went to work at the Merchandise Mart in Chicago, which houses the largest wholesale home furnishings center in the world, all the pieces of design background began to fit together. It was immensely satisfying to see my hard-won aesthetic principles turn into business profits, although that took some time. It was a logical next step for my new public-relations firm to lean at first in the direction of home furnishings. Along came the task of handling the Burlington House Awards for Burlington Industries, and this project meant I would be able to satisfy my thirst for an ongoing relationship with the interior-design field. Through it I have remained aware of how Americans are living, what they have in their homes, what colors, textures, gadgets, hobbies, and "looks" they cherish. It's like having a candid camera inside all kinds of American homes, snapping pictures of kitchens, bedroom-window treatments, bibelots on the bookshelves, handmade quilts, waterbeds, hi-fi sets hidden in fireplaces, bicycles mounted on walls like art objects, and billiard tables used in dining rooms. The great variety of American life styles is endlessly fascinating to me.

When the Burlington House Awards began, America's swing away from fashion and toward the home had already begun. In the late 1960s clothes began to lose their star status because people realized that although how they dressed was important it was no longer all-important, whereas how their homes were arranged affected the whole spectrum of their families and friends. And so I was given by Ray Kassar of Burlington Industries the assignment of structuring an award program for home interiors, a project to include all kinds of budgets and all kinds of life styles—and that means a lot of Americans. It didn't take long to assemble a judging committee, headed up by Mrs. Harcourt Amory, Jr., and called "The Burlington House Board of Governors." By the summer of 1968, everything was all ready for our first judging, except for one factor: we had no entries.

We had reasoned that the only way to spot homes and to obtain photographs of them would be to solicit entries from newspapers and magazines. The decorating magazines had already spotted, photographed, and published homes of distinction across the country. The family sections of newspapers across the country had already done many stories on local homes of interest. We decided to ask them for clips and photographs of their interesting home features from the past year, or to ask them for as yet unpublished stories. We would also gladly welcome any entries sent in by individuals themselves. The first set of rules I compiled and enthusiastically sent out to the press elicited either a total silence or a ruffle of protests about the ambiguity of the rules. With an injured sense of authorship, I went back to the drawing board and simplified the rules.

As our September deadline drew near, we still had only twenty-five entries, hardly a showing worthy of a national program. So I got on the telephone and called the editors of a hundred major newspapers throughout the country. In dealing with a program of such a large scope, the only real pulling power is the long-distance telephone, the person-to-person plea. It's the "We're desperate for your entry; we're all sitting in New York on pins and needles, waiting, waiting" approach that works. The warmth and urgency of the human voice is worth fourteen letters and telegrams sent to any town, be it Albuquerque, Seattle, or Miami.

The first judging of the Burlington House Awards was not a paragon of smooth functioning. We did not know how to categorize entries, for one thing. The governors tended to evaluate homes by comparing them with their own beautiful domiciles. Also, it was (and still is) very difficult for the governors to judge on the same level homes splendidly photographed in living color by *House & Garden* or *House Beautiful* and those of equal quality, badly photographed in black and white.

After the first bout, we restructured the judging and briefing procedures, learning some new lessons as we went. With each new rotating group of judges, we widened our geographic representation and the kinds of homes submitted to include as many styles of decorating as we could find. In the meantime, the editors continued to improve the quality of entries submitted each year. With the increase of interest in the home, more stories were being written on local homes. Editors knew that a good decorating story offering readers some ideas they could try in their own homes was a real service to those readers.

As the economy began to suffer seriously in the early 1970s, the governors moved away from choosing so many luxurious mansions and high-budget apartments as winners, and began to put emphasis on the homes of the budget-minded families who used imagination and elbow-grease in their do-it-yourself projects. The women also began to train their judging eyes to see good design in spite of mediocre black-and-white photography, to examine the story of a home with thoroughness, and to distrust an interior that looked as if a professional designer had been hired to do the whole job, from sofas to bath towels, without one bit of participation from the owner. It was exciting to watch the judges learn to understand and admire decorating idioms far different from their own. One governor, who lives in a totally French Louis XV apartment, was able to appreciate a simple adobe home in New Mexico with Indian artifacts, Spanish furnishings, and inexpensive Mediterranean reproductions. Another judge, who lives in a magnificent contemporary home with a great collection of modern art, selected as a winner a young couple who used brightly painted cut-out plywood room dividers and put green terry-cloth-covered mattresses on the living-room floor until they could "afford good contemporary furniture." She used a magnifying glass to identify the reproductions of lithographs on their walls. "They have good taste," she said with a broad smile. "I hope they make some money, because they would enjoy buying good modern art."

I was quite logically most interested in how young career women decorated their homes. Some of our entries came from women who earn five hundred a month, others from women who earn two thousand a month, so we broke down the category into different budgets. Likewise, we established categories according to geographic regions, because a nineteenth-century restored home built in the days of frontier Oregon life should not be judged against the elegant salons of a nineteenth-century Savannah house. Both restorations were equally good, but the work involved obviously very different problems and solutions.

The variety of homes submitted each year kept us from becoming blasé about the field of design or bored by the awards program. In the same morning's mail, for example, we would receive a solar-energy house sent in by our Southwest governor and a posh Florida house sent in by *Palm Beach Life*. A young couple's home in Kankakee, Illinois, the pop-art apartment of a young Wisconsin university student, and a reconverted church in Maryland would arrive in the afternoon mail.

It's exciting to see how many eighteenth- and nineteenth-century homes are being restored in every part of the country, because these structures are such an important antidote to the architecturally sterile buildings that have sprung up in so many parts of our country. My entire staff turned into amateur preservationists, cheering each house as it was saved from the bulldozer, or each decayed neighborhood as it sprang to life, thanks to the families who restored the old buildings and moved back in. We passed around for "reading at home" the descriptions of the early 1900s ranchers' bunkhouse in the middle of Texas that became a retired couple's home, and the late nineteenth-century migrant fruit workers' bunkhouse in California that became a beautiful pad for a bachelor. We watched people ingeniously convert everything from a water tower in San Francisco to a silo in New Mexico into gracious homes, and we watched people converting seventeenth- and eighteenth-century mills into stunning solutions for modern-day living. I asked one of these owners what it took to undertake such a project, and he replied, "Nothing but guts, time, and money, just about five times as much as you think you'll need."

We also watched the rise in the late sixties and early seventies of modest "second homes"—beach houses, motor homes with ingenious interiors, A-frame houses perched lakeside or mountainside, even houseboats. They all share a major feature: easy maintenance. As one winner wrote me in answer to my request for more information on her ski chalet, "It takes me ten minutes to clean this house every day before I hit the slopes. Who the hell wants to spend her time with a mop and pail?" I agree, because, as I said before, my dream house has a robot who comes out of the walls at the press of a button to do the chores. (It also does the job without benefit of salary, Social Security benefits, or unemployment insurance.)

We have seen a continuous flow of new ideas in the treatment of modern apartment space—limited as it always is. Boring, rectangular, unmolded, and low-ceilinged interiors can be made exciting by imaginative owners. People paint graphic designs up their walls, over the ceiling, down onto the floors. A well-organized silver and china closet, with everything safely wrapped, resides under a sofa, well hidden; a round table is covered to the floor with a decorative cloth which, when raised, reveals a TV set on one side and three wig stands covered with wigs in tissue paper on the other. The only clear space in a tiny apartment is the wall above the refrigerator, so it is filled with a homemade but handsome lacquered shelf, brimming with books. (The occupants refer to the space as "our kitchen-library.") A piano fits into the bedroom of an eighteenth-century house in Connecticut. The owner, when questioned, says that there simply wasn't room to put it any other place, and just why shouldn't a piano be in the bedroom? Suddenly, it seems very logical to have it there.

We also witnessed a renaissance in American handicrafts through the years that may even make the folk art of the nineteenth century look dull. (All of this is particularly awesome for someone like me, who can do none of it.) People are making exquisite pieces of handcrafted silver and other metals and wood, bed quilts, crocheted afghans; they are making their own ceramics, weaving their own blankets and stunning wall hangings on their own looms. They are hooking rugs, reviving the sampler, making banners of abstract art and bed hangings of crewel work done in an eighteenth-century technique but with a twentieth century feeling for design. The medieval world left us great needlework wall tapestries; we are going to leave future generations great embroidery, too, plus some needlework pillows with some very puzzling sayings upon them.

There are a great number of people making their own furniture, as well as doing their own upholstering. During the Great Depression, people were ashamed to admit that something had been made at home, or that they had a Murphy bed which pulled down from the closet. Today, handcraftsmanship in every medium is bragged about to anyone who will listen. And the Murphy bed is reappearing as a space saver, too. Americans are becoming adept at reconditioning old furniture and restoring antiques. It takes many hours to strip, rub, and oil a piece of furniture in order to bring it back to life, but the Awards show that it is being done in all parts of the country by nonprofessionals of all ages and life styles. And they're doing it in their spare time. We have marveled, too, at the ingenuity of some young marrieds. One young couple furnished their entire apartment in Indianapolis for $153. The wife, an artist, sewed the bedcovers and painted murals on the walls and on the burlap curtains she had made, while the husband refinished and painted all the beat-up furniture they had purchased at Good Will Industries. The result was original and sparkling.

Our country's current preoccupation with ecology is manifested everywhere in homes, too. People haul great rocks indoors to make their fireplaces; greenery grows everywhere, mineral and rock collections are displayed, and there is an emphasis on natural materials in decorating (wicker, straw, rattan, baskets, dried flowers and weeds, stones, slate, unfinished wood, and so on.) One of our favorite entries was a young family from the state of Washington who utilized the flotsam and jetsam on their beach to help build their house. They polished beautiful stones to make their drawer pulls, and made pieces of furniture out of large blocks of driftwood found just outside their front door.

I have been in middle-income houses in many foreign lands, and it is surprising how often these homes lack imagination, serving mainly a single function: shelter. One wonders why middle-class Americans are so much more design conscious than middle-class people of any other country, particularly since most of the really great design in home furnishings since World War II has come from the drawing boards of Italian and Scandinavian designers. Somehow Americans have learned the knack of how to wake up a tired room, even when the budget is tight. It may mean buying or remaking a simple thing like pillows for the living-room sofa, or replacing a small area rug. It may mean making new lampshades for the room, or introducing some new accessories, or simply recovering one worn-out chair. It's a question of a modest outlay of imagination, work, and money.

When Mrs. Albert Lasker, a woman famous for her philanthropy and her support of medical projects, became chairman of the Burlington House Board of Governors, we established a new category in her honor, "Institutional Awards." These were for buildings serving the public, such as hospitals, homes for the aged, schools, colleges, libraries, and the like. The prizes for these institutions were modest but meaningful: framed embossed plaques that stated that the institutions had utilized good design to benefit the people served within those walls. We received entries from all over the United States in this category, from nursery schools, universities, homes for the mentally retarded, and rehabilitation clinics. The sheriff of the Bergen County women's jail won an award for his jail, which had been submitted by *The Hackensack Record*. The inmates had been allowed to use donated paint, sewing machines, and fabric remnants to fix up their cells and meeting areas. I spent hours pouring through the exciting new design concepts for these institutions, particularly the children's wards and clinics, where fabrics, graphics, bright paint, and special injury-free play areas greatly lessen the frightening experience of a hospital visit or stay for young patients. We met and talked at length with such talented young designers as Paul Curtis and Roger Smith, who design and build themselves, without benefit of extra workmen, preschool environments of bright-colored plywood and plastic. They build multi-level structures within a room, with bridges, tunnels, portholes, and other enticing things for a little body to crawl through. In fact, a child would enter such a room and learn just by making his or her way over, up and down, in and around the constructions that make the classroom.

Mary Lasker was succeeded as chairman after three years by Mrs. Lyndon B. Johnson. Because of Lady Bird's unflagging efforts to enhance the environment of this country, another category was initiated in her honor— "The Burlington House Awards for American Gardens." Since I knew nothing about gardening, it was like opening up a whole new world. Unaware even of the difference between laurel and poison ivy, I was suddenly confronted with pages of descriptions of gardens, all peppered with endless, misspelled Latin names, all of them meaningless to me. My colleagues and I learned to spy over picket fences into gardens wherever we were, carefully investigating everything from many-acred wild-flower pastures to minute window boxes. One summer I photographed a "green garden" in Edgartown. My visiting sister-in-law, Nancy Baldridge (from the family branch that spells our name with two "d's") had gone into raptures over the "green garden on North Water Street." Since Nancy is a garden expert, I sped off on my bicycle three times, armed with a camera, but I couldn't find it. Finally, she led me there by the hand. Where were the flowers? There was nary a blossom in sight. The O'Briens' green garden won a top prize, of course, amid rapturous praise from the garden experts on judging day, but it still looked like somebody's front yard without flowers to me.

We greatly enjoyed working on the "Community Gardens" category, including everything from a vegetable garden in Seattle on land loaned by the city and tilled by families to provide food for the poor to small plots of flowers and vegetables in low-income-housing developments, which are carefully tended and guarded against vandalism. Once I was on a TV show in Southfield, a suburb of Detroit, and noticed that the employees all left the studio after the show was over to "do some gardening." That station had turned a neighboring field into a garden plot, giving any employee the right to a section to grow vegetables for himself and his family, and sometimes the employees were joined by their families in the tilling of the soil. Because of the daily exercise they were all in good physical shape and so were their family food budgets. "Being out of doors with a purpose," as one secretary said, "gives me a good feeling about life." I persuaded the station to enter its garden in the 1975 Burlington House Awards for American Gardens, and it won an award.

Corporate executives are growing gardens on office rooftops or on their window sills; some people manage to grow vegetables very successfully on small city balconies. One woman in Maryland made a lovely roadside garden out of an ugly ditch bank just to please passersby; another beautified a wretched run-down urban corner by planting a charming garden in a plot at the gas station. In order to obtain the owner's permission to garden there, she grew the flowers in the same design as the Sunoco sign overhead.

Some people have found the way to plant gardens on their house porches; they then cover the porches with plastic in the wintertime to protect their plants. One girl loves her plants so much that she moved out all the furniture in her small apartment to give full room to her "friends." When she goes away on vacations, she loads the plants on the back of an old pickup truck and takes them with her to be sure they will be properly cared for.

Because the garden awards category grew so fast, we invited a panel of garden experts to come to our office each year to survey all the entries and to help spot the superior gardens—in short, to help us separate the weeds from the plants. Sometimes, as the entries poured in by the hundreds, it seemed as though anyone who ever grew a patch of dandelions had photographed it and submitted it to us. Lady Bird went over them all, remarking diplomatically,

"There are so many gardens here that are not great in themselves, but are great in matters of the human heart." We gave special recognition to special gardeners—a painfully crippled arthritic woman who works among her thriving plants and flowers six hours a day; two high-school kids who grow flowers so successfully in a wild field that they have gone into the flower business to pay for their college educations; gardens for the blind; "Enid's Garden," the tending of which is effective therapy for the physically handicapped; gardens for senior citizens to please their eyes but also to keep their muscles active; and gardens like the Children's Adventure Garden at the University of California at Berkeley, where children from five to twelve learn the discipline and the rewards of proper gardening. All of this marks a genuinely positive development on the American contemporary scene.

I still don't know any Latin names for the flora and the fauna; and I still don't know a green garden from a front yard, but I have tremendous respect for the professional and amateur horticulturists throughout the country. And thanks to the decorating ideas that flowed into our office through the awards for home interiors, all of us in my office became aware of the vast changes in the American way of living in the past decade. It's all for the better, even if Americans are feeling the pressures of recession, overpopulation, energy crises, shortages, pollution, and lack of space all at once. They are coping with it. They are constantly improving their interior environment and demanding better products from manufacturers with which to do so. I have to keep reminding myself of this very encouraging trend when I go home at night and find another piece of veneer on the floor from my peeling Italian antique fruitwood commode. There is nothing I can do about it, except perhaps turn it into flotsam and jetsam and let somebody else, like the young family in the state of Washington, recycle it.

6

In Defense of New York

New York is so used to existing in a state of eternal emergency, the fact that the city is still standing at all is a testimony to her own intrinsic guts. The melancholy truth is that the worse the city's troubles become, the more absorbed in themselves her citizens become. A New Yorker might be defined as the most selfish of animals, unable to sacrifice anything for the common good. Therefore, although my affection for the collective city is steadfast, my feelings toward her average citizen are the opposite. But then again, is there any average citizen on this teeming island? New York is the kind of city which, when on the brink of total financial collapse, has to endure the sight of her well-paid city workers demonstrating and their unions complaining to the Almighty in righteous wrath because the mayor, in an economy move, wants them to work each day until five o'clock instead of being excused at four. (The old law dismissing workers one hour early during the summer months was passed in the days before air-conditioning, and in typical bureaucratic fashion, it has not been changed.) New York is the kind of metropolis that sees its sanitationmen striking so effectively that a new title is won, that of the "smelliest city in the world." Perhaps we should return to the acceptable method of coping with garbage before the mid-nineteenth century, when New Yorkers threw their daily refuse into the streets and the pigs were let loose from their communal sties to collect it in their own enthusiastic manner. The pigs were nonunion; they never went on strike, and the service was very inexpensive. Maybe what New York needs is a return to the simpler life and less complicated solutions to problems.

I become feisty when outsiders attack our city. New Yorkers have a right to criticize her. No one else can. The first question inevitably asked of a New Yorker by a non–New Yorker is, "How can you *stand* living in that city?" I always want to respond, "Because it makes *me* fascinating and *you* dull," but, of course, I never do, because if I did my verbal opponent would say, "You see? You're snarly and you feel superior. That's what happens to you when you live in New York." If I have become defensive about our city, I will probably go to my grave bravely exhorting her good points. One has to believe that the affirmatives outweigh the negatives, or one could not survive. New York's negatives are any city's negatives, but a lot more so. Likewise, New York's affirmatives are fantastic ones; no other city can approach her. I feel it would be difficult to be effective in public relations far removed from the center; my business ear is finely tuned to the beat of the action in this city. In fact, I quite thrive on it. Where else does a taxi driver begin a loud and continuous diatribe (if he is over the age of thirty) against the mayor before you get to the first stoplight? He never stops until you reach your destination, but in the meantime you learn a lot about the taxi industry and city politics, whether you want to or not. The more you try to read your papers in peace, the louder the harangue. The passenger cannot ignore such speeches. He must mutter phrases of agreement every so often, or else he will be forced into verbal battle. The passenger is not permitted to remain silent or to read. He must say, "Yes, you're so right," every so often. The taxi driver is always morally and factually right, and he demands your recognition of this fact. No matter what the issue or who is in office, the mayor is the scoundrel responsible for the trouble in Cambodia, an argument with one's wife, the unfavorable balance of world trade, the recession, and the national increase in gonorrhea. He is the universal voodoo doll for all taxi and transit-system members over thirty. The taxi drivers in their twenties, on the other hand, have long hair, are polite, and despise talking or being talked to. Their only problem is that they don't know the city and can hardly find Rockefeller Center. My favorite taxi in New York is festooned on the inside with a collection of three hundred campaign buttons, a veritable museum collection of seventy-five years of slogans. Furthermore, one can enjoy them while licking one's choice of lemon, lime, or cherry lollipop, because this particular cab driver offers lollipops to every passenger. Other cab drivers offer you hot coffee, the morning paper, or canned sermons on "How Jesus Christ Is Coming Again."

One out of every ten cab drivers is unpleasant and surly and infuriating. I prefer to think of the other nine when I'm considering them as a group. They have seen it all, heard it all, been through it all. They typify New York, after all. They're either up or down, like the city itself, whose people are creating, designing, making deals, conniving, producing, selling, *doing.* New York is a city of people who are alive. Even Bowery Bums (who have been displaced from the Bowery and are now becoming Sixth Avenue Bums) have something to say when they're able to speak.

It's the humanity with which one copes during daily living that really makes it all worth while. In the constant pushings, shovings, and confrontations of all kinds that occur, we touch or are touched by other human beings. There is constant physical contact, which is good, not bad. I have a chance to let out all my hostility in my own way. That's why I could never live in the suburbs; I would not wish to be deprived of nurturing my love-hate relationship with my fellow man, even if he is a selfish New Yorker.

I stood talking to a Cincinnati friend on the sidewalk at Fifty-fourth and Sixth Avenue the other day, when an ordinary-looking man walked right between the two of us, pushing each of us back rudely without saying a word. He used his arms in a fast, hard upward chop, throwing our arms into the air as though he were making a path through us with an ice-cutter. The woman from Cincinnati just stood there stunned, hurt, and bewildered at this unexpected and uncalled-for attack. I wheeled around and let loose after the retreating male figure a barrage of juicy Italian expletives, having a marvelous time letting them all out. He turned around at my shouting, so I had "gotten to him," as we say in New Yorkese. Passersby ignored me as just another loony New Yorker, and I simply returned to my calm conversational tone, feeling much better for the outburst. I never would have used those swear words in English; if our ice-cutter had been Italian, he would probably have finished me off.

More often than not, I can summon more self-control to deal with these encounters. It makes one feel very proud to be in control. But it's actually a winning feeling either way—to be in emotional control or to be out of it. "Let it all hang out" is a cliché that describes perfectly a survival technique of many New Yorkers. In my own opinion, it would be very harmful to our collective psyche if we were to exist in a society of hypocritical manners and non-confrontations. In our city, we *confront*. Otherwise, we explode. Every individual is possessed of his own delicate mental balance, and if we lose our balance and are pushed too far, the overload switch is turned on. We had better know what our own thresholds are and face up to them. Each of us has his own way of facing up. My way is to use will power. I may not have it for food, but I have it when I get energy enough to begin contemplating homicide. The other day I successfully staved off a nervous breakdown in the Fifty-ninth Street Lexington Avenue subway stop, known to most of us as "the Bloomingdale's stop." My office day had been particularly arduous and depressing. My arms were laden with heavy things, and I still had the market to face before going to the apartment. Nevertheless I went to Alexander's department store to fight the crowds for what seemed like a reasonable purpose—to purchase color film on sale. But of course there was none left when I arrived, and I descended stoop-shouldered with the weight of my own fatigue and self-pity into the subway. Close by me on the platform I watched in disbelief as three young punks roughed up an old woman, stole her purse, and cuffed two small children standing next to her. It all happened in a few seconds. A subway guard took off after them, but the young men melted professionally into the crowd. Finally, after four of my uptown trains went by (I could neither shove nor hit hard enough to bully my way aboard), I felt a sudden sharp tug on both my handbag and my briefcase. It was one of the young punks, who looked up angrily at me because I wouldn't let go of my bags. "You little twerp," I muttered, forgetting that he might have a knife. But he didn't, and since I far outweighed him, he could only retaliate by spitting in my face and hitting my lower chin. His aim was terrible, and I told him so. I wanted to clobber him with my briefcase, just as the little woman used to hit her "attacker" in the park with her bag every week on television's "Laugh In," but it was so crowded I could not possibly have raised anything over my head. He escaped, leaving me exhausted and depressed. I felt as though the entire world had pushed and manhandled me. I felt as though the entire jigsaw were coming apart.

I took a big breath of what passes for air in the subway and began chanting quickly and silently to myself, "Shrinks take time and money . . . shrinks take time and money." By the time I had repeated this about twenty-five times the thought of giving in to a breakdown was absolutely out of the question. There was certainly no time in my life for it, and I would much rather spend the money for other things—color film, for instance, at full price for a change.

It is very difficult to exist in New York without being constantly aware of humanity. This is good because it breeds compassion, along with a desire to learn judo. Stacked up against the incidents of cruel "noninvolvement" of bystanders who refuse to help someone in case of trouble, there are thousands of examples of kindness and assistance that no one ever reads about in the paper. As you brush by millions of people each day you begin to notice that there is sometimes personal tragedy written on the faces of strangers close by. Just in one subway car, for instance, it is statistically possible that someone has just found out his wife has terminal cancer; someone else has just been told her child is hopelessly retarded; another has just lost his job; another has just learned her husband is leaving her; another has to have a quick "fix" and must find the money for it somehow. Other faces show utter personal defeat etched into deep lines that read like a news story. These are the ones who know they can't "make it." They have no self-esteem, no hope. They may never have felt personal triumph, the satisfaction of achieving, being praised, respected, appreciated. Some of them will never even feel love in their whole lives. It's all there on those faces. It makes one take a count of one's own storehouse of blessings and advantages. It makes one feel somehow singled out in life. If I lived in Portland or Santa Fe or Topeka, it would be different. It takes a city like New York to force me into making a mental checklist of blessings, and it happens nearly every day.

As to the humor that permeates this city, thank God for it. There is no place, with the possible exception of Paris, where there is so much intellectual irony, so much dry wit in the air. Art Buchwald makes Washington sound wittier than it actually is, but nothing beats New York. Even when the wit is sardonic, like Russell Baker's column in *The New York Times,* there is a pleasure sensation in its bite. I remember the admiration I felt in my youth in Paris for the Chansonniers de Paris, those singing geniuses who never read notes but who interpreted the news events of each day in songs drenched in political satire. I always considered them the cleverest of men because their material changed nightly. But then so did Hervé Alphand's material when he was the French ambassador to Washington during the Kennedy Administration. Relaxing after a formal, stuffy dinner party, he loved to mimic the world leaders of the day, and no one of importance escaped the sword's edge of his skits, including his own boss at that time, Le Grand Charlot de Gaulle.

None of this is surprising, for the French are traditionally known for being intelligent and witty. But so are New Yorkers, though we also have to listen to people from other places point out that one cannot be intelligent and prefer to remain in this city.

If New York's brand of humor is only a defense mechanism for survival in the city, what of it? The French often say that wars created their national wit, and perhaps we are fighting our own war in Manhattan. But does the reason for wit really matter? If life weren't so tough in our city, would the people be as interesting, as humorous, as gifted? The varieties of our city's humor are many, because it is both ethnic and class-conscious. There is the Jewish, both upper and lower class. Black humor has its upper and lower classes, too; then there is the humor of the Irish, the Italians, the Spanish-speaking, the Greenwich Villagers, the few Germans left in the old Yorkville area; the Madison Avenue ad agency humor, the newspaper humor, the Beautiful People humor. There are bright clowns of different political faiths—the Jimmy Breslins, Gene Shalits, Russell Bakers, and Bill Buckleys—who make us all laugh. It takes a New York to spawn such an incredible mix.

Each of the residential sections of New York is its own small village, a situation that hotel visitors rarely understand. We know our shopkeepers, and they know us. They cash our checks; they hide "goodies" for us in their cellars; they find extra help when it's needed, whether it's for cleaning, baby-sitting, serving, or typing addresses on envelopes. They pass on to us other customers' recipes so that some inexpensive cut of meat can be made more palatable to our families. They lend us money, console us when we go through the check-out line with runny noses. All the tradesmen in my section, which is Manhattan's East Side, have their own brand of city wit. Even the greengrocer on Third Avenue produces political wisecracks as he weighs one's tomatoes and lettuce, though I suspect that he became a fast talker in order to distract the customer from his prices.

There are forests of skyscrapers in New York, and they do not make for the coziest of environments. In fact, one tends to become very impersonal about one's fellow man inside these sealed glass boxes. But occasionally a touch of humanity shines through. My office used to face the Hilton, and once someone actually cut through that cold façade to establish contact with me. I had the habit of sitting facing the window in my bright-colored office (rather a conspicuous blob on the dark landscape of our side of the building, they tell us), cogitating over office problems and staring absent-mindedly outward. The slate cliffs of gray glass windows of the Hilton across the street was a view I quite loathed; no amount of fresh green plants growing in my window could soften it. The wall of glass was always the same shade of gray. It did not change according to weather conditions or the time of day. One could not even tell if the sun was shining. One day a tiny figure moved into the center of a hotel window on the upper right. People do not come to their hotel windows on a viewless street like this; they avoid their windows. So this figure caught my eye. Suddenly there was movement on the gray mountain. The man was waving and grinning at me. He was probably from someplace like Tulsa. Here he was in New York, establishing contact. I burst out laughing, and waved back, first awkwardly, then enthusiastically. He laughed in response and waved with yet more vigor. We continued this silly behavior for about a minute. Then we both turned away, he to leave for his day's appointments, I to return to the papers on my desk. The short encounter was over. I hope he felt better because of it, I know I did, and I chuckled over my papers for a long time. Two strangers had waved at each other, from one skyscraper to another, across Fifty-fourth Street. In Tulsa there is no need for this kind of behavior. In New York there is.

New York is a great city for "taking lessons." There simply is not a pastime, hobby, sport, craft, instrument, type of self-defense, self-improvement, or mind-sharpening for which there is not someone somewhere giving lessons. If you want to play a lute, do transcendental meditation, learn how to jitterbug, use an alpha biofeedback machine, or discover the secrets of growing herbs in your bathroom, instruction is available. When Clare was taking classes at Anita Zahn's classical dance school, I would occasionally visit, since it was appropriate for the mothers to show every once in a while. There was always a celebrity mother or two in attendance, such as Charlotte Ford Forstmann, to watch their daughters perform. Miss Zahn's classes are very chic: the little girls wear pink or blue Grecian-type tunics and are barefoot, with long floating scarves, in the Isadora Duncan manner. Everyone must take the whole thing very seriously, for Miss Zahn is a formidable institution in New York (and in the Hamptons in the summer), and as a former student and friend of the late, great Isadora, she looks askance at anyone who might poke fun at her leaping charges, including my sometimes clumsy daughter.

"Be a star, Clare, a joyous rising star, climbing in the heavens!" she would intone rapturously. "Jump for joy, star, high, high in the heavens!" And with that, Clare's jump would take place, the crystal chandeliers would begin to shake in tinkling rhythm, and the piano player would take off in enthusiastic arpeggios.

If the kids on Thirty-ninth Street in Omaha had ever caught me in a class like that when I was Clare's age, I would have been run right through the stockyards on cattle-slaughter day. But it's all part of New York culture.

Clare is now involved in ballet and tap, and I rather miss the sight of the tunic-clad, leaping figure galloping through our apartment, "making like the rising sun." I also cannot stand for one more minute of her practicing tap steps on our polished front-hall floor. She is going to have to do her tap practicing outside, on the Fifth Avenue sidewalks. I keep reassuring her that with all the nutty New Yorkers wandering around, doing their own thing, no one will even notice her.

Weekends with the children are easier spent in Manhattan than in any other place because there is such a variety of things to do. In the spring, there is the wonder of walking among the cherry blossoms of the Brooklyn Botanical Japanese Gardens. There is always a lot of animal action at the Bronx Zoo, and even the fish seem fishier somehow at the Coney Island Aquarium. Central Park is inevitably a Brueghel-like scene of little figures scurrying around in different activities. There are bicyclists racing each other, joggers of both sexes running around the reservoir. There are people riding horseback, baseball or football teams of both sexes, and all races, colors, creeds, and ages. Iceskaters twirl on the two big public rinks; artists are staging impromptu exhibitions of their work on easels; the story teller weaves tales by Hans Christian Andersen for little people gathered in front of the master's statue. On summer evenings the park abounds with humanity attending the free concerts and plays. On just an ordinary day, one might see a male dancer clad only in a "snood" (or, as Malcolm described it, "He was wearing a hairnet on his thingamajig") as he dances on top of a mound. There are always a few crap games around, and perhaps a man training a dancing dog or an acrobatic team working out. There is, of course, the inevitable prone couple nearby, in any season, madly embracing. They are usually both in jeans, both with long hair. It is difficult to tell which is which sex. Maybe they are both of one sex. It's all the same to the children.

Neither R.H. nor I is exceptionally good at group athletics in the park with our children. R.H. feels he gets enough of the park with his morning jogging. However, Malcolm's Excess Energy seems to inflate every weekend, and it is a problem for which a solution must be found. During the week he works off steam in school. On the weekends we are in New York a young boy shows up in the morning to take Malcolm to the park for a hard two-hour workout with a football, soccer ball, street-hockey set, or baseball and bat. Malcolm's sitter truly earns his money, but he is also given the award of Malcolm's hero worship, for he happens to be a big-shot athlete in the eighth grade and that's what impresses third-grader Malcolm.

The part of the weekend I enjoy most is taking Clare and Malcolm to lunch after the morning park activities. (Sometimes Malcolm goes off with R.H. for a "man-to-man hamburger lunch.") There are museums to be visited, children's plays to attend, exhibitions of items like minerals and rocks in the stores. Where else could there be thirty-one museums beckoning, two hundred and thirteen art shows running simultaneously, twenty-two photography exhibits, seventy-four plays and musicals, free concerts and dance exhibitions in the street, puppet shows in the parks, and twenty-three special theatricals for children— all taking place in the same weekend? The creative vibrations are everywhere.

I have taken the children to "little people's" musicals in dark basements on the West Side that turned out to be professional productions worthy of Broadway, featuring original music and outstanding child performers. Even though the costumes may have been made out of bargain-basement remnants, they are delightful, and the lighting and the orchestra are invariably first-rate. The musicians are often music students, always dreaming of "making it big," always grateful for the chance to "pick up a little bread" by performing at these children's theatricals.

It's hard to imagine how Manhattan can absorb so much talent, because it is everywhere. The determination of young artists to be seen and heard is so real that one can feel it in the air. Struggling students and seasoned professionals all walk the streets together, contributing to the special pace of the city, to its feeling of aliveness. Yes, New York is alive. It may not always be well, but it is always alive.

The negative aspects of the city cannot, of course, be dismissed simply with a flourish of rhetoric. High on my list of negatives is the tragic plight of the aged and infirm. So many of them are alone, tucked into miserable holes in the city and afraid to come out. They are easy targets for muggers; they suffer from malnutrition. But most of all they suffer from sheer loneliness. This is a city for the strong and vigorous; everyone runs, not walks, in the course of the day's activities; and anyone who can't keep up with the pace is overrun. A big city can indeed be a cruel place for the elderly. We expend much energy in worrying over the young; perhaps some of it should be directed toward the old. What is wonderful is the energy the senior citizens summon themselves when they take over baby-sitting chores, participate in volunteer programs, such as reading to the blind, and become active in community centers.

One has to be fatalistic about the crime rate in a city like New York. One must move with care, remaining ever watchful, and teach one's children to do the same. But from then on, it is in the hands of fate and our overworked guardian angels. When John Kennedy's new superbike was stolen from him in Central Park, it made the front page of every newspaper in the world. If seventy-five bikes belonging to other children had been stolen the same day, it wouldn't have merited a line of press coverage, but would have been dismissed as another fact of urban life. Our children have been taught not to resist if a gang asks for their bikes. Our children know about walking in the streets at dusk, how to act if they think they're being followed. They have seen real cops and robbers in action near our home, and have even heard shots exchanged. If you want to be positive about it, you can be glad that the children *are* being toughened up, that they are learning how to cope and are becoming "city-wise." They learn that it's not the end of the world if an addict takes away their money. And in at least one case I know of, there was actual justification for a positive attitude. The thirteen-year-old son of a friend of ours was a puny boy for his age, with thick glasses and a great number of complexes. One day, while he was riding in the park, three young toughs stepped into his path and demanded his bicycle. When he didn't respond, they knocked him off it, and for a little added pleasure broke his glasses right on his face. The boy went through a long ordeal with the doctors and the hospital, but his eyes came out all right. The story has an even happier ending. As a result he became determined to develop his body as well as his bruised self-esteem, so that he would be able to defend himself in the future. He took special instruction at the YMCA and became an excellent boxer and a fine all-round athlete. He will always be short, but his body has developed into a strong one, and his self-respect has improved enormously. An unfortunate incident in the park changed his life for good.

We pray for more policemen; we cheer the heroic ones and mourn for those who are killed in action. We begin to care very much about the local politicians we elect and what they plan to do to combat the reasons for crime. In a faltering economy, we can only see it getting worse, and we begin to nurture a sense of fatalism about our families and their safety. The pope took away Saint Christopher, the patron saint of travelers, by down-grading his sainthood a few years ago. I pray to him regardless. Many of other religions do, too. Then there are the children's guardian angels, and perhaps the New York children's guardian angels have to work overtime. Anything I omit or overlook in praying for the safety of the children, Nannie takes care of. After all, she's always going to Mass.

One July I sent a "Dear John" letter to Mayor Lindsay. "I have always respected New York policemen," I wrote, "but now my respect goes even further, especially for the men of the Nineteenth Precinct."

The night of July 13 had been a blessedly cool one by New York standards, because one could sleep without turning on the air conditioner. In a way, that was too bad, because if the air conditioner *had* been operating, I never would have heard "him" at three-thirty in the morning, when his noises woke me out of a sound sleep. I was alone in the apartment, which normally does not bother me, because the building security is excellent. But when I heard a great deal of fumbling with a key in the lock on the back door, and when I heard the door open, I quickly became alert and alarmed. R.H. was in Florida on a business trip; the children and Nannie were in Edgartown. "Dear God," I prayed, "let that noise be R.H., coming home unexpectedly." Like a woman timing her labor pains, I waited for a few minutes before calling the police, but when I heard heavy footsteps which were definitely not my husband's, I felt certain they must belong to an intruder. The footsteps moved from the kitchen into the dining room, then slowly back into our front hall. "He" moved clumsily, and I could tell exactly where he was with each step.

I grabbed the telephone and slipped way down under the covers with it. The dial light never worked on this instrument, and for once I really needed that light. I could not even find the emergency numbers 911 on the dial, but finally my finger found the o. I asked the cheerful "May I help you?" voice to connect me with the police, and the operator did. My heart was pounding so audibly and so fast that I tried consciously to slow it down. A heart attack on top of rape and bludgeoning would make R.H. an instant widower, and my will was not yet properly drawn.

I had a bad case of laryngitis and a throat virus at the time and this, coupled with the muffling blanket I had pulled over me, caused the dispatcher to call me "Sir." I was in no condition to correct him on this point of mistaken sex.

"He's here," I croaked.

"Please speak louder." I tried, but I had three frogs in my throat, not one. Again he could not understand, so I said it again.

"A man's here," I whispered, very slowly and very emphatically. Sarah Bernhardt could not have done it better.

He understood this time and asked for my address, which I whispered three times before he could decipher it.

Then I heard those lovely, reassuring words, "Don't worry. We'll be right there."

I checked the time and slid as silently as I could from the bed into the bathroom, hoping the intruder could not hear my movements on the carpeted floor. Then I realized that the bathroom was hardly a haven; I had removed the locks from all doors because of the children. I decided to leave the door slightly ajar, so that I would know when he reached the bedroom. The largest nearby weapon was a giant bottle of mouthwash. Perhaps I could scratch his eyes out with my long-handled bath brush. Could I blind him by throwing baby powder in his eyes? Could I stab him with my cuticle scissors?

Within eight minutes of my call, the police arrived outside the front door of the apartment. I listened to their urgent whispers, feeling immensely relieved. But then I heard them go into the Russells' apartment, our next-door neighbors. In those days the Russells often left their door unlocked, and ours was usually locked. I decided the police had used logic and figured that the intruder had entered the unlocked door. Then I heard the terrified voice of their maid, who had been awakened in her bed and was protesting in Spanish. I had to do something. One of my hostess gowns was hanging on the bathroom door. I threw it over my nightgown and, armed with the mouthwash bottle, made a beeline for our front door, past the living room where the intruder was lying in wait. I ran right into the arms of the policeman in the front hall. "It's *my* apartment, not theirs," I cried.

They, all six of them, quickly crossed over to my apartment. I felt so grateful that six brave men had come to save *me*. I remember thinking how much I must have impressed the police radio dispatcher with my under-the-covers emergency call. The men made a thorough search of the apartment and silently began to write on their report sheets. They had found no one. My emotions changed from hysteric fear to embarrassed relief, and finally to just plain embarrassment. I could tell that two of the officers were making an appraisal of me, looking at my eyes, checking my breath, watching my movements to make sure I was not drunk, drugged, or dangerously deranged. I became more and more chagrined.

As if to save my face for me, one of the men had an idea. "Could it have been your next-door neighbor, lady?" The other men nodded in agreement. The policeman continued.

"I mean, he might have come home late, with too much under the belt, and mistaken your apartment door for his?"

The idea of Tuck Russell doing that was totally unthinkable. Then I had an idea. The Russells' college-aged children had a constant flow of houseguests. Yes, that was it, a houseguest who didn't know which apartment was theirs. He had tried the key in my door, found it unlocked (though that was improbable), had entered, looked around, realized the mistake, and left, closing my door behind him as he went.

Right then and there the police wanted to find the person in the Russell apartment who had done this, to prove to me that I had not been suffering delusions. They went next door again, and I heard the maid protesting outside of her employer's bedroom door. She would not let them open his door, so I entered the argument. "No, really, officer," I protested, "Mr. Russell is not the drinking type, and he's not a houseguest either." If only his wife and my husband had been in town to witness this summer bachelor's scene, and to hear my impassioned and accurate defense of Tuck's temperate drinking habits. The policeman finally relented, and we walked back to my apartment again. How Tuck slept so peacefully through it all, behind his closed door, is still a mystery, for the maid was so upset by the incident she took to her bed for two days. The police began to pack up and four of them left, but as the last two were preparing to walk out of my apartment, the noise of the clumsy footsteps began again. It was eerie.

The sound this time came from directly overhead. A summer tenant in the apartment upstairs was obviously inebriated, falling against the furniture and wandering around. The carpets had been removed from the floors for summer cleaning, I learned later, so that the footsteps had come through the wooden floors as clearly as if they were in my apartment itself. One of the policemen kindly patted my hand. "It's okay, lady. If I had heard that noise in the middle of the night, I would have called the police, too."

I had to laugh. "You mean, you would have gotten your gun and gone to investigate, rather than 'call the police,' don't you?"

"Yes, that's what I mean."

"I'm terribly sorry for all the trouble I've caused you," I said, and with that the last two of New York's Finest disappeared into the elevator. Even with all the rush and the confusion I had caused, it didn't occur to them to make fun of me. I wonder how many people in panic dial 911 every night?

One of the important ways in which we can help in the fight against the destruction of our environment through pollution is to set the right example for our children. We can teach them to file away in the city trash bins every scrap of paper they may drop on the street. In this gung-ho spirit I have even urged my children to file other people's paper in the corner trash bins. And I have taken Clare and Malcolm on several Saturday mornings to Central Park when the big volunteer clean-up drives take place. On these occasions the Parks Department distributes large plastic bags to each adult and child, and we comb for trash in all directions, returning only when the huge bags have been filled and are ready to be dropped at the central pickup place.

One Saturday we worked particularly hard at our tasks, the children and I, taking particular delight in what we had collected that morning. My haul was one small oil painting (not very good and probably thrown away in disgust by the artist himself); a packet of letters addressed to "Sara," to be read "only after I've killed myself" (I, of course, read every word, and found the young lover had been playing this threatening game for many months); one real-hair wig, an excellent brunette fall that Marc Sinclaire might have put on a client for a Big Evening. . . . One wonders what Big Evening caused this young woman to lose it in the park; a dollar bill (which each of the children claimed, but which I as finder kept); and a professional ice-cream scoop (which ended up in our kitchen). Later on in the day the children and I carried a picnic lunch back to our clean Central Park spot, seating ourselves upon a blanket to enjoy the fresh green meadows around us, devoid of tissues, bottles, cans, paper, and shiny litter. By the time we had polished off the last deviled egg and drop of milk, the grounds were full of teen-agers, out to enjoy the spring sunshine. We packed up our things, folded the blanket, and looked around us again. The entire area was littered once more. It looked as if it had not been cleaned up at all. In one hour, these young people had negated our entire effort. The children were heartsick. My attempts to console them were inadequate. If they had been adults, I would have described their feelings as those of bitterness.

"Look, those weren't our New York kids . . . those were out-of-town kids. They won't come back here again."

We walked home rather slowly, still picking up larger pieces of litter and depositing them in the big park wire baskets. "Mommie, will I do that when I'm a teen-ager?" asked Clare. I told her of course not. Then I thought to myself, Clare baby, I only hope that is the worst thing you do when you are a teen-ager.

One must have a positive attitude to keep these events from overloading the psyche. To love New York is to understand her. After all, there are always objects of beauty to behold while walking along—a person, a car, or even a whole sidewalk full of unbelievably beautiful autumn leaves that drift over to the streets from Central Park. Clare and I collected some of these one Monday morning on our way to her school. They were far more splendid and jewel-toned than the ones we had gathered that weekend in the Berkshires. Clare tossed the Connecticut leaves into the trash bin on the next corner, and placed the Madison Avenue ones in her schoolbag to show at her "autumn foliage" science class that morning. Let no one speak ill of our city's trees.

Just when one is feeling particularly hostile to and frustrated by this city, for good reason, something usually happens that's delightful, something nice occurs that could happen *only* in New York. . . . Like the maintenance man in a midtown office building who parks his ancient car on a side street and goes to it at lunchtime to practice his hot, very sweet trumpet, in perfect accompaniment to the jazz playing on the tape of his cassette player. . . . Or like the two young men, strangers to each other, who sit laughing on the edge of a water fountain, comparing their long top-knot coiffures held in place with rubber bands. One is a college youth clad in blue jeans; one is a Hare Krishna disciple garbed in saffron robes and sandals. . . . Or like the two robust older ladies who catch a young man in the act of stealing a handbag at the greengrocer's, and who then bop the young thief on the head with their umbrellas, shouting in both Italian and Yiddish. They finally push him to the ground and straddle him, and I fear for his life, he is so close to being crushed to death. When the thief is finally carted off in handcuffs (having been grateful for the arrival of the police, believe it or not), the greengrocer celebrates by getting out a bottle of brandy, three glasses, and gallantly toasting the two ladies and himself. To each of the rest of us he offers a lovely free apple. This is the side of New York that never makes the papers or the six o'clock TV news.

New York's museums are terrific. With the cost of keeping their doors open far outpacing their income, they struggle along against impossible odds. There is no greater treasure-trove in the world than New York's museums. For those of us in business, they are also an endless opportunity for research. The Cooper-Hewitt, when it has opened all of its portals to the public in the Carnegie Mansion across the street from the Sacred Heart Convent, will form the greatest repository of design information in the world for anyone interested in can-openers, Art Deco, bridge spans, underwear, bassinets, lighting systems, or railroad ties. Museums such as the New-York Historical Society are not usually on the list of Manhattan "musts" for tourists, but they should be. One could spend a fortnight poking around its exhibits and still not become familiar with all its secrets.

What one appreciates most is that institutions like these have hearts. For example, one day I learned at three-thirty in the afternoon that a bank would allow us to make a presentation at ten o'clock the next morning on what our firm could do to further community relations in small upstate New York towns when that bank was allowed by law to open new branches in the following year. It had taken us so much time to see the proper bank officer that we had not even formulated our proposal. We had nothing down on paper, but by ten tomorrow we had to have *everything* down on paper. We knew only one thing: that utilizing the history of New York State was to be the basis of our "learn to love the big New York bank" project.

When I called the New-York Historical Society librarian, he was at first stunned by my request. I told him I needed a capsulization of New York State history by the time the museum closed.

"Surely, you don't mean its history from the beginning?"

"From the beginning," I answered.

"You mean, right from the Indians?"

"Unfortunately, yes."

"And how much time do you have for this research?"

"The rest of today." There were now one and a half hours left for the rest of this day.

The librarian, obviously a scholar and an intellectual, suddenly donned a businessman's no-nonsense hat.

"Hang up and come up," he said simply.

We hung up and came up, arriving there at four o'clock. By five, closing time, using just the books he had waiting for us, we had the basic periods of New York history documented in an outline form. We would now be able to go back to our office and write all night. We would be ready for tomorrow's presentation.

It's too bad there aren't more people in the world who say, "Hang up and come up."

In my children's eyes, one can carry the cultural benefits of a city like New York too far. Clare and Malcolm at one point became culture-shocked and went on strike, flatly refusing any further encounters with cultural matters. I think this was probably the result of one October Saturday when the rain was coming down in plastic-shower-curtain sheets and there was nothing to do. I dreaded the inevitable: two children bored, pugnacious, and unavoidably in my care.

The telephone rang early. It was Betty Pollock, an old college chum, who announced that she had a present for me and the children. If it had been a generous gift certificate from a toy store, it would not have been more welcome.

"I've ordered a car and driver for the day," she said. "Let's go to the museums."

The prospect was enticing. The children were delighted. We put on our rain gear and headed into the dry confines of the chauffeured limousine. Clare and Malcolm found all the buttons in the back seat which controlled windows, partition, radio, and air conditioning—which turned out to be the most intriguing items we saw all day. There were great delays in finding the Brooklyn Museum, our first destination, because the driver thought we should know where it was, and we thought he should know. (If one lives in Manhattan, a trip to one of the other boroughs can be a major event, not to be taken lightly.)

When we finally reached the museum, it was well worth the wandering. There was a superbly mounted exhibition of Navaho blankets and textiles. We also went upstairs to see the costume exhibit. Since we were the only ones seated in the little theater with its carpeted stairs for seats, we had our own private audio-visual show. The history of New York women's dress styles unfolded itself as mannequins glided across a stage on tracks, to the accompaniment of music and a commentator's voice on tape.

From here we sped back to Manhattan, went to a distinguished exhibit of rare Buddhas (which Malcolm constantly referred to as the "Boodies") at Asia House, then stopped by the Museum of Modern Art for a tour, had lunch at Betty's apartment, and ended up the afternoon until closing time at the Museum of the City of New York, right in our own neighborhood. Malcolm concentrated on the fire engines there, and Clare sat quietly on the floor through yet another audio-visual presentation, this time on the history of New York City.

By the time we had reached home again, after eight hours of concentrated study and feasts for our eyes, we were tired in our bones, our feet, and our minds. We could not have looked at one more thing. We thanked Betty for a very special day. It was my kind of a Saturday.

But the children reacted differently. As a result of this museum exposure, they refused to enter another one for an entire year. They would not even accompany out-of-town guests to see the dinosaurs at the American Museum of Natural History, which heretofore had always brought out the budding curator in both of them.

I shall continue trying to instill a love for certain things in my children, the things that have given me so much pleasure through the years. Yet the more I try to imbue them with a thirst for foreign languages, for music and art, the more they resist. Perhaps I should take the opposite tack and pretend to disdain the things that are dear to me; pretend to adore baseball and hate the opera. At times I have purchased tickets "as a surprise," hoping to creep up on Malcolm's growing love of sports with a parallel interest. When I got us tickets to the New York City Opera at Lincoln Center, I chose the best of the fairy-talelike operas, *Madame Butterfly*. I had first wept from emotion at it when my mother took me to the Metropolitan Opera when I was seven. The music of this opera is so melodious, and the costumes and sets are so magical, that I felt sure this would be a performance that would appeal to Clare and Malcolm (who at this point were seven and five). It would have to be a meaningful experience for them. It even had the United States Navy to appeal to the male part of the team.

By the end of the first act, two elderly ladies sitting next to me said that either I must take Malcolm home, or they were going to ask the usher to eject us. He had indeed been a bundle of squirming noisiness. I was worn out trying to "shh" him; I had tried digging my fingers into the flesh of his thighs. Nothing had worked. I gathered up our coats, and, in humiliation, led the children from the theater.

In need of a little balm to pour on my wounds, I turned to my daughter for support.

"Clare, *you* must have thought it was sensational!" It is very easy for me to put words into other people's mouths. I do it all day. Silence greeted my enthusiastic question. I asked again, "Well, didn't you?"

"Mommie, they didn't even speak English," she replied. "I couldn't understand one word."

"But Clare," I protested, "you don't have to understand the words. I told you the story beforehand. You're supposed to listen to the music and feel it."

"I don't feel anything when I don't understand the words."

Luckily for Puccini, there aren't too many Clare Hollensteiners in this world. I sat back in the taxi and relaxed. Both kids were just like their father. I might as well not fight it. I canceled right then and there my lofty ideas of saving money to send Clare to Florence for a year before college. Give Malcolm a Chicago Bears football game and give Clare a teenybopper to watch on the tube, and they'll be happy. When I was their age, I was thirsting for great cultural experiences. Where in hell were *my* genes in these kids?

Food is still one of New York's greatest assets. Where else in one block can one buy the biggest, longest hero sandwich, find an assortment of one hundred and thirty-five cheeses in one store, and then be able to select from among ninety-two types of sausage? Where else can one lunch at McDonald's in a space-age efficiency trap and then be taken to dinner and be served an excellent *osso bucco alla Romana* or a spicily hot Szechuan duck or an exquisite *soufflé au Grand Marnier?* Of course the fact that someone else is picking up the check is a very important part of this enjoyment.

I care a great deal about good food and wine. (Years of living abroad can spoil one for the pleasures of the table.) Even after the demise, for economic reasons, of some of the greatest restaurants in New York, there are still some exceptionally good ones. There will still be better places to eat in this city than anywhere else long after the Chicago steak houses and the Dallas club and hotel food have disappeared into the new world of fast-food pancake houses and fried-chicken and burger chains. R.H. and I have our own lists of restaurants to which we lead our out-of-town friends. The service and food are always good; the atmosphere is passable. (Good conversation at the table is far more important than the atmosphere of a place.) The bill is also payable.

It is fascinating to observe the manner in which certain New Yorkers operate in certain expensive restaurants. It is a status symbol of their success in business. Some people feel they *have* to lunch at La Grenouille, Orsini's, Elaine's, La Caravelle, La Côte Basque, Le Cirque, or La Goulue every day in order to be seen, discussed, and written about in the fashion or gossip columns. Some people, particularly out-of-towners, regard being recognized by the headwaiters at the "21" Club as the only proof positive they need to believe they are important people. I would love to know the sources of the incomes of such restaurant habitués; they must be endless. A fifty-dollar bill for two is the common denominator for such lunches, but it is something that I cannot in all conscience charge back to a client. However, when I am someone else's guest, then I always feel a warm surge of relief and gratitude.

There are certain restaurants to be seen in at one o'clock; others to be seen in at nine in the evening. The proper attire is the most important element of such an evening. The little Halston or Adolfo—the proper jewelry—the proper dark suit for the man are all part of the "to be seen syndrome," to some much more important than eating.

When I am lunching in an elegant bistro, I cannot help looking over at the incredibly thin, chic women all around me who are picking at their grapefruits, omelets, or lettuce leaves. This is all they ever seem to eat. I keep wondering if they sneak home in a taxi cab and lace into a hot-fudge sundae. But it's a thin, thin world in New York. Even if they don't eat, of course, those people are charged the same price as if they had waded right through the *coquille St. Jacques,* the *foie de veau à l'Anglaise,* the salad and fancy dessert.

There is an exquisite dessert offered by all such fancy restaurants that I would love to order, but I do not. I could never bear to be the object of all those disapproving glances from all those thin women. The concoction is usually served in an oval dish and looks like puffy round clouds of meringue, criss-crossed lightly on top with threads of burnt sugar, everything adrift on a smooth yellow custardy sea. Some people call it Floating Island. It never looked that good when I was a child. Like all the succulent fruit pastries and the Napoléons, it is included in the price of the lunch, but it remains untouched by the thin, beautiful people. They just pay for it. (Surely the waiters must enjoy it after they have gone.)

I absolutely loathe the business of "being sat" in just the right place by the maître d'hôtel in restaurants. (*Women's Wear Daily* has probably delineated more "in" and "out" areas in more important restaurants than any other social force in existence.) The New Yorkers who care nervously check their geographic location when they are seated even before they look to see if they sat down with the right group of friends. The management of La Grenouille works itself into a Gallic lather keeping the needs of editors like John Fairchild satisfied. Over at Orsini's, Michael Coady, publisher of *W*, peers through his horn rims almost every day to see who of the fashion and social worlds is lunching with whom. Chaucer would have had a good time dropping in on the scene, and might well have compared it all to the daily procession at Bath.

Eugenia Sheppard, whose syndicated fashion column makes her a national power, rules like the queen of fashion when she lunches. Her companion is usually a Cecil Beaton, a Princess Grace, or another member of visiting royalty. Aileen Mehle, the warm, sexy syndicated columnist of jet-set doings, includes a lot of zesty fashion reporting, too, in her "Suzy" column. However, she is a night owl, and leaves the lunch scene to Eugenia and *Women's Wear Daily*.

A lot of people will never meet Oscar and Françoise de la Renta, Egon or his former wife Diane von Furstenberg, Nan Kempner, Chessy Rayner, Gloria Vanderbilt, or Bianca Jagger and her walking stick. Yet they will rush with breathless haste to their newspapers each day to relish vicariously what their heroes and heroines ate or wore or said the night before. When a fashion superstar confides to a reporter that she is tired of fashion and wears only blue jeans now, the entire garment industry on Seventh Avenue shudders in an immediate reaction. Dress sales will be down at once. The industry depends upon the show horses to generate publicity about their new wardrobes, their new furs, their new hundred-and-seventy-five-dollar boots. How else would Mrs. Miller in Highland Park, Illinois, know she had better get cracking with her own wardrobe?

My influence with La Grenouille, one of the finest restaurants in New York, has always been nil. My regular business acquaintances, my friends, and my husband all share something in common: they can't afford to take me there. I am certainly not going to take *them* there. Many of my richer business colleagues prefer to invite me to their corporate dining rooms, where one lunches easily, quickly, and well, without wasting time on transacting bills. One day, however, I made a reservation for seven at the Frog Pond (a *Women's Wear Daily* synonym for La Grenouille). We had decided to shoot the wad for lunch that day, since the festive occasion was a reunion of Farmington and Vassar classmates. It was a pretty star-studded cast, headed by the mayor's wife, Mary Lindsay, and her newly engaged daughter, Kathy. A wedding in Gracie Mansion, the mayor's home, was to be the biggest social and fashion news for months. The press followed Mary and Kathy Lindsay right into the restaurant, but they were shooed away. The owner was stunned. Here was the mayor's family, the place was full, and there was no table for Mrs. Lindsay. Sheer panic was written on the late Monsieur Masson's face, and I loved every minute of it. Mary saw us at the worst table in the place, all the way back. Gasps of disbelief arose from the velvet banquettes around the room as the Lindsays strode to the back of the room. Even the lovely anemone flower arrangements seemed to perk up and bristle with excitement. *Quel horreur!*

We all enjoyed it to the hilt. We had more in store for the management. When the bill came, I was appointed treasurer. I did some fancy mathematics on the back of it and came up with an equal sum for all, including tip. Six of us absorbed the bride-to-be's lunch, but not her mother's. The wife of the mayor had to ante up like the rest of us. Ten-dollar bills and piles of change were soon stacked up by my plate, croupier-style. The scene was faintly reminiscent of my student travel days in Europe when, while paying the check, boys and girls alike, we would count the exact number of glasses of mineral water or wine each of us took and charge accordingly. Since La Grenouille is used to big spenders, hundred-dollar bills, and important people sitting in important places, the restaurant will never, I'm sure, forget our college-reunion lunch.

I enjoy grabbing a quick buffet lunch at the Colony Club, if I'm on business in the neighborhood of Fifty-fifth Street, and I like to meet friends at a bastion of old-world New York, The New York Exchange for Women's Work. Here the food is delicious and the atmosphere unchanged since the time of my great-grandmother, it seems. One runs into other habitués such as Billy Baldwin or Truman Capote; and they sell the best salad dressing in town in a bottle that looks like a urine specimen and bears a drugstore-type label.

Another joy of New York is that it is, always has been, and always will be the crossroads of the world. I run into Omaha friends and Rome friends at the same traffic light on Fifty-seventh and Fifth. All the people one has ever known in any of the periods of one's life are constantly walking around one small area of a very big city. There are so many coincidences that one can even become quite blasé about it.

This certainly holds true for encounters with old Kennedy Administration pals. One does not need a November to roll around, with its anniversary of the President's murder, to make any of us remember White House days. The other members of the "Kennedy team" are everywhere. Jacqueline Onassis lives "down the street" from us. Jean and Steven Smith and Pat Lawford have apartments here,

too. Professor Arthur Schlesinger, Jr., lawyer Ted Soren-
sen, National Basketball Association Commissioner Larry
O'Brien, Ford Foundation President McGeorge Bundy
and their wives live here. The Shrivers, Ethel Kennedy,
and close friends of the President's like Red Fay, from San
Francisco, come into New York on business frequently.
Pam Turnure Timmins, who handled Mrs. Kennedy's
press, is an interior designer here; Nancy Tuckerman, who
took over for me with Mrs. Kennedy and who has remained her close associate all these years, works for a big
publishing house here. Pierre Salinger and his cigar pop
in and out of town from Paris; his former assistant, Andy
Hatcher, is with a big public-relations firm here. If we all
have new lives now, we all did share a very special time in
history together. There is an unspoken bond between us,
one that neither time nor distance will eradicate.

Upon occasion I run into McGeorge Bundy, one of the
brains of J.F.K.'s staff, at the A & P in our neighborhood. I
have tried to stress to R.H. that if the president of the Ford
Foundation can tackle the Bundy family marketing on Saturday mornings, perhaps he might be able to do the same
with the Hollensteiner marketing. It makes no impression.

The Kennedy family members who live in New York—
Jean and Steven Smith and Pat Lawford—circulate around
at parties. Pat does some work for the French couturier
Jean Louis Scherrer, and is consequently gowned in one
of his latest creations.

One sees Ethel Kennedy in New York when she's rally-
ing around her pet causes, particularly the Robert F. Kennedy Memorial Celebrity Tennis Tournament held every
August at Forest Hills. If I'm sitting in a restaurant and
hear a "Hey, kid!" I know it has to be Ethel. The last time
I saw her husband was when he was playing tennis with
her, the spring he was killed. She has not aged since then;
she does not show the strong emotional scars that must be
there. Eunice and Sarge Shriver also come to New York,

he on legal or political business, and she for her mental-retardation projects. She has devoted her life to this cause and is immensely effective.

Whenever I catch a glimpse of Teddy Kennedy, he is surrounded by hundreds of people, lost in an adoring crowd. It reminds me automatically of other Kennedy brothers in other times and in other crowds. I also think of what his wife Joan has been through. She is one of the nicest of the family in many ways, and some day her real story will be told.

Yes, the same old faces are still around, scattered between here and Washington, but with new lives, new goals. Because we all shared a very special time in history together, there is an unspoken bond between us, a bond that neither time nor distance will eradicate.

As for the one whose memories are the sharpest, Jacqueline Onassis, she is very much a part of the New York scene in spite of other residences abroad. When her first husband died in Dallas, the American people seemed to feel that she was their mass inheritance, to mold as they wished. They thought they could select her American marriage partner at a date suitable in their own eyes, as well as dictate her interests, her charities, and her daily schedule of activities.

They were very wrong indeed. Jacqueline Kennedy belonged to herself, as always, on that November day when her husband was shot. She pulled herself together with a majestic dignity to walk through a state funeral the likes of which this country will probably never witness again in history. If she had been a widow in any other country, even a backward country, she would not have been forced to conform to public opinion. She could have been retired from the public eye and public responsibility. But we are all star-struck in this country. We want to know what our stars buy, what they eat, when they brush their teeth, what they say to the salesgirl. We want all the Grace Kellys of the world to marry only the Prince Rainiers of the world, too. We like our fairy tales.

The American public would not loosen its hold on Jacqueline Kennedy. First they criticized her for the lavish clothes she bought; then they criticized her for appearing too informally in pants, sweaters, and a trench coat. They had a head of state or the chief executive officer of a major corporation picked out for her next husband. What they failed to realize is that when she moved out of 1600 Pennsylvania Avenue, she was no longer the wife of a public official. The American people had no right to expect her to act as if she were a public official herself. She was *not* the one who had chosen to run for public office. She was not beholden to the voters any more. She could damned well do what she pleased. . . . And she did.

Those of us who knew this extraordinary, independent young woman were delighted over her marriage to Aristotle Onassis. He had charm, a love of living; he represented power and wealth. Life with him meant independence for her, privacy, travel, freedom—all the things she had *always* cherished. She had served her country well as wife of the President; now she wanted her own life back again. During the years Ari Onassis was alive, she was able to give her first priority its proper attention: the raising of a pair of children as best she knew how.

Like all of us, I know she remembers fondly the good things about the White House days. One day we stood impatiently waiting for our respective baggage at the Eastern Airlines terminal after a flight to New York from Palm Beach. We had been talking for twenty-five minutes. Still no baggage.

"Jackie," I said, "if only Air Force One had taken us here. We wouldn't be waiting for any baggage in a mob of people."

She laughed that wonderful, throaty deep laugh of hers. Then suddenly our expressions changed. We were thinking about all the times we used to fly around on the President's own plane, Air Force One. Our bags would mysteriously be transferred from the plane right to our rooms well in advance of our reaching our destination. It had always fascinated us to know the secrets of the White House baggage handlers. How comfortable and luxurious it had been to fly the world on Air Force One! But the last time Jackie had taken it was November 22, 1963, on the return from Dallas. It had already become Lyndon Johnson's plane by then.

7

Entertaining Requires Only Time, Money, Energy, and Heart

Entertaining is certainly not all food and table design. Some of the worst parties given are the most lavish ones. In all the years I spent at parties in embassies and in the White House (which meant work for me, not fun) I noticed that what mattered more to the guests than the physical surroundings was the spirit of hospitality extended to them by the host and hostess. I remember one night being a guest at a glittering ball in a Roman palazzo where we all tried to have a good time *in spite of* our hostess. She was an aloof woman of royal blood, whose hand, when shaken, felt like a chilly plastic bag of creamed onions. As she circulated among her guests, she never seemed to see them, and, whether from acute shyness or outright hostility, her manner gave a cold edge to the elegant scene that had been set in her magnificent Baroque palace. It should have been a great party. Rome's best band was there; the champagne was flowing; candlelight flickered on the frescoed ceiling and against marble-paneled walls; footmen in green-velvet livery looked after our every wish. My wish almost immediately was to be out of there.

The John Kennedys "unstuffed" the White House parties, so to speak, by having the Marine Band play as soon as the first guest arrived and by offering cocktails before dinner. Traditionally, the Marine Band had not been allowed to play until the First Family came down the great staircase to begin the receiving line just before dinner. In the past the guests had been left to stand musicless and drinkless for a full half hour in an atmosphere that could only be described as formidable. Luckily, the Presidential couples who followed the Kennedys did not try to revert to the colder formality of the past.

Watching Ambassador Bruce and his wife at work during their embassy parties was excellent training for me. At diplomatic entertaining, they were both the smoothest of professionals, for they understood its importance in the carrying on of embassy work. They would brief themselves thoroughly on all their guests, who often numbered well over a hundred. As each one came down the receiving line, they would catch the name and say something pertinent, such as, "So you're going to the United States with the France-États-Unis? That's a very fine organization. I hope you will enjoy your trip to our country." . . . "I'm told you are a very good painter. I hope to come to your show when it opens here." . . . "So, you're a member of our Olympic team. We are all expecting great things of you. Good luck!" Each guest, of course, felt flattered that the distinguished-looking man in the striped pants and the dark jacket and the elegant woman by his side knew who they were and that the Bruces had cared enough to find out about them.

I learned from them the importance of a good introduction, with the name and title, if there is one, correctly and audibly pronounced. When an introduction is mumbled, everyone is embarrassed to ask for a repetition of the names and therefore awkward gaps in conversation abound. When a third person joins the group, the embarrassment increases because no one can introduce him. Bravo to the person who has the courage to admit that he hasn't heard any names and asks to have them given again, loud and clear. If a host or hostess can add some compliments and information to each introduction, any party has a good chance of success, because then shy people can find something to say. When guests who are strangers to each other arrive in our apartment, I like to introduce them to each other in an exaggerated but good-natured manner in order to get a good conversation going while I seek out R.H. (who is inevitably still in the shower) and get them a drink. "Mary and George Parsons, meet Barbara and Dick Soames. Barbara, by the way, is the best woman tennis player on the East Coast and Dick is the top heart surgeon in the whole country. As for the Parsons, they live in a nineteenth-century house filled with a wonderful African art collection!" Having thus given them four things right off the bat to talk about—tennis, hearts, house restorations, and African art—I can leave the room.

If we are giving a dinner party for someone from out of town or from another country, everyone is likely to be a stranger to the honored guest. I always send a "briefing list" to the guest of honor ahead of time, giving him the biographical information that he might want to have about the guests. If, for example, he is a French banker, he may well prefer to seek out his American colleagues in conversation rather than someone in another field. If he is visiting New York to meet businessmen to learn the American financial picture at present, he will be grateful to know which guest is on Wall Street and which is a department-store executive or a university professor. I am so obsessed with the importance of proper introductions, after years of social secretarying, I have been known to introduce women to their ex-husbands at large social gatherings, brothers to their sisters, employees to their bosses. I am forever giving the wrong married name ("No, dear, that was my husband's name two husbands ago"). I can't even stand a short elevator ride without introducing all of the occupants to each other, if I think I know them. My record for *faux pas* is quite unchallengeable, for instance the time I introduced the Indian ambassador to everyone at a White House reception as the Pakistan ambassador. No matter. I keep consoling myself that for every error, I get fifteen right. I really believe that people like to be introduced to each other—whether they're standing around at a press party, talking in the street, or clustered in the elevator. I long ago overcame feelings of acute embarrassment when I come out with the wrong names. It is not the end of the world, not even of good friendships. Trying to introduce people is a mark of good manners, so one should be forgiven one's inaccuracies.

If the host enjoys people, then a gathering can't help but be a success. If he does not, like our Roman princess, then no amount of fancy catering or beautiful décor can make the party go. The mood of the person directing the show is what matters. Sometimes I think that people get married with this factor in mind. Many couples I know include one partner who is ill at ease with people while the other is relaxed and outgoing. Their household will invariably be warm and welcoming because at least one of them knows how to operate with guests. It takes only a few sentences from one person to put out the welcome mat.

We have one friend who is completely disorganized in the kitchen but who greets her guests so warmly at the door that it doesn't matter if we don't see her again until dinner is served. She literally hugs us all and makes us feel as though she has been waiting all her life for this night. She sits us down in her living room on comfortable seats with our drinks and leaves us feeling good about ourselves. We must be pretty terrific to deserve such a lovely welcome, we say to ourselves; the evening has begun on the right note. She, in the meantime, can be heard dropping things and swearing in the kitchen. Like me, she will not allow a guest to step into her kitchen, even when we hear the sound of breaking glass—it would only make matters worse. She is almost helpless in the culinary department; yet she gives dinner party after dinner party because she loves to and because everyone loves coming there. Once the food is on the table, her face is flushed with victory and relief, and she never returns to the hated kitchen until we leave.

If there is no staff—or blessing of teen-aged children around to help—it is good traditional manners for a guest to offer to help one's host and hostess. If the answer is a firm "No," and in my book it always should be, then one should not make the offer again. I frankly don't enjoy trooping into someone's kitchen to scrape and rinse plates in my evening pajamas, because it breaks the entire spell of a party. (Like every rule, there's an exception, and that exception is when I help out my sisters-in-law, both great hostesses, in their respective kitchens after a party, on a Golden Rule basis.) When hosts expect me to help, I know it in advance, wear a less than beautiful dress, and troop out into the kitchen with the other wives. The men, of course, are all smoking cigars in the living room during this ritual, but my interior anger is soothed upon realizing that the younger women do not stand for this sort of thing. Onward equality!

There are many ways of thanking a host or hostess for a party, some good, some not so good. Occasionally the thank-you appears in advance when a guest arrives with flowers in his hand. This is a European custom, dating from the days when there was always a servant to whom the hostess handed the flowers and said, "Here, put these in water in a vase, and bring them into the living room." If I am giving a party I don't much like to be confronted at the front door by a large bundle of difficult-to-open stapled paper, which must be dealt with immediately. It is much more thoughtful to send flowers the day after the party, or even better, the day before, so that they will enhance the home and there will be plenty of time to arrange them properly. A bottle of liquor or wine is always a welcome gift, but a present is really not necessary. Some form of thank-you is necessary, however, and the written form is best. The time-consuming process of putting pen to paper, saying something nice about the party, and addressing, stamping, and mailing does add pressure to one's day, but it is also a mark of respect and a much-appreciated gesture in this day and age. A telephone call the day after the party is not half as good as the written note. It is too easy and too often made at an inconvenient time, whereas the note can be read, passed to one's spouse, and enjoyed together. If one has been a guest of honor at a party, a written note is not really sufficient; a gift for the host is in order. I have had appreciative guests send everything from a poem written just for me to a whole imported Italian prosciutto, enough to last for six months. The poet was impoverished, the prosciutto-sender was well heeled, but their presents were appreciated equally. Other inexpensive but thoughtful thank-you presents I have received and cherished were a packet of closet sachets; four seedlings planted in clay pots, with a note giving watering instructions and adding, "These will surprise you, so I'm not telling you what they are"; and two loaves of fresh home-baked bread, wrapped in silver foil and plaid ribbons.

Everyone has his own criteria for the perfect guest. Mine are three: coming on time, leaving on time, and giving at the party, either by making good conversation or by listening appreciatively. The best kind of party combines both conversationalists and listeners. At a certain moment during any dinner party there can be a sudden silence, usually caused by an accident of coincidence, when several conversations wind down simultaneously. The host will always be grateful to the guest who jumps into the breach and quite naturally begins a new topic of general interest. The easiest thing to throw into a silent gathering is something from a recent headline that smacks of scandal or great controversy. Depressing news is a poor idea, for a damper will eventually descend on the group. But subjects that elicit strong opinions on several sides are always good for a conversational launch. Jokes are guaranteed to flop during lulls; they are successful only when they enter naturally into general conversation.

I am not beyond jumping into any and all breaches whenever there's a lull. If no one gives a toast, for example, and I feel that the occasion warrants one, I stand up and give one, often to R.H.'s mortification. He figuratively buries his head in his hands when I jump to my feet. The only toast I ever heard him give was at our wedding luncheon. He obviously believes that one toaster in the family is enough.

One year the Aristotle Onassises celebrated their wedding anniversary at El Morocco, the only large private party they ever had on that annual October date. This was a very elegant evening, with over sixty guests dining and dancing in the private Champagne Room of the club. The guest list contained many familiar names: Mrs. Joseph P. Kennedy, Doris Duke, Mike Nichols, Mrs. Danny Kaye, and many unfamiliar ones, including some Greek business friends of Ari's and some leading Iranian oil executives. It was truly a mixed bag and many people didn't know each other. Jackie looked magnificent in a long, rustling white-silk skirt, a black-cashmere pullover, and a heavy, jewel-encrusted Moroccan belt. The caviar served during the cocktail hour was fresh and plentiful; so was the chilled Russian vodka that went with it. George Moore, a retired bank executive and then president of the Metropolitan Opera, gave the only toast. It was short and sweet, devoid of flowery phrases. We all arose and joined in this simple toast, and I then expected the rest of the men in the room to follow suit and that a long, jolly session of toasting would begin. It did not happen. During and after dinner, Stephen Smith emceed the entertainment, which consisted of Paul Mathias singing Hungarian songs, Adolph Green singing a witty ditty about England and France, and Pierre Salinger playing "Sometimes I Feel Like a Motherless Child" on the piano. Bill Buckley made us all laugh with a witticism in French about Watergate, and a South American woman did an amazing takeoff on the Kabuki theater, with appropriate gestures and garbled Japanese. All sorts of nationalities seemed to be represented, but what about something Greek? What about the country of our host? And where was the toast to Rose Kennedy, the oldest and one of the handsomest people there? I longed to take over the microphone and the proceedings, to instigate some kind of sentimental tribute to Jackie's happiness with her husband. It was, after all, their wedding anniversary, and the guests, except for George Moore, had ignored it.

Finally, I could stand it no longer. It looked as though the evening would soon come to an end. Women are not supposed to leap to their feet at a large party like this when no one is toasting, but I was going to do it anyway. I was going to toast the Greeks, and "all the great lovers in the world," beginning with Adam and Eve. I arose and went to the standing microphone. Although I could not see him in the darkness, I could feel the negative vibrations from R.H. across the room. He knew me well enough by this time.

Suddenly the spotlight was on me. I knew exactly what I was going to say; it would be a good toast, funny but sentimental. I got as far as "Ladies and gentlemen" when a male voice interrupted me. I couldn't see who it was because I couldn't see anyone with the bright light on me.

"Tish, Tish—don't!"

"Why not?" I whispered at him impatiently, my hand covering the microphone.

"Because Jackie and Ari aren't in the room!"

It was true. Jackie was powdering her nose, and Ari was out of the room talking to the headwaiter. I had been on the verge of giving a rather long speech in front of more than sixty people, the rousing climax of which would have been a toast to two empty seats. It would have literally finished off the evening.

At least one of the morals of this story is Don't make a toast until you see the whites of their eyes. It could have been one of the most embarrassing moments of my life, and I have had many. And R.H. would have moved to another hemisphere.

Guests who talk about their work to the exclusion of everything else are bores; so are people whose only mission in life is to criticize. But a celebrity or person of achievement who refuses to discuss his work can be irritating to the extreme. I usually tell such a person that he has an ego problem, which generally shocks him into loosening up. The greatest conversational pitfall for anyone is any personal subject of great interest to the speaker and of little interest to anyone else. It is particularly important for parents to avoid discussing their children in front of people who do not have children. It only convinces them all the more not to have children.

Being a good conversationalist, even if one is not in a particularly happy mood, is really nothing more than good manners. With the pressures of today's life, manners are more important than they ever have been. We may be dropping lots of fuddy-duddy rules of etiquette (such as the wearing of white gloves and the leaving of engraved calling cards on silver trays in people's front halls), but we should not abandon considerate behavior. Unlike etiquette, good manners are never out of style. Kindness is important no matter how free and informal our lives become. I am a bug on the subject with our children, because I know they will be happier adults if they have manners. Nannie and I urge them to do something special for a classmate who is ill; they have to write thank-you notes the day after receiving a present, attending a birthday party, or spending the night at a friend's home. When they complain that I insist too much, I revert to my social-secretary days in Paris, Rome, and the White House, trying to sound authoritative and official about the whole thing. They have always been rather awe-stricken when I mention the words "White House." It's nice to know that something can make an impression.

I tell the children about the beautiful thank-you note I received from Mrs. Harry Truman when she paid a visit to the Kennedys; I show them samples of Jacqueline Kennedy's artful notes, and Lady Bird Johnson's, and other special letters that have been saved. If the children can get it through their heads that the famous and the overly busy take time out to be thoughtful, perhaps they will not find such actions such a terrible chore.

When Clare and Malcolm were invited to the White House by Mrs. Nixon, I knew that would make an impression, too, even if they were only four and six. As for me, every time I go back to the Presidential mansion and the East Wing (where the First Lady's Secretariat traditionally resides), it is always a sentimental reunion. Many of the White House regulars who were employed even before my time are still there—White House guards, Secret Servicemen, police, gardeners, laundresses, footmen, the ushers'-office staff, the butler. Many of my old team are still plugging away in the social office, including correspondence assistants, calligraphers, and protocol specialists.

On this particular occasion Mrs. Nixon had invited our entire family, Nannie included, to witness a State Arrival on the grounds of the South Lawn. (Translation: the head of a foreign country and his wife arrive from Andrews air base by helicopter on the South Grounds, to be greeted by the Presidential family, to receive military honors, including a review of the troops and a twenty-one-gun salute, and to participate in the welcoming speeches.) As the Nixons' social secretary, Lucy Winchester, explained, Mrs. Nixon had read in one of my books how much those ceremonies had meant to me. She felt that "Tish's children should share in what she had seen and enjoyed so many times." (This was a marvelous chance to give the children a little sermon on the subject of thoughtfulness.)

R.H. was away on a business trip, but Nannie, Clare, Malcolm, and I arose at five-thirty one rainy, foggy December morning to catch the early air shuttle for Washington. The children had not slept all night in anticipation; the weather, of course, forced us to be very late. Clare kept trying to throw up from nerves, but I talked her out of it. I regaled them on the flight about a White House reception my family had attended one Easter Monday afternoon when my father was in Congress. I was only four, which was Malcolm's age at this point. My older brothers, Mac and Bob, ran a race in the East Room to see who could drink more glasses of orange juice and eat more of the cookies being passed on elegant silver trays by white-gloved butlers. Bob won, if I remember correctly, with a total of twenty-four orange juices and twenty-two cookies. I considered my brothers' behavior so unpardonable (having already become a social snob at four) that I pretended not to be related to either of them. Little Malcolm could not understand why I had criticized my brothers, a fact that gave me a sense of foreboding. I could see him mentally patting his stomach, trying to measure its capacity.

By the time we arrived at the White House, the president of Brazil was already on his way, not by helicopter, alas, but by car. Because of the steady downpour, all the military ceremonies on the lawn had to be canceled, and we sadly watched the big military buses and trucks leaving the South Grounds. Lucy Winchester assembled us in the Blue Room to await the arrival of the heads of state in the East Room. We were closeted in the familiar oval-shaped room with Secretary of State and Mrs. Rogers, Mrs. Emil Mosbacher, wife of the Chief of Protocol, and the Commandant of the United States Marine Corps, whose medal-emblazoned chest fascinated Malcolm for a thankfully long period of time.

But Malcolm was not to be consoled. "You mean, no soldiers at all, Mommie? No cannons?" I had had him well briefed on the military pomp, marching bands, and the rest, but it was not to be. Life was no longer worth living. His travel fatigue began to show.

The two presidents, followed by their wives, walked slowly into the East Room to the familiar strains of the President's own march, "Hail to the Chief," played by the red-coated Marine Band, who sat in their traditional corner of the big marble foyer. How I love that band, and how many superb memories the sight of them gave me—including one of the toughest moments in my years as social secretary when I had to face all of them and tell them that one of them needed a deodorant, and would whoever it was please shape up? (He did, by the way.)

Representatives of the armed services then presented and posted the colors in the East Room. Malcolm perked up a bit at this. I remembered how we always had to practice the color guard over and over so that the flags dipped just enough to avoid hitting the top of the doorway into the East Room. The welcoming speeches were made before a battery of microphones and television cameras. Henry Kissinger seemed to be everywhere at once. "Clare!" I whispered in the same tones I would use in pointing out Snow

White, "there's Henry Kissinger!"

"Henry WHO?" she retorted in a voice that carried right up to the portraits hanging on the wall. I gritted my teeth, certain she was going to call out, "Oh, Henry Kiss-Kiss?" our pet name around the house for that gentleman. Luckily, she did not. Everyone now began to talk at once as the Diplomatic Corps and State Department officials walked through a fast-moving receiving line, helped along by Bud Mosbacher, the Chief of Protocol. I chuckled to myself as I saw the man first in line. It was, as it had always been, the Nicaraguan ambassador, Guillermo Sevilla-Sacasa, who as doyen of the Diplomatic Corps always goes first. Many ambassadors have waited in vain for many years for him to retire. Several of the distaff side of the White House Press Corps saw me, and we had a reunion in the hall. One of them whispered, "Good to see you, Tish. Anything about today's way of doing things you would have done differently?"

"Oh, no, you don't," I shot back at her with a smile. She started to laugh, too. She would have liked nothing better than a quote from Mrs. Kennedy's former social secretary criticizing Mrs. Nixon's social secretary.

All of a sudden, the crowd magically disappeared. The ceremonies were over. The Presidential guests departed for their quarters in Blair House across the street. The President, Mrs. Nixon, and Lucy were in the Blue Room alone with Nannie, Clare, Malcolm, and me. We talked for a couple of minutes and then the President moved off to his office. The children's and Nannie's faces were devoid of emotion over being alone with the head of our nation and his wife. Nannie does not show her emotions in any case; Clare was experiencing curiosity rather than awe, and Malcolm was obviously still miffed about his soldiers.

Mrs. Nixon ushered us into the Red Room, where we sat down together with Lucy for a twenty-minute chat. The Red Room had very special memories for me, being the first room to be opened up in Mrs. Kennedy's White House restoration project. I looked down at André Meyer's gift of the Aubusson carpet and at the Douglas Dillons' Lannuier Empire furniture with renewed admiration.

We talked about everything from the new decorating changes in the public rooms to Jackie's official portrait, recently hung downstairs on the ground floor. We talked about the complexities of state visits abroad and the pressures on the distaff side of the Presidency. Talking to Patricia Nixon about Tricia and Julie was exactly like talking to Lady Bird about Lynda and Luci. They were two concerned mothers watching their children cope with life in a goldfish bowl and worrying about their lack of privacy. (The White House is the only residence of a head of state in the entire world where all the movements of the family, in and out of the house, can be witnessed at all times by the public and the office workers.)

Orange juice was passed on a silver tray, and Malcolm downed his one glass with dispatch, looking with disappointment at the retreating figure of the butler. He would have liked another twenty-four glasses, but soon he gave in to his fatigue and sprawled down, face first, pretending to sleep on the historic rug, right next to Mrs. Nixon's chair. I was embarrassed, and Nannie went white with mortification, but Mrs. Nixon merely laughed and bent over him.

"Malcolm," she said soothingly, "what are you going to remember most about this day?"

"Where are the cookies?" was his answer. "The President is supposed to have cookies."

I was humiliated. Mrs. Nixon laughed heartily and stayed my hand as I reached down to yank him up off the floor.

"I know children," she said, still laughing. "He's just being a boy. I'll have cookies for you the next time, all right, Malcolm?"

"All right," my son agreed reluctantly, and he pulled himself up and sat on a chair for the last few minutes of our visit.

The President's house is a very special place. My fondest hope for Clare and Malcolm is that they grow up to see it again, as did I, in some sort of close and personal way. It is, after all, not just a house. It is a seat of power. I also hope that Malcolm's manners will be better the next time. Clare, of course, considered Mrs. Nixon's remarks sexist.

"Mrs. Nixon said Malcolm was 'just being a real boy,' " she sputtered. "I guess the reason I couldn't behave that way," she added sarcastically, "is that I'm a *girl*."

To me, the White House has always represented the epitome of entertaining ever since I was a little girl. I don't care who is in office. I have watched and been part of parties there ever since the 1930s, but the best in my eyes will always be the private ones given for and by the staff. I remember so vividly President Kennedy's birthday parties, when the staff "roasted" him, much to his delight. A picture of Mrs. Kennedy's good-by party for me, with the Marine Band playing in their scarlet coats and singing "Arriverderci Roma," hangs on my wall, laden down with its memories.

Sanford Fox, who worked under me and all the social secretaries anyone can remember, finally decided to retire during the Gerald Ford administration. He had been seating official dinners and overseeing the calligraphy of menus, place cards, and invitations for three decades. I took the shuttle to Washington during a day of client meetings and spent exactly one hour at his good-by party, given by the Fords in the movie theater of the White House. All the social secretaries came back to honor him, the Fords made speeches, there were toasts and a cake, and many sentimental memories were invoked. I left Sandy with a memento to take with him into retirement. I had bought him a gold-tooled leather "table plan"—an oval-shaped object into which one sticks little white cards with the guests' names written on them in the order that they will be seated, according to protocol, around the table. Sandy had been making these table plans for years for the President's state functions, so I made one for him and his wife's future dinner party at their little home in Virginia. It was going to be some dinner party. Sandy's wife, Lucile, had the pope and the President on her right and left; Sandy sat between Queen Elizabeth and Indira Gandhi. The other guests at the table did not descend beneath the rank of a chief of state or a prime minister.

Because of the hectic pace, there is a certain amount of bluff in my world of entertaining at present. I can no longer be the perfectionist hostess I once was. Before I had my own business, before R.H. came into my life, I was a women's-magazine dream. Inspired by years of great cuisine tasted in the dining rooms of world-famous embassies, I would spend days preparing delicacies to titillate the palettes of my dinner guests. I learned dishes from the embassy chefs in Paris and Rome, and from chef René Verdon at the White House—and only their best ones. My easier recipes appeared in several cookbooks published in America (all of them plagiarized from the world's great cooks, of course). My table settings were memorable, too, because I had been influenced by the magnificent table designs used by my ambassadorial and Presidential employers in their official residences.

Those days are gone, probably forever. Now my principles for entertaining are organized entirely according to how much can I do in the shortest possible time, with the least amount of effort. This is hardly a motto for "*une femme de grande distinction,"* which is what I have always wanted to be.

When things are really frantic and it's too late to do anything but set the table for a party, I close my eyes and call one of those services that will deliver a delicious main dish like *blanquette de veau* with rice, salad, and rolls on the side. All I have to do is heat them up and transfer them to pretty serving containers. I would never admit the source of the food, of course, and I always make the dessert, just to save my own face. Importing the main dish is expensive and not as good as one's own cooking, but sometimes it is the only alternative open. Once in a while I will hire a waitress to serve and clean up, but usually I call her too late and end up saving a bit of money by having the guests serve themselves from the sideboard. R.H. and I make a good KP team after dinner. We share a mutual dislike of leaving one ash tray dirty after a party, and we can't face a disarrayed house the next morning.

No matter how easy one's menu is, giving a dinner party is unquestionably an exercise involving a great deal of effort. The "casual" hostess is a myth. If she exists at all, she is a disorganized plan-as-you-go creature who is not thoughtful of her guests. *She* may be relaxed, but chances are that her guests won't be.

There never seems to be enough room in my house to make lavish preparations. How can I possibly think great Cordon Bleu thoughts in my kitchen when the sink is filled with Nannie's orange-juice squeezer, when Malcolm's Civil War soldiers and cannons are in battle array all around the canisters, when Clare's Girl Scout cookie boxes are stacked on the counters, waiting to be delivered, and when the fridge is filled with eight of Nannie's bowls of instant chocolate pudding? Even R.H. seems to be out to persecute me. Four cases of wine just delivered are blocking my entrance to the worktable, to be put away "when he has time." This is not the moment to complain. I must find my way around this obstacle course and force myself into action. Tonight is the big work night, because tomorrow I am having a party for eight guests. They are invited for seven-thirty, and they will come on time, because they know me. They know I will manage, diplomatically enough, to send them home by eleven at the very latest, much to R.H.'s embarrassment. (This early curfew is for the benefit of our guests as well as our own.) R.H.'s and my mopping-up operation after the guests leave takes until at least twelve-thirty, well past our regular bedtime. Since regular sleep is one of the principles by which I physically survive, and since a six o'clock wake-up time always seems close at hand, I refuse to let guests who want to drink too much enjoy their excesses at our expense.

Since our friends have learned by experience that there is no dillydallying over cocktails at our house, they always arrive at our apartment no later than seven-forty-five for a seven-thirty dinner invitation. By eight-thirty we are in the dining room, and *le dîner est servi*. Long cocktail hours only result in unbearably boring conversation as the drinks take their toll and destroy every guest's ability to appreciate my food. R.H. would be delighted if the cocktail hour were to continue forever at a relaxed pace, but I have noticed when this happens in other people's houses that I begin to crawl up the wall with boredom and hunger and he is in bad humor, and worse physical shape, for forty-eight hours thereafter. Some people always have a long cocktail hour, so we generally arrive an hour late to avoid a good part of it. I always call the hostess in advance to explain that we will be late, but no one ever seems to mind. They just cocktail merrily away without us.

In spite of my own regimented, short-cocktail-hour dinner parties, our guests keep coming back—much to R.H.'s surprise.

It is now nine o'clock and the party is tomorrow. The children are reading in bed and it is time to face the kitchen. The menu will be simple: *bœuf bourguignon* with rice, French string beans, salad, rolls, and *crème brûlée*. I made the dessert last night, preparing its three separate cooking stages in between helping Malcolm with his reading and doing my floor exercises. The splendid *crème* in its crystal serving dish is balancing precariously right now on top of four of those damned pudding bowls. I know what will happen tomorrow unless I prepare a defense now. Malcolm will head like a homing pigeon at suppertime for the refrigerator, will remove one pudding bowl, and my beautiful dessert will come crashing onto the floor. I know him well, so I admonish him at bedtime, refusing him admittance to the refrigerator for tomorrow, no matter what. His big blue eyes fill with tears. "Not even for a soda, Mommie?" "Negative." Hard, cruel Mommie.

Yesterday morning I had already made a careful checklist of things to do for this party on the bus. So far the only things crossed off are the marketing items, the wine, and the dessert. I now wash, drain, and dry all the salad fixings, the job I dislike the most. I make a fresh jar of dressing. In order to get the plastic bags full of salad things back into the refrigerator, I must rearrange the bowls of pudding and my *crème*. I split the dinner rolls, put a small pat of butter in each, arrange them in a baking pan, and return them to the fridge, covered with a sheet of foil. They will be ready to thrust into the oven tomorrow without any additional steps.

I listen to a news broadcast in Spanish while I polish the silver. It would have been nice to have been able to ask Juana to polish the silver. I resolve again to improve my Spanish. At this point R.H. arrives in the kitchen to make his one contribution to my advance planning for the party. He puts the table pads on the table in the dining room. Bless you, R.H., but when are you going to move those wine cases out of my way? Thank God for my long arms, which can reach over the stacked cases to work on the table.

The main course, which I will now prepare and refrigerate tonight, is easy to make but time consuming. I do all the browning and sautéing of my beef dish, throw everything into the pot and simmer it for a while, meanwhile lacing it heavily with red wine and herbs. I turn off the fire and clean up the floor, which now looks as though I had rather carefully thrown down on it about a quarter of everything that went into the pot. It makes me feel better to mutter in a constant low undertone about why someone who works as hard as I do can't have a fabulous chef doing all this for me. The radio is now giving the weather report in Spanish. I am beginning to understand it. Why can't I understand Juana?

In half an hour I can put the cooled Dutch oven with its *bœuf* contents into the refrigerator. There is a moment of crisis when I realize that I have to make a choice between the eight puddings or our dinner party. The latter has to win. The Dutch oven with its lid goes in, and the eight little dishes come out, to die a horrible death in the kitchen sink. I'll hear it from Nannie tomorrow, not to mention two outraged young Hollensteiners.

There is no more cooking to be done. In fact, once our guests arrive, I will have to spend only eight minutes in the kitchen away from them to get dinner into the dining room. Tomorrow night's pans for the rice and beans are placed in position on the stove; I prepare the tray with demitasse cups, spoons, sugar bowl, and creamer, and balance it on the Girl Scout cookie boxes. Where there's a will, there's a way. All the serving bowls are placed inside the oven, where I hope they will remain until tomorrow night. Nannie can do her cooking on top of the stove tomorrow. The radio is now playing Spanish love songs. It's too bad Juana and I can't sing to each other. Maybe we could finally learn to communicate.

The table is next. Our Louis XV dining-room chairs are, surprisingly enough, upholstered in a red-white-and-blue-striped raincoat fabric. I enjoy alternating the linens for the table, an easy way to be creative. I have a store of table linens that includes many-textured tablecloths, colorful place mats, queen-sized bed sheets (they fit our table perfectly and make wonderful tablecloths), and napkins in different solid colors. Tomorrow's party will have a "country look," thanks to an abstract-patterned red-and-white bed sheet and wooden accessories. I arrange my wooden candlesticks on the table with matching salts and pepper mills, and large wooden place plates, which serve no earthly purpose other than being pretty to look at. As for the centerpiece which I thought up on the bus this morning, but which I will prepare tonight, I shopped on my way home for some big shiny red apples at the fruit stand and some little white flowers at the florist's. I now pile the apples into our large wooden salad bowl (we'll have to use our enameled Swedish bowl for tomorrow night's salad) and put the sprigs of white flowers into a glass of water to keep them fresh for tomorrow. Just before the guests come, I will tuck them into the little spaces between the apples. I have put red candles into the wooden candleholders, but then change my mind and replace them with white ones. (This is an exercise I go through regularly; I constantly buy colored candles which I never use. Somehow white ones always look better to me, except at Christmastime.)

A plain crystal cigarette urn filled with cigarettes goes at each place; so does a matching ash tray holding a navy-blue matchbook. The sterling flatware is put into place, as are the oversized crystal burgundy goblets. Then I place hot pads and serving pieces on the dining-room sideboard (which is really a hall table) and straighten up the living room, putting cigarettes and matches here and there, hoping few people will use them. I check on the guest towels and soaps in the front bathroom, weed out the coat closet in the front hall and leave room for six empty coat hangers. It is midnight and I'm exhausted. I find R.H. snoring peacefully in our bed, obviously tired from his one job of placing the table pads in place. I'd be glad to challenge to a duel right now anyone who says entertaining is easy.

The next evening, party night, I'm home at six-fifteen to find the children anxiously awaiting the chance to sit in the kitchen, watching Mommie cook. This is exactly what I don't want. I chat with them through the bathroom door while I take a quick bath, and then I do something I should not do. I let them watch a TV program they are not usually allowed to see, one with lots of violence, blood, and gore. This is their prize for staying out of my kitchen.

By seven sharp I am in the kitchen, wearing one of my dressy caftans with a long apron over it to protect it. Hair done; make-up in place; trusty little mirror ready on the wall. This I use while getting dinner together—just to make sure during my trips to the kitchen that there will be no telltale signs on my chin of having tasted the salad dressing or sauces, no drooping curl that got caught in a waft of steam or a flying sizzle of grease. *Madame la Cuisinière* must look her well-groomed best. After all, she wants everyone to pretend that there is a large staff in the kitchen.

Half an hour until the countdown, guesttime. The kitchen action is speeded up like a fast-action film. Coffee cream goes into the pitcher and back in the fridge; sugar cubes into the sugar bowl. Oven is lighted, kept low for warming up earthenware serving bowls and the rolls. The salad greens look magnificent. I dry them in paper towels once again, blanket them with herbs, and stick the big enamel bowl into the refrigerator for its last crisping. The Dutch oven is reheating very slowly. No need to bring the mixture to a boil until just before serving. More red wine goes into the pot, more spices. I shake a little in, taste a little, and shout *"C'est ça"* in triumph when it tastes just right. I make the rice and keep it hot by placing the saucepan and its contents in the top of a double boiler. I make the coffee, throw out the grounds, and wash the inside parts of the coffeemaker, just one less thing to worry about after the party.

R.H., of course, has just gone into his shower, so I prepare the bar, open two bottles of red wine, and put them where he will find them for his wine-pouring ritual. The ice bucket is readied; the lemon peel is sliced for martini drinkers; and mixed nuts, our only hors d'œuvre, are placed in the living room. I would rather have our guests appreciate my cooking than stuff themselves on fattening, elaborate hors d'œuvres.

A flying leap around the dining and living rooms tells me that everything is prepared. There are a few awkward moments when I tell Malcolm to remove his football pads and wet paintings from the front hall, or else. I light a Rigaud candle to make a lovely scent in the living room and await the front doorbell, reading the last page of *Women's Wear Daily* in that split second before the doorbell rings. R.H. will be late, but he'll do his bartending efficiently when he does arrive on the scene.

The above may be a typical dinner for eight, but most of our parties are somewhat less typical. I can hustle up Spaghetti alla carbonara (a recipe from Rome days) for a Sunday night supper or a *quiche Lorraine* with salad and white wine for a weekend brunch with no difficulty. One of my best dinners, impromptu, to put it mildly, took twenty minutes to prepare. It consisted of two frozen packets of lamb stew, heated with lots of wine, a package of frozen peas, heated with some well-chosen herbs, and, mixed into the stew, some noodles with butter and cheese. These happened to be items that were in our larder, and this happened to be a night when we completely forgot we had guests coming to dinner until they walked in the door.

They were from out of town and would have been very hurt and embarrassed had they ever known the truth. I hope they still don't. We bluffed our way along beautifully. I happened to glance at the kitchen clock as I clandestinely set the dining-room table. The time elapsed for that job was one minute, thirty-five seconds.

Although I do not have the time to design elaborate table settings any more, I still like to experiment. Sometimes I take our casual blue-straw place mats and flowered napkins and combine them with a very formal all-silver centerpiece. Or I'll use a piece of Nantucket driftwood on a dark blue gunny-sacking cloth. Or my mother's formal eighteenth-century Dresden centerpiece on an informal red, white, and blue checkerboard cloth. I like to use all kinds of things for the center: our household plants, an abstract sculpture, "hollyhock ladies" floating in a silver bowl, or a large, decoratively arranged bowl of salad. When I can steal some lilies-of-the-valley from someone's garden in May, I put sprigs at each guest's place in the little crystal cigarette urns. My favorite of all is a collection of red clay pots of geraniums clustered in the center of the table. Sometimes I mix little white votive candles in red clay pots among the geranium plants instead of regular candles.

Happily, the days when plastic flower arrangements were plopped in the center of the table are gone at last. Creative entertaining is here instead, and the younger generation is responsible. One couple in their twenties, both working and living on a very tight budget in a restricted space, give some of the best dinner parties I've ever been to. They make do in their one-room apartment by using a red-lacquered coffee table with a tatami mat and floor cushions as their dining area. Guests are served expertly cooked Chinese dishes, jointly prepared by them both. A simple, beautiful Japanese flower arrangement is always present in the center of the table. (She managed to take an Ikebana course in night school.) The food is served in decorative but inexpensive lacquered bowls, complete with chopsticks for the indoctrinated. It is all very simple, lovely, and well planned.

The older generations have been hidebound for so many years with the stereotyped flower-bowl-between-the-silver-candelabra that these changes are indeed welcome. Whether it's chili con carne or an Indonesian curry, the different foods served at parties today call for new colors and textures in table settings, even in shapes of serving pieces, plates, and glasses. People also seem to be eating in every room of their home, except maybe the bathroom. The new vogue of the "super family kitchen" (like the old vogue of the family kitchen) removes the need for a dining room. "Dinner in the kitchen" no longer means tunafish sandwiches for the kids at a formica-topped table in the breakfast nook. It means wonderful gourmet food served, perhaps, on a large butcher-block dining table, where the cook(s) can participate in their guests' cocktail hour as they work. I envy them greatly. I am a messy cook, and would rather not have people see how I operate; also I need to give total concentration to my cooking and can't afford to be distracted.

But regardless of your style, the secret of entertaining is simply to take a little time to show your guests that you care, and if time is at a premium, then a little creative bluffing can come in very handy. One night we gave a dinner party for eight, and I tried out a friend's dessert tip—a "fabulous chocolate mousse" made from instant chocolate pudding, lots of rich cream, and some crème de menthe. I made it and gave a sample to Malcolm to see if his growing taste buds would appreciate the concoction. I was unprepared for his answer:

"It's good, Mommie. It's butterscotch pudding. It looks like chocolate, but it sure doesn't taste like it. It's butterscotch."

Then I tasted it and decided it wasn't chocolate *or* butterscotch, but just odd. So I used gamesmanship and presented the concoction in a spectacular way. I took my delicate crystal brandy snifters and crammed the stuff down into them. The necks of the glasses were very small, and only the smallest spoon would go inside, so the procedure took a very long time. I added some whipped cream and some chocolate shavings. Later, while we were consuming our fabulous mousse, everyone was so involved in using their tiny spoons in the tiny openings that no one thought to question the flavor.

The dessert mess was minor in comparison to the time I purchased a large eye round roast for a dinner party but absent-mindedly forgot to roast it. I tried to grill it like a London broil, just before dinner, and the result was a meatless dinner, a very difficult situation to explain to non-vegetarians. I have also been known to leave a bit or two of paper towel in the salad when I've dried it too carelessly and fast. The messiest mess I ever made was when I dropped a beautiful strawberry ring mousse all over the floor. I scraped it up with a large spoon, praying that no one would enter the kitchen at that point. I stuck it in the electric blender, added a strong shot of cognac, some leftover strawberries, and some vanilla ice cream, then served it in glass bowls as a "new kind of strawberries Romanoff." I even ate some myself; it was excellent.

I have had my share of disasters in the kitchen, each one the result of having to hurry too much, but fortunately, the culinary successes have far outweighed the disasters.

Entertaining for children involves a lot of the same principles. We try to make each child's birthday very special, and if I have to be away on a birthday, we celebrate it as soon as I return. If I'm in New York on a birthday, no matter what arises at the office I rush home at lunchtime for the party (for which I've stayed up at night preparing). The planning has, in fact, begun at least three weeks before the event. I buy some invitations from the dime store, and the birthday child fills out the correct information, using the model I have given him. If more than a dozen are invited I have the invitations run off on a duplicating machine at the office.

The party is usually a lunch, and I state explicitly in the invitation that party time will be exactly one and a half hours long. Because there is no room in an apartment for body-contact games, the children play cerebral games for a while before the meal. Thirty minutes are plenty for Mommie, because little boys and girls quickly start to roughhouse in a living room filled with fragile objects. Prizes for the winners are given out by my children, who have also wrapped them (which accounts for the third-hand look of each prize). One of our favorite games is to have the children look at a card table full of common objects for three intense minutes. Then they rush to their pads and pencils to list as many of the objects as they can remember. Another game that requires some advance preparation (although once made, the props can be stored and reused for other parties) is the passing around to a circle of seated children of a series of objects, each encased in a numbered nontransparent bag made of fabric remnants or bits of old sheets. Each child writes down on her numbered list what she thinks is inside each bag after she feels it, and passes it on to the next child. It is amazing to see, for example, how many different things a cluster of twenty-five rubber bands can feel like when you can't see them. (Adults have as much trouble as children in guessing the contents of the bags.) We have enclosed in bags items like a group of paper clips, a light bulb, small strainer, book matches, bookmarks, rubber erasers, a scouring pad, a shower cap, elastic bandages, and so on.

Although we live across the street from a park, I simply

won't take on the responsibility of leading a large group of children to play in a New York park—unless I were to be assisted by a battery of baby-sitters and the entire police force, which I'm not. Besides, one and a half hours of noise and excitement is as much as I can take. Enough is enough.

I was utterly intimidated by the thought of twenty-two of Malcolm's Saint David's classmates who accepted his seventh-birthday-party invitation. Each year the boys seem to grow more obstreperous (or is it that Mama is getting older?). I devised a battle plan for organizing absolutely every minute of their prelunch leisure time. I typed detailed instructions in several copies to hand to my helpers, including Clare and one of her friends. The sequence of the games, the rules, and the number of prizes were all specified. (R.H. sauntered in, listened to the din for four minutes, and retreated gratefully to his post by the hot-dog broiler in the kitchen.)

We managed to get through "Push the marbles by the knees from one end of the room to the other," "Pin the wart (a fresh raisin stuck on a pin) on the monster's nose" (the monster was left over in a Halloween poster, and I did not have time to organize a donkey and tails), "Drop the clothespins into the tomato juice bottle" (there was quite a bit of cheating here), "Draw the best animal," and a "Guess how many paper clips there are in the plastic box." The apartment damage was minimal; the glass in only one picture frame was broken; an antique Italian porcelain cup fell into pieces; a telephone book was torn; two ink spots were imbedded forever in a yellow chair seat; and seven large wall markings became a new feature of our décor.

We resort to a save-the-apartment plan whenever we are planning to entertain a large group of little boys. We begin by pushing the big table in the dining room back against the wall and removing the chairs from the room. The whole room thus becomes a nice big empty floor space.

Then we spread the children's printed animal (or fairy-tale or comic-strip) sheets all over the floor. Each child removes his shoes before entering the room and is told he can sit with a couple of friends on the sheet of his choice. Many of them rush to find seats under the tables pushed against the walls, because, as one seven-year-old explained it to me, "It's my own private dining room." Since they sit on the floor, we don't need to set the table with costly or time-consuming decorations. The sheets protect the floors, and crumbs and spilled messes are easily disposed of when the sheets are picked up after the party.

My menu is tailored with two goals in mind: to please the children and to make things easy for me. We have always used festive paper plates, cups, and napkins, although with the rising prices of such items, we will probably be back to reusable dishes. With R.H. tending to his duties of wienie-roaster, I organize Nannie and Miss Wenzel (our Nannie's day-off substitute, who is always a part of our children's parties) into an assembly line. As the frankfurter is passed from broiler to heated roll, some potato chips and a dollop of mustard and catsup are added to each plate. (This alleviates the problem of the boys throwing sauce bottles around the room to each other.) Nannie also passes a big platter of egg salad and peanut-butter-and-jelly sandwiches she has made for non–hot dog consumers. The platter is usually depleted in record time, constantly amazing us, since she always makes twice as many sandwiches as there are guests. Along with birthday cake, I always serve ice-cream bars (thus avoiding having to give the child a spoon or fork.) If anyone asks for a fork for his cake, I answer, "Let's see how few crumbs you can find in your napkin after eating it with your fingers." Miraculously, there are never any crumbs left.

One year as an experiment I took a group of Clare's fourth-grade classmates to a relatively inexpensive French restaurant near my office, one that is surrounded by skyscrapers and caters to a business clientele. Normally, the cost of feeding several children in such a place would be astronomical, but because I eat there so often I made an arrangement with *Monsieur le Patron,* and the cost of feeding seventeen little girls came to about the same as lunch for four adults would have been on a normal day. I brought in a large birthday cake from a nearby bakery. The girls came directly from the convent in taxis at their regular Wednesday-noon early dismissal. They walked in single file to the back of the restaurant, startling the blasé business crowd with their diminutive size and their gray convent uniforms. Right in the middle of lunch, one of them had to go to the bathroom, so of course all of them suddenly had to go to the bathroom. Back through the narrow tables to the front of the restaurant snaked all seventeen. One heavy martini drinker shook his head in disbelief, certain he was seeing triple instead of double. Everyone behaved beautifully, and, of course, they delighted the French waiters by singing "Happy Birthday to You" in French, followed by a snappy reprise of "How Old Are You?" in English.

One of the little girls had apologized to me before lunch: "I don't want you to be embarrassed, Mrs. Hollensteiner," she said with a worried frown, "but I-er-I don't eat French food." She spoke the words as if she were facing her first plateful of octopus and squid, for like most of the others she was a McDonald's habitué, and this was her first experience in a French restaurant. But she soon forgot her fears and ate heartily of everything, so I doubt she will ever be frightened of *la cuisine française* again. To Clare's classmates, it would be *poulet à la crème* and *petits pois au beurre* from here on; forget the creamed chicken and the peas.

The New York Times runs an article every so often about children's birthday parties—lavish ones costing over a thousand dollars, complete with special entertainment, fancy food, and expensive presents. But kids need only one thing in order to have fun: a group of other children. Give them a game or two to play, give them a birthday cake, and they will enjoy themselves thoroughly. A friend told me about two of her college roommates who had come to lunch one day to admire her new baby. One, a young woman of great wealth, brought an enormous, terribly expensive stuffed animal from the F.A.O. Schwartz toy store. The other, who was living on a very strict budget, had painted three empty baby-powder cans, each one with a different motif. The large stuffed animal evidently spent its life gathering dust in the corner of the nursery, pretty but admired only by adults, not by the child. The bright red, blue, and green baby-powder cans were clutched one by one all through infancy, and were still enjoying a prestigious position on the bookshelf years later—loved and remembered.

Although I do not have to decorate the birthday table because I use sheets on the floor, each guest goes home with his own "loot bag" inscribed with his name. I give one to each child as he leaves, so that the contents will not be spilled forth in our apartment, perish the thought, and the chocolate kisses and other gooey candy won't destroy our upholstery.

I always seem to be buying party favors on my business trips, since there is more time for personal shopping when I'm away than when I'm home. Bargains are always easier to find when the party isn't the day after tomorrow, and the favors themselves tend to be unusual and more fun for the children, too. One year I brought back some tiny wooden shoes from Holland and another year I found some little painted roosters in a Lisbon shop. When I was in Helsinki, lecturing, I discovered in the big local department store a group of tiny, inexpensive ceramic animals, made in Russia. Another year I found twenty little painted paper fans during a Chinese New Year's sale in San Francisco's Chinatown. When I get home, everything goes into the "gift closet" in which I keep a running supply of birthday presents for the children to give to their friends, goodies to give to children who are sick or in the hospital, and an advance-guard attack on the Christmas season. I also buy children's get-well and birthday cards by the dozen, so that we are always prepared. I purchase wrapping paper during the big post-Christmas sales, and keep it on hand, as well as a plentiful supply of the colored yarn Nannie taught us to save from incoming presents. (Nannie also gives an assist by ironing all gift ribbons so that we can reuse them.) I really envy such creative people as Molly Newman, who has a daughter in Clare's class. Molly handmakes every gift from her family. Even the gift wrap is a work of art—such as plain brown wrapping paper emblazoned with hand-painted tulips all over it. When a birthday present comes for Clare, it isn't something purchased; it's something personal like a bed pillow made of white piqué and gingham, with Clare's monogram in the center. God obviously passed me by when He was handing out the do-it-yourself talents; He passed by R.H. and our children, too. It's all we can do to get a piece of ribbon tied around a package, and the package always looks as though someone had wrapped it in the dark.

I wish I had time to carry out some of those delightful "party themes" presented in the women's magazines. They are all so pretty and tantalizing-sounding, but I believe that what really counts is having the right guests at the party, giving them plenty of food, and sending them home with a nice reminder. We have long since abandoned the idea of decorating the apartment for children's birthdays and of giving out unsavable favors like those paper snappers and party hats. Party decorations invariably go unseen; the children look at the apartment, the presents, and each other—not at the party décor.

Having grown up in a household where we could always

have our friends over, I am determined that our home will be the same. The children know that they can always invite their friends to visit and that I will always provide extra food and drink for impromptu lunch or supper parties. The apartment inevitably takes a beating, but possessions just aren't that important to R.H. and me any more. I hope that if Clare and Malcolm can learn how to become good hosts at an early age, they will keep this attribute all their lives. They will have learned the fundamentals of good manners: how to entertain, how to share, how to put other people at ease, how to think of others before oneself. These are simple lessons, and can be learned only at home.

The entertaining of male business acquaintances has never been a problem. I have taken men to lunch on business matters for some twenty-five years now, and in all that time there has never been an embarrassing episode. One reason is that when I'm picking up the tab, it's an arrangement definitely understood in advance; there is no mini-wrestling match when the bill comes. All a woman has to do is be prepared with her credit card (with which she can cope by stopping off to see the headwaiter on her way to the ladies' room); or she can have a check all written out to the restaurant except for the amount. It takes one second to fill that in, and there's no embarrassing waiting. If she has a charge account with the restaurant, better still. Taking a man to a meal at one's club is also a smooth way to handle it, but a woman who takes a male business acquaintance to a woman's club for lunch is, in my opinion, asking for it. The typical man is ill at ease lunching at the typical woman's club.

I took an old friend to lunch on business one day, and I noticed two people next to us on the banquette staring in fascination as I paid the bill. They were speechless with curiosity, a fact of which both my friend and I were acutely aware. Partly to alleviate my own feelings, I said in a tone my neighbors could not help but hear, "Well, I wish every business lunch were as pleasant as this one." My friend had a mischievous look in his eyes when he answered just as loudly, "But darling, when your business with me is *love*, it is always so wonderful. Where do we go this afternoon? Is the hotel room all ready for us?"

I laughed all the way down Fifty-sixth Street, certain that our shocked neighbors on the banquette were still discussing the rich nymphomaniac at the next table and her lover.

Time is so precious there is often none available for lunch outside the office. I prefer to transact business in someone's office, anyway. One does it faster, more efficiently, and better than from a dining table. I am inevitably ill equipped for serious talk in a restaurant, and end up taking important notes on sugar packets, matchbooks, or the back of a blank check. I have never had a business lunch yet at which I didn't suddenly need my briefcase; of course, the briefcase is checked with my coat.

My staff and I like to "brown-bag" it to the office. Our small office refrigerator is stuffed with yoghurt, carrot sticks, hard-boiled eggs, grapefruits, soda, and apples. We could open a health store. These lunches, which came into style with the recession and with diets, are satisfying for their taste, economy, and the feelings of virtuousness they invoke. Sometimes I invite a close friend, the nonworking kind, to come to my office for lunch. This is entertaining, too. It requires an invitation, planning, and cleanup. I make the sandwiches at home, prepare fruit, and pack a bottle of wine, some glasses, and napkins in my tote bag. During our office picnic we sit discussing old times and the future of our children, while I continue to answer important telephone calls or handle urgent business as it comes along. My visitor is usually delighted to catch me in my own office milieu and be able to observe the action. I notice the look that will cross her face every so often, perhaps a pang of remorse that her college education, the same as mine, had overeducated her for the life that she has been leading. Perhaps not. We sometimes talk about starting to put that education to use, going back to school, taking a typing course, learning accounting, acquiring a marketable skill. It may mean that she will have to take an apprenticeship at a salary far beneath her worth to gain the most precious asset of all, experience. A friend of mine who had her doctorate in the history of art but had never worked for money in her life looked out of my office window one day, sipping some white wine from a crystal wine glass I had provided for the occasion. "Tish," she said rather sadly, "I feel so inadequate going out on a job interview. All this foreign travel, all this education—I feel like a bouquet of herbs bobbing around in a pot of stew—only there's no meat in the pot!"

She has now put the meat in the pot. She began as a secretary in a small international business organization and rose to an executive level within fourteen months. She is so busy she now invites *me* to a sandwich with wine at her office.

After spending so many years both having guests and being one, I have accumulated some very strong opinions on the subject of "houseguestery." Whenever I visit someone for dinner or the weekend, I always, for some reason I would not care to have analyzed, experience anxiety if the bathroom is messy. I get upset if the water glass is one of those used plastic things that looks as if it has been rimmed in someone else's toothpaste. I just can't drink out of it, because even constant rinsing won't help its appearance. I also have an aversion to those arrays of pretty bottles filled with sickly-sweet cologne that the hostess obviously never uses herself.

I have always believed that every hostess should sleep

in her own guest room at least once. How else is she to know that the window screen is not properly set and is admitting a bunch of mosquitoes? How else is she to know that spending the night on her mattress is as smooth an experience as riding down a pot-holed Manhattan street? One of the most thoughtful hostesses I know always keeps a supply of new plastic-encased toothbrushes in the guest bathroom for forgetful friends, with a rack of twelve different kinds of toothpaste, all neatly squeezed from the bottom by the grateful guests. I have learned to love the hostess who keeps the guest bathroom supplied with a box of facial tissues, an extra roll of toilet paper (it's inevitably down to the last piece when the guest arrives), and some plain nonallergenic face soap for guests who can't use the pretty scented guest soaps. Every hostess should also try to put on her make-up in the guest bathroom, and every host should try to shave there. The light can be very bad, unflattering, misleading, and maybe even dangerous. When I stayed for the first time with Ambassador and Mrs. Bruce in the embassy residence in London, my hostess, one of the most accomplished there is, came in to see me as the footman brought me breakfast on a tray.

"All right," she said, laughing, "what's wrong with the guest room?"

"Nothing," I replied, surveying the beautiful porcelain breakfast set on the wicker tray. "How could there be anything wrong in such unmitigated luxury?"

"No," she said, "I want the truth. I haven't slept here yet. Something has to be not right. What is it?"

"The bathroom light," I said, my mouth now full of croissant. "I couldn't get my make-up on properly last night. I had to bring it to the bedside table and use a compact mirror."

A week after I had left, a friend of mine stayed in the same room. When I asked her about the visit, she told me how beautiful she thought Winfield House was, what a wonderful time they all had had, and how fascinated she was by the big new illuminated cosmetic mirror in the bathroom.

On the subject of electrical things, another common fault in the guest room is the bedside reading lamp. I do all my reading in bed in a sitting-up position, and if the lamp holds a forty-watt bulb (which belongs in an oven, not in a reading lamp), my evening is ruined. The hostess who leaves a large wastebasket in her guest room also knows what she is doing. Houseguests have to unwrap things, throw away packing tissue, plastic bags, and the old newspaper and magazines they were carrying. There should be one top drawer cleared in the bureau if it's an overnight guest, two drawers if the guest is staying longer. The closet should have empty hangers and some space to hang things. (Otherwise, one can use the shower-curtain rod in the bathroom.)

Having guests in an informal summer vacation house is a different matter. Rather than load the bathroom with scented bath powder, I stock it with plenty of band-aids, suntan lotion, after-sun medicated spray, and take-your-own containers of insect repellent for the flies and mosquitoes. Once I stayed in a house in Palm Beach where the host left in my bathroom the morning after my arrival a small, handsome thermos jug. The label read "medicine to take upon arising." Inside was one very chilled, very delicious Bloody Mary. (I didn't have a hangover, but was delighted that he had thought to anticipate my needs.)

I always manage to leave a bouquet of fresh flowers in each guest's room, but I've never been able to duplicate the opulence of a weekend I spent in San Remo, Italy, where I found a note awaiting me on the pillow on my bed. It read, "Gardener working beneath your window. Please call down from window to give him your flower order." I spent the next five minutes leaning on my elbows over the window sill, talking to the gardener, Luigi, who memorized my final selection of five flowers and delivered to my room ten minutes later a magnificent bouquet, beautifully arranged. Gardeners like that are a rarity these days, but I get the same kind of pleasure when one of the children comes in bearing flowers, even if it is a healthy bunch of dandelions in a jelly glass. (A bunch of dandelions looks very pretty in something black.)

The perfect houseguest is one who knows when to help and when not to. Houseguests who insist on interfering in a carefully planned schedule in the kitchen when one tells them to sit down and relax are more of a hindrance than a help. There are always things that can be done when a guest leaves, though, such as finding the linen closet, stripping the guest beds, and making them up with clean bedding for new guests as a surprise for the host and hostess. My favorite houseguests also remember to bring presents for the children; for us they bring items like an enormous *pâté de maison* or a wheel of Brie cheese, which require no preparation on my part but which provide hors d'oeuvres for the household for days. They do things like swim with the children when we're too busy. They write us thank-you notes the day after they return home, and later on they remember to send us color snapshots (the flattering ones, if any) of us and the children.

There is unfortunately very little written on the "art of being a houseguest." And most of what there is in book form is very out of date. In this era of telephones, it is rare to find written advice from parent to child as was once a regular custom. I was therefore delighted to come across a letter one day in Bob Wickser's house on Nantucket Island that he had written to his older children. He let me read it and I copied it to give to my own children when they are old enough to spend time in other people's houses without me breathing down their backs and telling them what to do. Bob had written:

"The first and most important rule is writing the bread-and-butter letter. My mother told me when I was a young boy that I must write a thank-you note within twenty-four hours of leaving my hostess. To forget, neglect, or put off too long writing such a thank-you note is to jeopardize your friendship, imperil your reputation, and lower your social standing in the eyes of people you like and respect (or why should you visit them?) Such a letter need not be long, flowery, or overly complimentary, and it should never smack of insincerity. Limit yourself to saying thank you for what you enjoyed. . . . Some people may think that when you visit a bachelor, it is not necessary to bother about writing because single men often seem careless and inconsiderate, gay or carefree; whereas older people expect conventional behaviour. I assure you that such is not the case. Everyone likes to be thanked and no one likes to think that his 'friends' take advantage of him. In truth, rich people like to think that they are liked for themselves and not for the luxury of their style of living, or the social and sporting pleasures which they can make available to their guests. [I only hope that such social and sporting pleasures will be available to Clare and Malcolm when they grow up.] I must remind you of the truism 'There is no such thing as a free lunch.' What you receive from others you must give back, and that really means giving of yourself, making an effort even when you don't feel like it."

The letter continues to warn against bringing a pet when one is invited somewhere, and discusses the giving of presents:

"I always fall back on my favorite rule of giving, which is to give something that I would very much like to have myself . . . a bottle of good wine or liquor, a delicacy, a good book, or something useful like a box of tennis or golf balls."

Bob continues with good advice on not accepting invitations if one does not feel well, the necessity of paying for one's telephone calls, tipping the maid (if there is one!), and he concludes:

"Remember that a desirable houseguest is punctual,

avoids arguments, gives as little trouble as possible, pays for whatever expenses he may incur, is polite to everyone in the house, is willing to engage in the activities planned for the day, and above all, says 'thank you' promptly."

There is indeed a lot of responsibility in being a good houseguest, just as there is in being a host or hostess. The thing R.II. and I like best about our houseguests is savoring the memories of the good times we had—after they have gone.

8
If You Think You Look Better, You'll Look Better

Like most other women with young children, I rarely have a chance to relax at home, to grab a few moments of refreshing solitude. Privacy and the opportunity to "save some of my day for *me*" almost disappear in a working woman's life from the minute she enters the hospital's labor room until the day her children reach maturity (whenever that is). When I hear someone incanting, "I want to find myself—to be ME—I want more time just for myself, to understand *who I am*," I know automatically she is not a working mother with dependent children. Self-analysis and introspection are incompatible with our station in life. Self-pity is not, however. There is always a little time for that. One can always sneak in a few precious moments of feeling put-upon while riding to work or waiting in line at the butcher's. But as for turning inward in any philosophical manner, forget it. There is no time for that.

One's mind-set upon arising is terribly important. One should start the day affirmatively, with a positive feeling that "good things will happen today." If they do, then one is a happy prophet. If they don't, then one can rationalize that "they'll have to be good tomorrow." It helps to wake up, sit on the edge of the bed, and give a big stretch with both arms, like a luxurious pussy cat. Then one should stand up and give some even bigger stretches, reaching from the toes high up in the air, one arm at a time, as if to say, "I'm all here, I'm awake and in good shape . . . the blood is circulating . . . the countdown is progressing nicely." If you don't know how to stretch properly, watch a dog or a cat in motion upon waking up from a long sleep. A nice half-minute wake-up stretch in an optimistic spirit puts one in the right frame of mind to greet whatever will be. (In our house "whatever will be" can be fairly mind-boggling, but one rises above it with an affirmative mind-set.)

The woman who can actually beg, borrow, or steal time for herself—even thirty minutes a day—is not only lucky but intelligent. Those thirty minutes are important. They can mean a recharging of batteries, the discipline of a helpful and necessary beauty routine, or the mental repose of reading or thinking about something unconnected with one's work. To shut the door on the world and to think about absolutely nothing at all is one of the most effective prescriptions one can write for oneself.

At least once a year I can do it. I can actually lie in my bathtub for an uninterrupted twenty minutes, relaxing every muscle in hot water, soothing my eyelids with cotton pads dipped in cool witch hazel or boric acid. The magazines have told me to do this, and it works. Obviously, no one else is in the apartment at the time. Obviously. My mind goes as blank as the white pads covering my eyes. Ten years suddenly drop off my life. I will be able to go out to fight the world again with vigor that night, looking clear-eyed and healthy, feeling warm and rosy, very aware of my own sense of well-being. I arise from my bath, Ariadne personified in flowing diaphanous garments (a caftan from a Tall Girls' Shop). My hair is clean, and it is brushed vigorously. I give myself a pedicure, a thorough tooth-brushing, and squirt cologne wildly from head to toe. Then I apply the same scent in a strong perfume to seal in the fragrance for that whole evening. (I do not put it on my face. I did that lavishly once and, as a result, spent several months wearing veils and visiting the dermatologist.)

R.H. will be unable to resist me tonight, because not even Cleopatra could have been cleaner and more lovable, sweet-smelling, relaxed, and *beautiful*. Then I remember that one of the very reasons I am so relaxed is that R.H. is out of town and I do not have to cook his dinner. The children and Nannie are also out to supper. There are only Dustin, Pierre, and myself at home. It happens about once a year. But thank God it does happen once a year.

There are thousands of women in this same predicament—a lack of uninterrupted time. When we finally make it to the hot tub, one of the children rushes in with an immediate problem to solve, or the telephone rings and it is always for us. I have a lucite gadget in my bath, something that looks like one of the metal milk-bottle carriers of old, in which I keep four different kinds of bath-water preparations. Based on oil, herb, or milk formulas, these magic potions help keep my skin soft, but, more important, they lift my after-office morale. Each night I alternate the kind of "bath junk," as Clare so poetically calls it, to keep that joy of total immersion in the hot water very real. The beauty experts in the magazines tell you to close your eyes "deeply . . . let every muscle go, start at your toes, relax, relax. Let every muscle, every bone, every piece of skin go. Relax, relax. Move mentally up the foot to your ankle. Relax the ankle, relax it completely." And so it goes, slowly but surely, until the entire body is in a totally limp state, utterly without tension. I usually make it just about to the ankle when a fight starts in the bedroom—which becomes the family room the minute I get home from the office at night. I arise from the tub, drip over our tangerine carpet, yell a few times, swat a pair of fannies, and return to the water, full of tension. The temperature in the tub has dropped twenty degrees. I put myself back into the exercise of relaxation anyway, beginning at the toes. I make it up to mid-calf when the next round starts. Malcolm wants to see a sports event on TV; Clare wants to see her teenybopper series. They aren't fighting each other; they're fighting the set. It's an expensive cable TV set, and the controls have already been broken five times this year. The last time the repairman came to fix it, he shyly asked me just what *was* the composition of my family. He must have been convinced we had King Kong living with us.

Clare is now sulking in her room (for five minutes), and Malcolm is crying from injured innocence in his room (for five minutes). I ought to be able to make the relaxation almost to the thighs this time before being interrupted. No such luck. The phone rings at the knees. Please, God, let no one answer it. Immediately, Nannie calls down the hallway: "It's for you, Mrs. Hollensteiner, it's for you." I shout back to her to tell the person I'll phone later, but Nannie has already disappeared into her room, not wanting to miss one second of her seventh viewing of "Masterpiece Theatre." I know she has not heard me, so I drip out of the tub once again. The tangerine carpet between the bathroom door and the telephone is beginning to look like a Jackson Pollock painting.

"Mrs. Hollensteiner," a young male voice pleads, "I am sure you could use some subscriptions to magazines. I—"

I cut him off politely but firmly, let the water out of the tub, lie on the bed for thirteen seconds, long enough to pound my pillow eight times from frustration. Then I am all right again. I put eye drops in my tired blood-shot eyes, since there has been no time, as usual, for those boric-acid pads. I call the children back from banishment from the bedroom. We have compromised on TV programing. We will watch fifteen minutes of shot-putting for Malcolm's sake; we will watch the last fifteen minutes of the teeny-bopper's agony over the school prom for Clare's sake. In the meantime, I will be reading *The Wall Street Journal* in bed, off my feet, for *my* sake.

Clare Luce taught me in Rome that it is very important for a woman to keep off her feet as much as possible in order to stay young and beautiful. Clare is now in her seventies, keeps off her feet a lot, and looks very young and beautiful. I am in my forties, still not beautiful, and still desperately searching for ways to stay off my feet.

For years I have been teaching women via the lecture platform how to relax and get rid of tensions, how to stay fit and younger-looking. Several large companies have paid me handsome fees to give courses to their women employees on how to look better, how to feel better, how to buy the newest fashions and assemble the proper wardrobe for the office (on a budget), how to develop good voice control, how to handle the telephone diplomatically and efficiently, how to adapt the new hair styles and cosmetics to oneself—and how to get it all together appropriately for one's job. Of course I have always felt, upon examining these companies, that their male executives needed a lot more help than their women employees, but I was never able to get that across. I have prattled endlessly about the advantages of lying on a slant board at home with the feet raised, or of reclining in bed, listening to gentle music and thinking beautiful thoughts, while the face lies coated in a complexion mask. But I've always told it straight.

"Miracles don't happen, but you'll look at yourself afterward in the mirror and *think* you're much improved, even if you're not. And in thinking you look better, you'll feel better about yourself and suddenly you'll look better." All those little attempts at pampering do work after all.

There is nothing that helps one's "look" more than a nice dose of self-confidence.

If only I had the time to practice what I preach! If only I didn't have to swing into action like a trained military division the minute I walk through that apartment door. There is one saving factor, however: office problems are of necessity dropped when I cross the threshold. The children take over, for one thing. Then there is the inevitable, formidable pile of mail to attend to. There are also three stages of dinner logistics with which to cope, a husband with whom to converse (thank heaven), and four newspapers to scan. And I still have my fifteen uninterrupted minutes of floor exercises to squeeze into the schedule somewhere.

One day Marjorie Craig, Elizabeth Arden's exercise specialist, made a cursory inspection of my silhouette when we were working on an Arden project together. She suggested subtly that I attack the floor more regularly. There really is no space in our apartment where a long outstretched body can make a vigorous movement without dislodging a television set from its stand, or breaking a toe on a metal bed frame, or hitting an antique table with a resounding whack detrimental to both furniture and body. I decided to take action anyhow. Our apartment would become my own personal gymnasium.

The very next morning I arose at five-twenty, determined to have a good half hour's thump on the living-room floor. This was to be the beginning of a new daily regime of self-discipline from five-thirty to six. Even for a morning person, it was a challenge. With great difficulty I rearranged all the furniture in the living room to provide clear exercise space. I put a cheery, rhythmic Lester Lanin orchestra tune on the record player, then stumbled out to the kitchen to prepare a pre-exercise cup of coffee. On goes the light switch—but what is this on the floor in front of me? Blood. A river of blood. Someone in the house has been murdered.

With an audible "Hail Mary" and a burst of courage, I summon the strength to look. The blood trail leads to our compact freezer. The door of the freezer is very much ajar. Someone had opened it early the day before and had not closed it. The entire expensive contents of the freezer, our meat and fowl supply, including a quarter of a cow we had just purchased in Maryland to save on our meat bills, is now pulpy, bloody, unfrozen, spoiled. Damnable carnage! I feel like becoming a vegetarian this very minute. It takes me a whole hour to get all the meat and chicken inspected and thrown away, to wash out the sanguine freezer interior, and to mop the desecrated floor. There is something very disgusting about squeezing blood out of a floor mop at six o'clock in the morning. I must also act on the eight pheasants. I plop their unfrozen, unappetizing-looking bodies into a large pot of boiling water. These were the birds that R.H., the great hunter, had shot a few weeks before. He had considered them works of art and, along with them, had brought me eight different pheasant recipes, each one more difficult than the last, as suggestions for our next large gourmet dinner.

The birds have taken longer than the meat to defrost; they are still at least cool and will be safe if cooked at once. So I will stew them like chicken before breakfast and we will have them for dinner tonight, reheated. There is obviously no time now to prepare a subtle *faison à l'orange* for the family. Besides, who would want that for breakfast? But if I leave them uncooked until tonight, they will probably give us ptomaine. Having thus passed my first exercise-shower period, I now make a quick breakfast, cope with the cooked pheasant, dress, and leave at the usual time with Clare for her school and my office.

You will never find my recipe for stewed pheasants in any cookbook. When the boiling of those birds was completed, they tasted like misguided chickens. Any Cordon Bleu graduate would have felt betrayed by the mere sight of them. I also swore that morning that I would never again attempt a five-thirty in the morning beauty routine. It was obviously never meant to be. I figured that after a few years of beauty neglect, I would cover my face with a veil and my figure with muu-muus, and R.H. would be forgiven for his marital wanderings. By the next day, of course, I realized that those exercises could and should be somehow worked into my schedule. And they were.

Even though I jest about my own failings, it is sadly true that the harder a woman works, the more difficult it becomes for her to find the time to keep up her physical status quo. Men are forgiven for going to seed, but women never. Keeping herself pulled together physically is important to a woman's husband, her children, her bosses and associates, and, above all—*to herself*. The most incriminating sentence that can be made about anyone is "she's turned into a slob," which can translate into "she's getting old ahead of time." If we grow better-looking with maturity, so much the better. Some of us do gain a serenity, a sense of oneness with our world, a kind of "character beauty" with the passing years. Others of us fade into lackluster colorlessness. I can't help but smile when I see those cute, tiny blond bombshells—the boop-boop-de-boop girls (who collected fraternity pins and got all the guys in my high-school years)—fade out in their forties like seven-year-old chintz. That is sweet revenge for all of us who were gawky wallflower adolescents.

Our faces tell a lot about our lives, whether we're happy, whether we like ourselves. Growing older is certainly not the death sentence for a woman's looks—not today with all the aids at her disposal and with the new positive attitudes toward aging. When R.H. sees a stunning older woman, he likes to borrow the quote, "Many a fine tune has been played on an old fiddle," and I like to remind him when I see an attractive older man, "Many a *great* tune has been played on a mellow guitar."

The combination of discipline and a mind that absorbs

experience and knowledge is the key to a woman's attractiveness. I'll never forget my first Christian Dior fashion show. The New Look had just been born. I was a young American, the only one in a salon full of chic French private customers. I sat in the rear, feeling shy, awkward, and very badly dressed. Monsieur Dior came back and talked to me in French, frankly curious as to who I was. I asked him in my best schoolgirl manner, "In your opinion, Monsieur Dior, what is the secret of a woman's beauty?" I could have kicked myself the minute the naïve words came out. His answer was direct and simple: "The Marine Corps." That was all. He arose and went to find his assistant because he didn't like the accessories on the last mannequin. Later, after the collection was over, I cornered him.

"What did you mean by the 'secret to a woman's beauty is the Marine Corps?' " Thoughts had been racing through my mind that made no sense. Could Monsieur Dior have meant that sex orgies at Quantico, Virginia, with the Marine Corps would make a woman beautiful?

"Discipline," he answered in his soft voice. "Flat bellies, firm muscles, quick reactions, beautifully disciplined creatures. Women should be like the Marines."

Of course he was right. Jacqueline Onassis today in her forties, and many more like her in their forties, fifties, even sixties and seventies, follow regimes of exercise, careful eating, rigorous beauty habits, and plenty of mind-exercising too.

Militant feminists decry any reference to physical beauty, any drawing of attention to a woman's looks. God gives us the raw materials of both our looks and our brains; it is up to us, men and women equally, to develop them. The development of a woman's brain is far more important than the development of her bust, but to one who can do them both I say *"Brava!"*

Keeping in shape does not require all that much self-discipline. Working hard at one's floor exercises for fifteen minutes (or ten, if there is absolutely no way to do fifteen) can always be accomplished somehow. In the summer I use a bit of hall space (cool, bare wood floor), and in the winter I manage to rearrange enough furniture to clear a place on the carpet to call my own for a few minutes before being interrupted by the children or the curious dog. I do the Air Force Exercises, which one can find described in detail in pocketbooks, printed on exercise mats, or by writing the Air Force. The exercises prescribed by the President's Physical Fitness Council are roughly the same. All good exercises, including Swedish gymnastics, yoga, or whatever are based on the same deep breathing, stretching, bending, pulling motions. The Elizabeth Arden exercises add a bit of thumping and bumping of one's posterior as well. A daily regime of a quarter hour renews energy, helps our shapes, reduces the flab, assists our blood circulation, makes our skins and hair look better, reduces the tension in our muscles, helps get rid of backache, and removes some of the aggression in our souls. Sufficient reasons to make the effort!

I find my own exercises less boring if I can do them to favorite television programs. The pace is fast when a detective like Kojak or Cannon is hot on the trail of a murderer; the exercise rhythm slows when Gene Shalit is reviewing books on the "Today" show; and I practically do them in slow motion when a depressing newscast or a bad weather report is being transmitted.

Schedule-wise, one of the toughest problems with which all working women must cope is the care of what is supposed to be our crowning glory. I envy with an emotion approaching fury those who can set their own hair. When I do my own, the resulting coiffure can only be described as a careful arrangement of scouring pads. I need someone standing over me with strong arms who can tug and pull my stubborn, thick hair into shape over those curlers. My hair-care bills are not a luxury; they are a necessity. Granted, I can perform certain maintenance operations such as oil treatments at home. It doesn't take too much dexterity to wash and rinse one's hair, apply a cream oil, don a plastic shower cap and then over that an electric heating cap. I never waste time during such self-centered activities, however. The thirty-minute oil-heat cap treatment is usually performed while I am working in my office at home. I sit plugged in with my electric typewriter and plugged in with my heating cap, silently praying the whole time that no one will see me—and that no one will spill water on me, for instant electrocution would be the result.

My dash to the hairdresser is made usually once a week, either very early in the morning or at lunchtime. Ralph, a handsome mustachioed Argentinian who works in a tiny shop near my home, has been programed to have me in and out in exactly fifty minutes on Saturdays, and Tom, who holds forth in a shop near my office, gets me out in forty-five minutes. The whole thing is done in such fast action half the clients of the shop don't even know I've been there. Since drying time is a time of peace and noiselessness (the hum-drum noise of the dryer is uninterrupted, so one can concentrate), I do my most intellectually challenging work at this time. My best press releases have been written at the hairdresser's.

Like many luxurious things in life, we require constant upkeep, not only to look well but also to perform well. We all have our own definitions of just what is the minimum upkeep of our physical selves. I have an acquaintance who has had so much plastic surgery, she knows everyone in the hospital surgery department intimately. She greets them like brothers and sisters before she goes under the anesthesia. She began having her face lifted when she was thirty-five, having discovered one incipient forehead wrinkle. She has now had it lifted so many times that R.H. swears they will have to reach down to her toes to pull up the skin the next time. When I suggested to her one day that she look for a job (she had never worked), she angrily demanded to know why I would mention such a thing. I explained that while working she would not have the time for excessive mirror-gazing, except on her lunch hour. It would save greatly on medical expenses.

Such narcissism is inevitably costly to one's bank account and one's self-esteem, not to mention one's brain development. My face-lifting friend is still unemployed and hospital-bound. Toni Kosover, in a *Women's Wear Daily* story some years ago, wrote that "some women are more concerned with keeping up their buttocks than their breasts." With that dazzling piece of news for an introduction, she went on to explain that the new rage in plastic surgery was for the female fanny—with the goal of making men's hearts pound faster. Of course, it does require the patient to spend eight days or more in the hospital, wrapped in elastic bandages and sleeping on her stomach for several days. It is a very painful operation, with some unattractive scars to show for it. She won't be able to climb stairs for a while, and it will be three weeks before she can sit on a normally hard chair. However, after six weeks of all this, supposedly she will forget the pain and the agony to rejoice in her newly streamlined backside. Meanwhile, I would imagine her husband has collapsed under the weight of medical bills and is in need of a hospital himself. Some of the contented recycles, such as Ira von Furstenberg, who has told reporters all about her breasts-and-buttocks operations, are happy people because they feel "perfectly up with today's image." When I read such items, I feel far behind in "today's image." Perhaps I should be spending the money saved for fixing up the apartment on *my* front and back, instead of the apartment's. But I don't think I ever will.

Tension is as much a part of our daily lives as breathing or inflation. Some of us have to deal with more of it than others. If one accepts the premise that people who have a minimum of tension are boring, rather than gelatinous creatures of no substance, then one will accept that it follows that people with a maximum amount of tension are interesting, dynamic people, very much alive and involved.

I embrace this philosophy simply because it would require a combined effort of the entire American scientific community to measure the extent of my tension. I *have* to look at tension affirmatively. Otherwise more tensions will be added to those already in my make-up, and medical science simply isn't ready for that.

Since tension is something we'll have to live with all our lives, we might as well learn how to recognize it and combat it as best we can. Like many happy people, I actually thrive on a certain amount of it; I couldn't live without pressures to goad me on. But I can't live *with* tension, either, unless I can grapple with it on a daily basis so that I feel it is being kept under control. Some of us take out our tensions in our stomachs, ending up with ulcers; some of us in our mouths, causing gum and teeth problems; some of us in our backs, which can involve tremendous pain. I am one of those who takes it in the neck and shoulders. No one would ever know this unless he were to ask me to turn around quickly to see something behind me. Suddenly it feels as if both shoulders have separated and my neck has broken.

Not being a doctor, I cannot dispense medical advice, only homespun remedies for neck and shoulder tension. This area of the body can stiffen with jabs of pain; the muscles knot into what feels like tangles of hair. Something like forgetting an accepted invitation can bring it on, or an argument with a department store, or the comparison of unpaid bills with one's bank account. One of the first things I do when the stiffness and pain occur is to rotate my head around, first clockwise, then counterclockwise, with my lower jaw hanging loose and relaxed. One should think beautiful thoughts while the exercise is going on. Be sure never to perform it in front of people who are not fully aware of why you are doing what you are doing. (The children, watching me perform this exercise one night, thought I was far scarier-looking than the vampire they were watching on television.)

Lying immersed in a hot tub up to your chin for a good long time, listening to music or thinking beautiful thoughts is a very pleasant therapy. Of course, you may well have a problem later with dry skin from all the hot water, not to mention an increase in your electric heating bill. An electric vibrator used on neck and shoulders for five minutes helps, too. One should hit hardest and deepest at the specially painful kinks. This is a form of masochism, like asking a dentist to drill your tooth without Novocain, but you'll feel better later. If you are really tightened up to the point where you feel as if a 240-pound tackle has just passed over you on the line of scrimmage, worry not. An electric wet-heat pad will help. Just lie on the pad on the bed for twenty minutes. If you are going out for the evening, there could be problems. The whole back of your coiffure, no matter how great the precautions taken, will be a damp, limp mess. If you have sensitive skin like mine, you might look as though you've contracted measles on your upper back and neck for a while, too. But your muscles will be relaxed, and that is what matters.

Yoga breathing exercises are great for tension. I have no time to meditate and have not been in a lotus position since one of my knees was badly injured several years ago. However, taking the time to lie down somewhere, to make the body go limp in sections until it is totally relaxed, and then to inhale in short, panting puffs, is very effective.

Tensed muscles seem to respond to the flow of oxygen.

When I feel suddenly "clutched" at the office, I do what Dr. Eugene Cohen taught me to do. I let my head drop all the way down forward on my chest. Then I contemplate the rise and fall of my chest as I breathe deeply, very normally and quietly, still watching the rise and fall of my chest. This should be continued for five minutes or so until the "clutch" disappears. It is best to close the door of one's office while doing this—in order not to be disturbed, but also not to cause one's associates undue alarm. If I were built more along the lines of one of Hugh Hefner's bunnies, there would be a more interesting view of the rise and fall of my chest. But, boring or not, this pull on the back neck muscle helps relax my whole head.

The greatest aid of all is "Miraculous Max," as his grateful friends call him. Max is a short, muscular man, dressed all in white, who puts you on a massage table and goes after your neck, shoulders, and spine with gusto. His fingers feel all the knots and kinks, and he kneads the muscles until they give way. He is a medically licensed masseur whose patients (many of whom are famous actresses and singers) are sent to him by doctors. If only everyone who suffered from tension had a masseur of Max's ability available to him or her, there would be many more happy, relaxed people in this world.

Another ailment from which I suffer along with millions of others is the reaction of my sensitive eyes to badly polluted air—for which New York is so famous. The interior air we breathe, however, is far worse than that of our sooty streets. The combination of people who smoke and badly ventilated rooms makes my eyes and consequently my state of mind quite miserable. Associates have learned to wear heavy wool sweaters to long meetings when I am present. I can survive heavy smoke from cigarettes and pipes for just about an hour, but then the windows, even on cold, snowy days, have to be thrown open in order to still my protests. If one is encased in a sealed skyscraper office, there are ways of coping with the problem, too. I dab at my weeping eyes and sniff as though trying to disguise my discomfort. I gently push away from me the ash tray holding someone's cigarette, the smoke from which flows toward me in a magnetic jetstream. If the smoke becomes quite unbearable, I excuse myself in a very chipper way (although feeling quite persecuted inside). "I'll be right back," I inform them, "just need three seconds to change the air in my lungs." It never fails. More and more cigarettes are extinguished prematurely and new cigarettes lie unsmoked in packages around the table. I have not suffered in silence, but at least I have not been a dictator. People are really quite considerate if they realize one is in the grips of a bona fide allergy.

I long ago had to give up eye make-up. One day, in the full bloom of the hay-fever season, the cameraman on a TV show held up a sign to me by the camera fairly early in the show. "WIPE YOUR EYES" read the sign. I could hardly wait for the commercial so I could be off camera and steal a quick look in my compact mirror. I had been sneezing and my eyes had been tearing. The eye liner and heavy mascara had run into dark gashes under both eyes. A black streak also ran down both cheeks. I looked like Marcel Marceau getting his make-up ready for his pantomime act. A few weeks later I ran into my amused TV host, who told me he had received a pile of letters from viewers asking what he had said to Miss Baldrige off camera to make her cry so hard.

Since the time I floated a lost false eyelash in my vichyssoise, much to the horror of my hostess at a posh dinner party, eye make-up has not been my specialty. For anyone whose eyes sting with smoke or pollution, or for anyone suffering from eyestrain, here's an old exercise trick that works beautifully. Pick a quiet moment, relax, close your eyes, and cup both hands over both eyes to shut out any light whatsoever for about five minutes. Open wide and then squint hard several times. Pretend that someone is commanding you, "Squeeze your eyes!" "Squeeze them, squeeze them!" During the course of these active facial contortions, eye fluid rinses down over the eyeballs and the eyes feel greatly rested and clear. This is again something not to do in front of your friends or office colleagues unless they know what you are up to and aren't likely to assume that you have just donned some sort of Halloween fright mask.

The best beauty recipe, the best tension-reliever, the best mind-renewer is to remove oneself from the action from time to time. For anyone having to live with the pressures of New York, being able to leave on an occasional weekend and during summer vacation is definitely the device that keeps the lid from blowing off the top. My family is blessed and we know it. We have an escape hatch when we really need it—the little eighteenth-century town of Washington, Connecticut, two hours away from New York City. My father has a small house there, one that miraculously adjusts from being just right for him to being able to accommodate the five of us, too, from time to time. I talked my father into converting his dining room into the children's bedroom. This was accomplished without carpentry or decorating, just by moving furniture and using a little imagination, such as turning the English sideboard into a toy chest.

Washington is a town that happily has changed hardly at all in over a hundred years. My father's house is perched on the Green, facing a white Congregational Church, and has a disappearing architectural treasure—a front porch. A noisy potpourri of Hondas, Rolls-Royce convertibles, antique cars, farm trucks, and Jeeps scoot by us at our crossroads. Everyone from the town of Washington looks up at our house as he rounds the curve and shouts "Hi!" When I am working on Grandpa's front lawn, rear end waving jauntily in full view, I pray that only strangers will pass by. One day when I was on my fifth hour of attacking dandelion roots, curved over in a pair of shorts like a thick hairpin, I heard a friend of my father's telling a visitor who lives where in town as they walked by.

"And here," he explained in a tone that changed from normal to one of amused disbelief, "is a place where—a place—well, let's call it 'Tish's Bottom'!" I should have felt flattered. I had just become a tourist stop in the valley.

Gardening is tremendous therapy for city-trapped people. In my single days, and before my parents had moved to the country, I used to invite myself to different friends' houses to work in their gardens and on their lawns. I would mow, rake, weed, prune, and trim. In return, I received room and board, or just board. I was usually so tired after seven hours of working with the earth that I always slept like a log. These excursions meant good exercise out in the sun and fresh air, and usually the improvement of someone's garden as well. It was also great psychological therapy, for I would take care of a few editors who had been nasty to me or my clients. Some people stick pins in voodoo dolls. Believe me, it is much more fun to pick up a trowel, take aim at a weed, dig deep, and think, Take *that!*

The town of Washington is laconic and slow-paced, just what New York isn't. It is medicine for us; it is an escape from people. The city people who weekend up here are fairly successful in hiding from each other, except when grocery-shopping down in the Washington Depot. People who have no place to go look upon a Connecticut hideaway as a sort of glamorous Shangri-la. In actual fact, our "glamorous" activities consist of nothing more than what suburban children consider very normal in their lives, like having stairs inside your house to fall down, charcoal-grilling hamburgers, shooting baskets through a hoop attached to the garage door, watching the worms in the earth after the rains, uprighting the garbage cans after the racoons have pushed them over during the night, and examining a dead skunk, from a respectful distance, to wonder why it smells the way it does.

When Clare was in kindergarten, I heard one of her classmates question her. "What do you do all weekend at your grandfather's?"

"Play with the garden hose," was her answer.

"All weekend?" asked the friend, rather awed.

"*All* weekend," replied Clare proudly. It's a simple matter to construct paradise for a big-city kid.

R.H. manages to shut the world and everything else out of his consciousness in Connecticut. I have always admired the way he sleeps. A fire engine could come into our bedroom, and he would not hear it. (I smell smoke from a bad incinerator eight blocks away; it wakes me up and I try to rouse R.H. to call the fire department.) On a Saturday in Connecticut he simply settles himself down on the living-room sofa for three hours at a time, with children and their friends rushing in and out, shouting, slamming doors, jumping on him. He sleeps. He is a good sport, however, about joining in with the children's athletic activities, such as playing tennis with Clare or supervising Malcolm's "hockey practice" on the Gunnery School ice rink.

I spend my entire time in the country organizing, marketing, and cooking for the family, but the change of tempo is there. And the change is what is needed. The air is pure, and the silence almost noisy. We all breathe deeply, for we know that the air we breathe at home is gray and thick by comparison. Pierre runs free, making himself all the more lovable to me by catching an occasional small mole, bringing it proudly to me, and then bouncing it up and down like a Ping-Pong ball. Dustin has long runs off the leash in fascinating places like the historic graveyard. There is a great sense of freedom for us all.

Our weekends are not prolonged; we are too busy for that. We leave at nine on Saturday morning, and are back in New York by late afternoon on Sunday. Just to gaze upon the scenery in that "other world" is worth the trip in itself. The minute we leave Route 84 at Southbury, we are in a world of shuttered wooden mid-eighteenth-century houses, painted in warm yellows, dark reds, soft grays, and olive greens, as well as the traditional white with dark shutters. Eighteenth-century fences made of heavy curved gray stones encircle the hills protectively; grazing animals are tucked away cozily in the rocky landscape. The nearby homes of celebrities—such as the Arthur Millers' and the Alexander Calders'—are just like anyone else's. The right to create undisturbed is as much a part of this land as the earth itself; and privacy, if desired, is rigorously preserved. Although everyone is friendly, there is a "Don't come too close" kind of spirit that denotes independence rather than coldness. For a New Yorker, this is like water flowing on parched earth.

The children love to go to Woodbury, twenty-five minutes away, to a beautiful old yellow-shingled house on several acres of land, inhabited by Uncle Mac, Aunt Midge, and cousins Megan and Molly. Along with all the fascinating barns, there are horses, steers, ponies, ducks, geese, and a calf-roping chute. There is a Belgian hare, a Scottish Airedale, an ugly bulldog, a clumsy mutt, and a giant black mastiff who fancies himself a puppy. There is always a "character" around the farm, such as Henry the Goat, who loves to eat cigarettes and old magazines.

Aunt Midge patiently teaches the children to ice-skate on the pond and takes them riding. Uncle Mac teaches them to lasso and lets them watch him rope cattle with his partner. They can also cheer him on in the professional ring every autumn when the rodeo, which is sponsored by the Scovill Manufacturing Company, of which Uncle Mac .s chairman, comes to nearby Waterbury. I have always puzzled over the fact that my suave, smooth-talking oldest brother metamorphoses every weekend into a Western-talking cowboy. Nephew Malcolm phrases it all very delicately in his own words. I once overheard him bragging to a friend, "I have an uncle who dresses up in a suit to go to his office, then he comes home, and you know what? He puts on blue jeans, real cowboy boots, and a hat just like mine. Then he gets on his horse and spits out of the side of his mouth!"

We spend many weekends right in New York City, recharging our batteries. I am up before seven on both Saturday and Sunday mornings because the schedule is frenzied and I have to take the dog out. I long ago gave up resenting the fact that I have no leisure on weekends, while my family has a great deal of it. One typical June weekend I spent my entire time at the grocery store, in the kitchen, in the dining room, and inside the closets. It was freakish weather, beastly hot, in the nineties for several days. We made the mistake of having a dinner party Friday night, and not having foreseen the heat wave I had only hot food. Saturday noon I was at it again, cooking a children's party lunch for six guests. After lunch we went to the park for three hours of torture, known as "baseball," in the intense heat and humidity. I played pitcher, the basemen, and the entire outfield, so everyone could bat and score the inevitable home runs. Every time I reclaimed the ball in the outfield from a pile of dog-do, I remembered that I was being a good mother, and smiled through gritted teeth.

R.H. was hungry, having missed lunch, so I cooked another big meal Saturday night. The next day was "closet day," which means that I burrow, molelike, into our insufferably disorganized, crowded closets to change from winter to summer wardrobes. There were fourteen separate piles of clothes in the front hall, each requiring special attention, labeled "Take to the thrift shop," "Wash when possible," "Wash—emergency," "Dry cleaners," and the like. No one could pass through the hall. I had to survey the scene and laugh, since the day before I had just finished and handed in an article for a decorating magazine on "The Well-Organized and Designed Closet—Our Biggest Time-Saver." If the editor were to see my closets, she would demand her money back.

Then there was Sunday lunch to prepare, with two more friends of the children's and a grown friend of R.H.'s whose family was away. Because it was Father's Day, I had to scuttle around finding suitable presents and wrapping them up. I moved from the big cleanup in the kitchen after lunch to the children's dining room-laundry-office and began working on a press release for "The Women of the Year 1974" awards. I wondered how Dixie Lee Ray of the Atomic Energy Commission, Congresswoman Martha Griffiths, Billie Jean King, and the other awardees had spent their weekends. My disposition grew worse. Here I was, supposedly one of the top-paid women executives in the country, examining hands ruined from baseballs in dog-do and from scouring pads in hot water. Where was my quiet time, those few moments to do what *I* wanted? Why was I scrubbing vegetables, baking chicken, roasting beef, setting tables, writing press releases all weekend? Why wasn't I at the Guggenheim Museum, or shopping in Madison Avenue boutiques, or having a facial and a pedicure? Or why wasn't I stretched out on a chaise, munching chocolates and enjoying a sexy French novel?

On Monday morning I felt much better. I unlocked the door to "Letitia Baldrige Enterprises" at eight-five. Thank God for the office. If it weren't for the office, I might have to do all week what I had just done all weekend. That *really* would be a disaster.

It is always written in very small print, but a working mother *does* owe something to herself once in a while. She should make a resolution to get away at some point for a period of self-pampering, even if it's only for two or three days. The period should be short enough so that she is not really missed at the office or at home, but long enough for the body to take at least one long, deep, beautiful, unpolluted breath.

I have done this only once—when we had already been married nine years. Larry and Bette Peabody invited us to Haiti at Carnival time in February. R.H. was unable to leave his business at that time, but I decided to go anyway. R.H. and Nannie told me they could cope well enough, and though it was a bad time at my office, it's always a bad time at my office, and my associates were willing to cover for me.

I took some of my recently earned lecture money and bought a round-trip air ticket. My friends were on hand to greet me at the Port-au-Prince airport. When they found a frazzled female with a bag full of caftans and a body full of enough aches and pains to activate an entire hospital, they rushed me home, gave me a large rum drink, and put me to bed, the perfect beginning of an emergency rescue operation.

My visit was five days long, which gave me time for a jump-shift in health directions but did not allow me to become a guest-pest. Although the only purpose of this trip was rest, I couldn't change the whole nature of my being, and had brought along a lot of writing materials and work to do. In the tropics, sitting around is the main activity, but I am physically unable to exist at that pace. I still got up at six in the morning, exercised, worked, and attempted to use up some of the supercharged energy God had suddenly given back to me.

In a place of physical splendor like Haiti, the creative muse seems to live just outside the window. On this mountainous island, filled with a tropical vegetation of incredible beauty and well over five million handsome people, one suddenly feels akin to all the world's great painters and writers. There's an urge to portray the beat, the feel, the smell, and the sensuality of the surroundings. After awakening early, I would stretch out on a wicker chair and hassock on the outdoor gallery outside my bedroom with my writing pad and pencil. At seven a young Haitian would appear with a large glass of freshly squeezed orange juice and a pot of strong, lovely coffee, the best I have ever tasted. Larry would appear at his end of the gallery and sit down at his outdoor desk; after a cheery wave of silent greeting to me, he would begin his day's design project, whether it was furniture, fabrics, lamps, or rugs. Soon Bette would appear, and that was the signal for breakfast to be served downstairs on the lower gallery. At the Peabody's, the table is set differently for each meal, with varying linens, china, and flower centerpieces, all beautifully coordinated with great thought. In the meantime, our "visitors," who had been waiting for our appearance on the gallery, would begin to arrive—these were Haiti's barefoot merchants, bearing baskets on their heads filled with flowers, fruits, and vegetables. The colors were blinding; an exotic mixture of flower fragrance, pungent fruits, and spices greeted our nostrils. The Peabodys would bargain in French with each one, buy a little from each, and the men and women would go away smiling and singing, flashing broad smiles that showed many gold teeth. After breakfast came long hours under an umbrella by the pool, where I would work, never unaware of my surroundings. The beautifully landscaped pool was on the lowest portion of the hillside estate, surrounded by a veritable jungle of deep red poinsettias, birds of paradise, palm trees, plants, and other flowers. I would lean back in my white wicker chair, writing pad on my lap, and gaze up every so often at the tall white plantation house festooned with lacy Victorian trim. The two stories of outdoor white-colonnaded galleries, with white wicker furniture designed by my host, were punctuated by big, round white Japanese paper lanterns, suspended from the ceilings on slender cords, which swung in the breezes by day like giant golf balls. At night these soft lanterns illuminated the white façade like the loveliest of magic moons.

There is a constant symphony of noises in the Haitian air, but no one seems to mind it. The dogs bark incessantly, around the clock. One can hear all day and night the sound of small-car motors straining up the mountainside. Horns blow in happy dissonance. Several times a day we would hear enthusiastic applause erupting in the street outside the estate, and the roar of a souped-up motor, with other cars following swiftly behind. That would be Papa Doc Duvalier's son, now in command of the country, going up to the house above ours in his special sports car, outdistancing the truckloads of armed soldiers who were always well behind the man they were supposed to protect. But soon my ear would catch a carpenter's hammer echoing down the hillside, or a rooster which would make its contribution to the confused mixture of croaking frogs, chattering children, snorting pigs and donkeys, and goats conversing in constant "yep-yeps."

But if there is never any quiet in Haiti, it is still a bouquet of noises quite different from the city's. Human beings and animals seem to sleep in shifts around the clock. The air is gentle, clear, touched with a melding of different scents, and filled with the beautiful colors of the cotton dresses and turbans of the women and the brightly hued shirts of the men.

Those days in Haiti were a much needed health cure. I

didn't have to worry about my family and my office. All I had to worry about was whether I would sit on the roofed terrace, by the pool, or in a bower of antherium. I worked hard doing my exercises both in and out of the pool. (Doing the same exercises at an American health spa would have cost me well over a thousand dollars a week.) Every time I saw a Haitian woman walking up an inevitable mountain road with an inevitably large load balanced on her head, I would automatically "tuck in and pull up" the stomach and fanny to improve my posture. I was soon rested, exercised, and mentally refreshed. I would now be able to return to the pressure cooker of life in New York again.

Before driving to the airport, I savored with my hosts a last mango and a last custard apple as the sound of Carnival drums, bells, and whistles faded into the distance. My next day's lunch in New York would be tuna-on-rye with buttermilk in my building's cafeteria.

Once again I told myself that if I could have this life in Haiti for long periods, I would never appreciate it so much. One has to keep telling oneself things like this. It's a very important part of survival.

9
An Extra Portion of Ham

Once a businesswoman gets up before a microphone, it's hard to get her away from it. It is not that she loves to hear the sound of her own voice, it's just that there still aren't many of us around and we receive too many invitations as a result. I am usually not paid for speeches that relate to business. One is supposed to do them for the prestige of the firm. In the middle of them I generally wish I were home in bed. (The one exception was the evening I shared the podium with Vince Lombardi at a Menswear Association dinner at the Plaza Hotel.) A man speaker, of course, has only to change into a dinner jacket and black tie at his office, and then report to the dais of the hotel ballroom. If he has a little five-o'clock shadow on his face, everyone is sympathetic with his lack of time for an evening shave. Let a woman speaker arrive with a hair out of place and there's instant criticism. She is expected to have her hair done prior to the event, no matter what crises may be perpetrating themselves in her office. She has to take off her old face and put on a clean new one, a process far more time-consuming than shaving. She has to change her underwear, shoes, handbag, and jewelry to suit her evening dress. Then she's supposed to saunter in punctually, perfumed and perfectly dressed. No one minds if the male speaker is wearing a shabby old dinner jacket. It is hard to tell what his dinner jacket looks like, anyway. He may have to buy a new one every ten years to keep the width of his jacket lapels in style. The woman speaker has to buy a new dress every year. She is supposed to be always "in fashion," and if there is press coverage of the event her attire will usually be part of it. Equality is not yet here.

Once when I shared the rostrum with a man (who was also a good friend of mine) at a banquet in a Southern city, we were asked to address our audience on the same topic: the responsibility of the home-furnishings manufacturer to the consumer. Our speeches were exactly the same length, fifteen minutes, and I felt they were equally substantive. My male colleague's remarks were reported in detail by the lone reporter who attended the dinner. My participation was described as follows:

> Then tall, striking, silver-blond Tish Baldrige made her appearance at the microphone. The former secretary to Jackie Kennedy was wearing a long-sleeved brown-velvet gown with a glittering turquoise choker necklace.

I wrote a note the next day to my fellow speaker, enclosing the clipping, along with a parody of what *could* have been his press coverage:

> Then medium-tall, bald, and skinny _____ made his appearance at the microphone. The former Good Humor Man from Lake Waramaug was wearing a well-pressed, rented dinner jacket, after-shave lotion, and spaghetti sauce on his shirt front.

I have admitted that I was born a ham, a true daughter of a speech-loving congressman father; I also admit that I was the kind who always gave the class graduation address and who entered all contests like the "Good Citizenship Essay" ones put on by the local newspaper or the Chamber of Commerce. I had the joy of reciting my prize-winning essays aloud to adoring relatives and parents' friends on more than one occasion. (My brothers were excused from these audiences, partly because my parents knew they would hate it, partly because my parents feared what they would do during their little sister's performances.) Dale Carnegie will disagree, but I believe it's in the genes. Public speakers are *born* speaking publicly. They don't have to learn how. They start giving speeches from their bassinets in the maternity wards of the hospitals.

The only fashion shows for which I enjoy doing the commentary are those out of town. Doing a fashion show for the Hartford *Courant*'s charity or for the Clarkson Hospital benefit in Omaha, or for a March of Dimes benefit luncheon in Flint, Michigan, is different from facing a blasé New York audience. I can relax at the microphone, forget the frivolity of the "filmy chiffon leg o' mutton sleeves which are a great new look this spring," and enjoy myself, knowing that those women out there at the end of the runway are my friends in spirit.

People like me are constantly being asked to judge something. I am too much of a feminist to accept judging a beauty contest, but something like the Penney Journalism Awards for the best magazine writing done by women professionals is a task I frankly enjoy. I take all these judging duties seriously, whether they entail pouring over essays written by the Girls' Club of America citizenship-award finalists or inspecting an endless array of dolls dressed by the Bankers Trust employees for poor children at Christmas.

My lecturing is an additional source of family income. Because of a terribly demanding business-cum-family schedule, I can only go out once in a while, say ten times a year. (I have to speak "for free" many other times during the year.) I fly out to the city the night before, appear on local television very early the next morning, have a press interview ("How often do you see Mrs. Onassis now, Miss Baldrige?"), give my lecture, then have lunch or tea with hundreds of people, answer more questions at the microphone, shake what seem like a thousand hands, and put myself on a jam-packed, inevitably late, unbearably uncomfortable evening flight back home. It is a brutal routine, physically and mentally.

I used to utilize the monies earned from these speaking trips for Bill Blass and Pauline Trigère clothes. Now they go for tutoring lessons and medical expenses for the children—not to mention the vet expenses for our menagerie.

Anyone with dreams of getting on the lecture circuit can get there, provided two elements are present: a name or a gimmick and the ability to get on one's feet and project to an audience. I could always get to my feet. I didn't have a gimmick, but I began to acquire a name at a young age. I first lectured when I came home from the American Embassy in Rome, after I had written my first book. Later on, anyone close to Jacqueline Kennedy in the White House automatically had a "name" (or a gimmick). (I valiantly protest, to seemingly deaf ears, that I had a name before those White House days.) When I am to speak to an audience even on such a topic as "Yes, a woman *can* start her own business," I am introduced by an awestruck voice that says, "Of course, Miss Baldrige is *best* known for having been" (and here the tone grows extremely reverent) *"the social secretary to Jackie Kennedy!"*

My name is so strange that once having been vocalized it lingers in people's memories. I constantly hear from women who come to town halls where I am speaking, "I didn't know who you were, but I came anyway, because I knew your name from somewhere." It's not very complimentary, when you analyze it, but I guess I ought to be thankful I wasn't born Mary Smith.

The logistics surrounding speaking engagements are normally appalling. Each appearance requires that the hair and wardrobe be coped with in advance and the family taken care of. Shoes and bag are shined; lecture costume is pressed; suitcase is packed. I have learned to use only one color of accessories, usually black, so I don't have to carry extra shoes or bags. My make-up kit is always ready to go, and I keep a fresh nightie and a pair of bedroom slippers in a plastic bag, ready to be packed. Everything fits into one carry-on bag, or a tote with a garment bag. When I leave town for more than a day, I do a big marketing ahead for the household. The night before, or even the morning of my departure, I will often roast a chicken and leave it behind. Then I depart for the office, lugging baggage, briefcase, *et al*, for I will leave for the airport from my office. I realize how much my feminist friends would hoot and holler if they saw me getting up early just to prepare the chicken. They would accuse me of treason against the movement.

Then, of course, the departure scene is always enough to set one back physically with cabs enroute caught in traffic jams, airport delays, messages before takeoff from the cockpit, "There will be a slight delay due to a minor mechanical malfunction." There is the inevitable question of lost baggage. I have learned through bitter experience to haul my luggage aboard with me if I am to make a public appearance soon after the flight's arrival.

During certain months, especially spring and fall, the speaking schedule is unbearable. Life is one series of saying "Good-by, I'll bring you both back a little present" (the traveling mother's form of child-bribery). In one such typical month I gave an address to the Executive Secretaries' Convention in Chicago; another to American Women in Radio and Television at Billings, Montana;

spoke to students at my niece's boarding school in Virginia; gave a decorating lecture to a women's club in North Carolina; spoke before the Lynchburg, Virginia, Women's Club; addressed wives of a bankers' association at Pinehurst, North Carolina; spoke to the wives of delegates to the Shopping Center Convention at the New York Hilton; gave a fund-raising speech to the Brandeis University's New Haven chapter; participated in the Washington Fashion Group Career Seminar; and made a fund-raising speech for the Christ Child Society at the Harvard Club in Boston. I received fees only from the Executive Secretaries, the Lynchburg Club, and the Shopping Center wives. The rest was done for charity or with a friend's gun pressing against my back. I am waiting for the Next Life, when "justice will be done." Then I will be paid back the pounds of flesh others have taken from me.

There are many national lecture bureaus, but only four or five top ones. Mine, Colston Leigh, is one of the oldest and finest. They also get one third of everything I make, which makes them less lovable in my eyes. One third is the traditional percentage, however. Many times I am asked to speak because of my own personal contacts, but I must refer them all to the Leigh Bureau anyway, and I thus lose one third. It's rough to earn what seems like a wonderful fee, one thousand dollars, for a town-hall appearance in the Middle West, only to have to shell out approximately $150 for airfare, $18 for taxis to and from La Guardia Airport, $50 for the hotel bill (including supper and breakfast), $5 to the dry cleaners, $15 for the hairdresser, and $10 in tips and incidentals. My expenses thus reach an average of $230 to the Middle West, the lecture bureau deducts its third, and I am left with a minor sum to show for a trip that took two days out of my life. My absence from the office for those two days requires an additional outlay of work time in the evening and on weekends to compensate for it. I also have to call my office twice a day while I'm gone to deal with the invariable crises. On more than one occasion, I have been talking to an agitated client on the backstage pay telephone while I'm being introduced onstage. That sort of thing makes for tension in the neck, leading up to a session with the wet hot pad that night.

Sometimes the travel itself is a major operation. When I spoke in Great Falls, Montana, I was gone three whole days—just for one speech. If one has to be gone three days because there's only one airplane in and out a day, Great Falls is a great place to be. I steeped myself in Montana history, spending hours in the Charles Russell Museum and poking around the fascinating nineteenth-century houses of the territorial governors in Helena. On such a trip I always manage to get caught up with my shopping. There is never enough time in New York to shop, so when I have even one hour free on a lecture foray, I rush to the biggest store to buy upcoming birthday and Christmas presents, underwear, stationery supplies, and anything else needed at home. (In Great Falls in October I purchased a pair of authentic cowboy boots to lay away for Malcolm's Christmas.) The only negative aspect of this efficient use of time is that I usually struggle back into the New York airport laden with shopping bags and feeling very put-upon.

If time would only permit, which it doesn't, I could earn a fair amount of money lecturing. The smart professionals, like Vincent Price and Art Buchwald, go out on tour and *stay* out on tour for weeks at a time, hitting one town after another in a logical travel sequence. Their expenses are therefore minimized and they clear a nice profit week by week. But I am unable to do this. My business won't permit it; my family life would suffer too much; and my mental health couldn't stand it, either. Saying the same thing over and over again, day after day, my voice would become as stale as yesterday's onion sandwich and just as welcome. A new audience always recharges one's enthusiasm, but when I am constantly repeating myself, I forget whether that story was just told in this speech, or in this morning's speech, or in last night's. Panic inevitably sets in. I gave the same talk three times in one and a half days in Dayton, in order to accommodate their town-hall crowds, but I could never do that again.

The same principles apply to dressing for lecturing as do to dressing for television appearances. The rule of unfussy, understated clothes and a minimum of jewelry works equally for both large and small women. I have great admiration for a woman in the Southwest who showed up on a local TV panel show with five of us, wearing a long, glittery gown and dangling rhinestone earrings. It was ten in the morning, and her face fell three feet when she saw all of us in tailored daytime clothes. She made a beautiful recovery, though, for she looked the camera straight in the eye when she was introduced, saying, "Oh, and I'm wearing the evening gown I'm going to model in our church's benefit fashion show next week. I thought you might like to see it." I loved her cool.

If there are clanking bracelets or a clinking necklace around one's neck, one will obviously play with them while speaking, and the noise of the movement of one's fingers touching the jewelry will be greatly exaggerated to the audience. Necklace microphones can cause atrocious feedback noise when hitting against gold chains or ropes of beads. When I was unconsciously playing with a long rope of pearls one morning while co-hosting a show with Jim Conway in Chicago, a crew member held up a scrawled sign at me from behind the camera, which read, "Lay off necklace. You sound like dentist's drill."

That was all I needed. Another thing a speaker should avoid is a neck scarf if she is going to yank it incessantly during her program. Wearing a scarf is like wearing a sari. Some women can; some women can't. (I'm not talking about Indian women wearing saris, needless to say.) A scarf must fit to the body and lie there at peace, quite naturally, without constant tuggings, shiftings, and rearrangements.

My aim in life, whether standing on the lecture stage or sitting in the TV interviewer's chair, is to look as slim as I possibly can. I wear dark, solid colors, never a pattern, which melts into the background. In earlier days we were not permitted to wear black on TV because of glare problems, but now, with color, we can. I often wear a very bright-colored scarf (which I have learned to pull into place with a scarf ring and never touch) with a black or navy costume. If there are reds, rusts, or pinks in the scarf, I take care to match my lipstick accordingly—a small detail, but it shows up on camera. Because my neck is long and scrawny, I wear either a high-neck dress or a scarf or choker to disguise it. All it takes is a good analytical view of one video-tape playback to see one's visual faults and resolve to correct them.

I marvel at the clothes worn by women who are going to sit onstage or who will be part of a TV panel. Everyone, before going to the auditorium or stage, should sit down first in front of a full-length mirror at home and see what happens to her legs and hips when seated in that particular skirt. She's simply giving herself a preview of what the audience will see. Flabby knees or thighs, partially exposed by a skirt that rides up when the figure is seated, are not an exercise of beauty, nor is the underslip, which is often exposed. My own knees, affectionately known as "The Bobbsey Twins" in our family, have long been a source of private embarrassment. I turn my body away from the camera front, a bit to one side, so as to slim them, and whenever I see a bouquet of flowers on the coffee table on the set, I manage to sneak it over to a position just in front of my knees, if I can get away with it.

I have three main lecture subjects. In one I prattle on about my career in Rome, Paris, Tiffany's, the White

House, and in "life today." This last is far less glamorous than the others, but my audience can relate to it far more easily. I inevitably finish off with a word about the women's movement, specifically geared to be conservative for women's-club audiences, but far more radical for women students. One theme that young and old alike can understand is that more women must be elected to government office—at all levels. I always give the National Women's Political Caucus and NOW a big plug in this respect because they are doing more than anyone else to get women elected. A typical town-hall lecture series, very popular in the Middle West, involves speaking for a full hour in a local movie theater around eleven o'clock in the morning. This is often followed by a question-and-answer period (this timetable is totally against my father's speech philosophy that if absolutely everything can't be said in thirty minutes, nothing should be said at all). These women, however, want their money's worth. They have gone to great trouble to attend. They have hired a sitter, made a hair appointment before, organized a car pool and a downtown shopping expedition—all centered around the lecture, which, incidentally, always benefits some charity. Several hundred of the women join me afterward at a nearby restaurant, organized by the town-hall committee, following which there is another question-and-answer period. By now my main mission in life is to survive the whole experience, but some lovely soul inevitably revives my flagging spirits by asking not about Jacqueline Kennedy but about my husband and children.

I have another lecture, on the subject of decorating, which requires the frantic pushing of two sets of automatic slide-changing buttons on a remote control. I project one hundred and sixty colored slides in pairs on two screens. It is extremely difficult to base one's entire talk on slides and then to be at the mercy of one's visuals, such as slides that stick, electrical wires that short, and projector bulbs that blow out. No matter how often I plead in advance with the people arranging my audio-visual requirements, the same things go wrong each time. But then, when they work, the slides are pretty dazzling, and make the audience want to go home, throw everything out, and start decorating all over again. I use the best slides from award-winning homes, plus good ones from my Sears, Roebuck days, and others purchased from museums and historic places, which illustrate far better than words the history of decorative furnishings in this country. I always sneak in a few slides of White House rooms for good measure, and occasionally some of our own apartment, which the audience always loves, particularly when I point out my own decorating mistakes. The slide they like best is the one of the impossible room off our kitchen, which is multi-purpose to a fault. It is the children's dining room, the laundry room, and my office. The combination in a small space of an electric typewriter on a stand next to a cluttered executive desk made of blue steel, with matching file cabinets and typing chair, a round table with four chairs, juvenile artwork pasted all over the walls, old gas dryers built into the wall, a washing machine, and a small electric portable dryer is not just an ordinary, every-day, run-of-the-mill room plan. I have a collection of what "not to do under any circumstances" slides to show to an audience who might have gotten just a little uptight about looking at all the superbly furnished award-winning interiors and those rooms done by those geniuses "with no money but lots of know-how." I show them rooms that will ease their inferiority complexes at once when they realize the mistakes they could have made but didn't.

My third category of lecture topic is the role of women today and their careers, which includes advice even to the very young (which they usually have no intention of following). Probably the nicest feedback I ever had from the "very young" was a whole book full of thank-you letters that an instructor from the Sears Charm School in Milwaukee sent me (from her pupils aged nine to eleven). I had lectured to them on the subject of manners, which is not the most popular subject for any age group. To receive a written thank-you note for discussing the topic is very notable indeed. A letter signed by "Your Friend Judy" stated, "I did not know that we shouldn't eat fried poultry with a fork and knife unless the hostess says we can. Now that I know I'm sure I will remember." (What I had actually said, of course, is that one should not pick up chicken with the fingers unless the hostess says one can; Judy's way was much better.)

An eleven-year-old in the same class wrote, "I liked what you said. Because a girl can learn to be ladylike. I can learn table manners, how to act at a party, what to do if a boy calls, and how to introduce people. When I grew up, I wanted to be a boy more than a girl. Now I can become a very nice girl. Thank you." (I wonder if she has become an ardent feminist today.)

One week-long absence every year is well worth the troubles it causes my family and business. I am a Woodrow Wilson National Foundation Visiting Fellow, which is a high-faluting name for those of us chosen to go out every year to spend a week on campus with the students of a small college. My mission is to represent the business world to the academic community and to talk to the girls about going into a tough job market, balancing family life with career, and coping with all of it as best as one can. Strangely enough, a number of boys turn up at all my class discussions and rap sessions. Sometimes I hold forth in the college cafeteria or in a faculty house in the evening, or in the dorms. I attend classes which pertain to my business experience and general knowledge; occasionally I'm allowed to teach a "Women's Studies" class. It all takes me back to my own college days. It is an absolutely exhilarating experience, and if the girls today are totally different from me and my peers at their age, they are also totally interesting and delightful. We first attack the problem of how each one feels about herself and about the necessity of having self-confidence. I try to get them off the subject of "Who am I?" because there isn't time in our competitive era to ruminate on such an egotistical subject. Instead, we talk about what we can all do to feel better about ourselves and how we can survive through tapping hidden resources in ourselves we never even knew we had. Today's students are a joy; they are so eager "to get out there and fight." They want to succeed so badly, and generally their desire is matched by their bewilderment in how to do it.

When we discuss the family role, I no longer raise even a quarter of an eyebrow when girls tell me they are living with boys now, have no intention of getting married, and have no desire for children. When I look such a young woman straight in the eye and ask, "You mean you have no intention ever of getting married, no intention EVER of having a child?" the student usually backs off and admits, "Well, maybe in the future." (The distant future for a twenty-year-old can mean five years from now.) In any case, I can sympathize with the ones who for very personal reasons do not want to have children. What's wrong with admitting one would not make a good parent? No one should have to have children. Some people just don't want this dimension in their lives. But on the necessity for legalizing their living-together situation, we don't agree. No matter how hard I try, for their sakes, to separate in my own mind their theories and what I feel is the key to my own survival in an extremely pressured world—a commitment to my husband and children and their commitment to me—I cannot. Without having my commitment to my family, I would feel no necessity to work as hard as I do to succeed. Most of the young women I talk to seem to be burning with a desire to succeed, too. The one who lives with a man yet rejects all sense of commitment to him may be something of a hypocrite. She may also be robbing herself of an extra measure of energy that such a commitment seems to bring.

With students who do not reject the idea of marriage, we naturally discuss the importance of sharing household and child-caring tasks. Today's young people do this so naturally; I envy them that.

With the economy in bad shape, it is easier to impart to students the necessity of "starting at the bottom" in all humility in the field of their choice. The era when a college graduate could insist on starting in the executive suite has vanished, at least temporarily. No one wants to hear it, but I tell them anyway that the way to get ahead in this particular time is to get the foot in the door, to accept a job that means dirty work no one wants to do. If you're in the company you would like to work for, a foot in the door can mean half a body in the door in a short time. When somebody gets moved up, is fired, or dies, there you'll be, with your proper attitude showing, ready to jump into the job. (Your roommate, who felt herself much too good for that receptionist's job, might well be still on unemployment.)

I never get off the subject of the importance of knowing how to type fast and accurately. This sermon is always met with derision and resentment by college students, as the feminist in every girl wells up in her soul at the very mention of that symbol of female slavery, the typewriter. Then I explain how in my own office, in this economy, I cannot afford to hire a secretary for any of my executives. I won't hire anyone in an executive capacity who can't type professionally her own letters, memos, releases, project write-ups, and client reports. Our one office "secretary," talented Lexie Tanner, does a little of everything *except* secretarying. The Boss does her own correspondence on the typewriter. My fingers have been trained to chase along after my brain. Collectively, we all save our little company a lot of money by doing our own work. My college audiences seem to take all this in eventually, and for the moment, at least, the typing onus is lifted.

I always look forward to these college visits, because I learn far more from the students than they do from me. God bless the foundations for funding the program, the purpose of which is to help bridge the gap between the business and academic worlds for students. Topflight representatives from the worlds of politics, finance, journalism, and foreign affairs are sent out to the smaller campuses that do not have a relationship to a large city. These visits are much needed, but the Fellows need them, too. (I also get to play a lot of tennis during my week on campus.)

In one way the students are just like the clubwomen I talk to. No matter what has been discussed during the previous hour, no matter what age or sex my audience is, when it's questions-and-answers time the first question is always, "What was Jackie Kennedy *really* like?" When Julie Nixon Eisenhower, whom I happen to like very much, took over for one week as moderator of Barbara Walters's syndicated TV show, "Not for Women Only," she asked me to be part of the panel for her first two shows. Just as we were about to sign off on the first show, she turned to me with a teasing look in her eyes: "Tish, tell me, what was Jackie Kennedy *really* like?"

I looked at her for a moment. "I don't really know, Julie. But tell me something, what are *you* really like?" With that, the show went off the air. *Touché*.

There is no possible way to develop a strong ego in my family about my public speaking, nor am I successful in inspiring my daughter to follow in my footsteps. One night in Edgartown, during our summer vacation, I informed eight-year-old Clare that I would graciously allow her to attend my lecture at the Methodist Church, a beloved Edgartown landmark, for the benefit of another sentimental spot, the Old Sculpin Gallery. This gallery is one of the eighteenth-century jewels on the island of Martha's Vineyard. I told Clare that people were paying to hear me, that she could stay up past her bedtime, and that she would not have to pay for her ticket from her ice-cream-cone allowance. She first asked me if she could stay home, forego the lecture, and still stay up until ten. When told this plan would not work, she declined my invitation, saying she was really not interested.

I had frankly expected a different reaction, since this would have been the first time she heard her mother speak in public. My advice-to-mothers book says that "one should not expect affirmative reactions from children in regard to one's public appearances." All right, book.

At seven the night of the lecture, Clare accompanied me to the church to test the mike, tramp around the platform, and line up things with the church custodian. Much to my surprise, she said, "I'd like to come back for your talk tonight, Mommie."

"You may come, Clare," I tried to disguise my pleasure at this change of heart.

"But you have to promise me one thing first, Mommie," she said very firmly.

"That depends. What?"

"That you won't mention I'm here, that you won't point me out in the audience. I'd be too embarrassed."

"Okay," I replied, "that's a deal. But you have to make me a promise, too, or I won't let you come."

She looked at me suspiciously. "All right, what is it?"

"Promise that you won't crack your knuckles during my speech."

She promised. She had just discovered some of the glories of being double-jointed, and had been on a knuckle-cracking binge that was driving us all to desperation.

The speech was given, a full house attended, and I referred to Clare only once, citing the fact that two children had been born. A crowd surrounded me afterward, congratulating me on doing a good job, for which I was thankful. It was a pretty tough audience, and the lectures which one donates to a good cause are always full of more "clutching moments" than are the paid ones, it seems. I asked my daughter what she thought about it as we walked the short distance home in the cool evening air.

"You went on too long, Mommie," was her only comment. "I wanted to go to sleep in the whole last part."

I cracked my knuckles in answer.

One reason I will never do a long lecture tour is that I am afflicted with motel-phobia. I stand accused of suffering from a persecution complex about motel rooms. I am also afflicted with an advancing case of claustrophobia, and am *always* the one who gets the room in which last night's occupant held an all-night sales meeting, replete with a marathon of booze and cigar-smoking. All the fumes hang in the air, mixed into one ghastly, pungent symphony of smells. I rush to open the windows. The windows, of course, do not open. There are three courses of action open to me: go crazy, smash the windows with a chair, or take remedial action. Naturally, I must pursue the last course, since the Hollensteiner family cannot afford the other two. I turn up the air-conditioning unit to its highest (even in the deep of winter); then I take out of my suitcase a spray can of room-freshener and go to it with a vengeance. I even squirt it into the hallway outside my room for good measure. I have been known in desperation to squirt it right into the faces of oncoming people in the corridor. No matter. The air they are breathing is foul, and they should welcome the change. My next act is to order dinner from room service, mostly hot things, because by the time the waiter arrives the room temperature will stand at twenty degrees. (I wear a winter coat to bed in these attempts to get rid of the bad air. . . . It is all in vain. The bad air simply recirculates in an ever-increasing colder temperature.)

My next act is to call the family to complain about my lot in life. Malcolm usually throws me off by telling me something with enormous pride such as he just "made the soccer All-Stars at school." (All-Stars in second grade?) Before I can complain to Clare, she complains to me about the fact she is the only girl in her entire school of four hundred and eighty students without a costume to wear in the Christmas play. By the time R.H. gets on the telephone, I am exhausted by family emotions. He is in an exceedingly bad mood because Dustin just did a Number Two in the hallway which he will have to clean up. I remark to him that it all makes me feel very missed.

I am sorry I have called home. The meal arrives cold from Room Service. It has a posh price tag attached to it, too. No matter. I must eat to stay alive, and it tastes no worse than if I were eating it by myself in the Ye Olde Oaken Bucket restaurant of the motel. I survey the interior-design scheme of the room. I don't know why it is, but the color scheme is always either a sickly olive-green-gold combination or a hideous "peacock blue" (that's the name they give to it, but a peacock would defoliate itself if it had to bear such a color in its tail feathers). Then there's often a combination color of rusting red in the room, the color of ten-year-old drainpipes. The mattress is always carved into the deep slopes of someone else's body, not mine. The telephone is usually across the room, far from my operating post, the bed. The TV is inevitably placed so that in order to see it one has to sit in a spine-aching chair over in the corner, facing the neon lights out the window. I sometimes think this is the way the motel saves on electricity. Some motels have a gadget I have christened the "Torture Wake-up." One asks the front desk for a six-thirty wake-up, expecting a telephone to ring the next morning at that hour. Instead, something goes off in the early-morning darkness in the room with a terrible noise, sounding just as though six seat-belt buzzers were sounding off together. There is no light attached to it, so one can't find the damned thing to turn it off. It is usually mounted on a wall, well camouflaged. By the time one has found it and turned it off, the day has begun wrong. Instead of arising slowly from bed and stretching into a "Good Morning, World!" affirmative greeting, my nervous system has been shattered.

There is never, of course, room in the bathroom, where the light is good, for one's cosmetic case. Or if there is, it's on a ledge flush with the washbasin, with the result that one's cosmetic case is constantly sitting in a flood of water. The motel designer probably thinks women will use the unattractive "vanity table" built in the bedroom between the two chests of drawers. The only trouble is, there's no water there, not enough light to see one's face, and it's cluttered with stand-up cards telling guests about all of the hotel's services and bars.

One might well ask why, if I hate so much being sealed in a smelly motel room, I don't stay with friends? The answer is that when one is "on the road" for business or lecturing, staying with one's friends is guaranteed to rob one of any sleep, composure, or chance to work on one's remarks. No matter how much one pleads beforehand, there is a cocktail party or a dinner. Exhaustion piles upon exhaustion. One goes to bed red-eyed, overstuffed, swollen-ankled, unprepared, and exhausted from answering the guests' questions about what Jackie was really like.

The guest of honor is always questioned so incessantly, she usually gives her full speech before she has to give it the next morning. Having to leave at seven for a morning TV show before the lecture is also a good way to inconvenience one's hosts, too, most cruelly. I have certain friends with whom I always stay, who understand my problems.

They never invite guests over when I arrive for the night. They give me an early dinner; we get caught up on each other's families with our feet communally up. I'm in bed at nine, after I've had careful instructions about making my own six-o'clock instant-coffee breakfast the next morning. I steal away before the house is awake.

Except for those few good friends, such as the Bill Witters in San Francisco, the Bennet Harveys and the Phil Wrigleys in Chicago, the Ken Boltons in Cleveland, and the like, the motel retreat is the answer at the end of an interminably long day after a tough trip from New York. Bathing, getting into bed, working *off one's feet*, talking to no one except the family are life-saving operations. For me it provides the letdown that allows me to go out the next morning with an "I'll knock 'em dead" attitude. I owe that, at least, to my audience.

On the subject of lecturing and traveling, I wonder if any airlines have ever asked a businesswoman about what she'd like on an airplane? I doubt it. All airplanes are designed for men, and very short ones at that. No one cares about what a businessman looks like when he gets off the plane. But when a businesswoman or lecturer is being met at the plane, everyone cares. She has to appear chic, carefully made up, elegant. She has to be lovely and sweet-smelling. If a woman has boarded the plane in a snowstorm, she must leave it with her boots glistening clean, free of all salt stains.

I always board a plane in a disastrous physical and mental state. I am always late for the plane, requiring the running of long distances, clutching heavy boxes of slides, briefcase, dress bag, tote bag, and handbag. I arrive breathless, shiny-nosed, mussy-haired, lipstickless, and bad-tempered. Somehow, during that flight, I have to pull a Cinderella-getting-ready-for-the-ball before I meet the group at the other end, which can include the officers of the sponsoring organization, their children, sometimes their dog, a woman's editor from the local newspaper, and a radio reporter clutching his tape recorder. I have to disembark looking as well as I possibly can manage for them. Every time I see the lavatory unoccupied and go in to do my "head-repair job," someone starts to rattle the door. I peer outside to find five people lined up, looking desperate, so I return to my seat. The airline that makes a tiny space for grooming purposes, separate from the lavatory area, will get my business. And the airline that makes some seat space longer for their taller passengers will not only get my business but will be placed permanently on my nightly prayer list.

One important reason that I continue to lecture a few times a year, even if it takes a great deal out of me, is that I am keeping in touch with my own sex by going "out there." I want to know what they're thinking, what they're buying, how they're coping, what they're enjoying, what their homes look like, and what they're hating about life in general. In the first place, I am genuinely interested. In the second, such information makes me much more effective in my business. New York is such an island of self-centered, pseudo-sophisticated egotists that it is easy to forget that the rest of the country is not like this at all.

It's amazing what one learns in another city even on those rides to and from the city's airport with the program chairman. There are all those revealing little conversations while waiting around in TV studios or standing in endless receiving lines, balancing limitless crystal punch cups on a plate full of little sandwiches. Then there are the predictable lunch menus of salad and potato chips, followed by pineapple sherbet topped with green mint glop. Knowing of my work in interior design, the women are constantly taking me to their homes to show off their own decorating and handiwork talents. This is an exciting education in itself. I probably see the inside of more homes than any decorating magazine editor.

"Out there" normal values are immediately apparent, and to a New Yorker, they are downright refreshing. Out there they couldn't care less about the latest gossip or a new Andy Warhol film or the fact that the wife of a much photographed young couple is supposed to be a lesbian. They've never heard of Orsini's, where the Beautiful People lunch and are photographed by *Women's Wear*, and they would consider a woman absolutely crazy who rushes to Yves St. Laurent's boutique to buy four pairs of his new pants at one time.

These women out there, of course, make a lot of sense. I have watched them wrestling with the women's movement for several years, too. They are still feeling uneasy about it. For too long now their daughters and granddaughters have been openly flouting the traditions they hold dear. I think that sometimes when they talk to me they feel comforted, believing that their female offspring can be liberated in every sense but still end up married, with a couple of children, a career, and a decent-looking wardrobe. One woman complained that her daughter and her daughter's friends refused to join her town's women's club, which had been the center of the community's volunteer aid and social life for four generations. She was clearly upset, because she saw her club eroding at its very base. I asked her what her daughter was doing for her community, and the mother answered, "Oh, well, of course, she does a lot in her own way. For one thing, she and two friends have set up a remedial reading clinic for the underprivileged children of our town." I then asked the woman whether it ever occurred to her that her women's club might very well go bust, with no new young members and with all the older ones dying off, but that her daughter would form a new association, even with her clinic as a base, which in time would have its own customs, its own clubhouse, its own lecturers coming to town?

If the young today refuse to follow their parents, they are developing their own new routes to social consciousness and they help society in their own way just as much. The end result is just the same.

There is no doubt but that the boat is rocking badly in the minds of my women audiences. Some are downright seasick from it. One does not have to be a Jet Setter to have a child involved way over his head in drugs, alcohol, or sex. Emotional family dramas are being played out in the same tragic manner just as often in the quiet Kansas farmhouse as they are behind the big stone gates of the estate in Greenwich, Connecticut.

There is a great deal of poignancy in the American woman's sense of confusion over the female revolution. No one likes to have one's entire life style and one's entire lifetime contribution to the family challenged, belittled, downplayed. These are intelligent women; they have been playing according to the rules. I do not blame a wife and mother for her resentment against her "militant sisters." But she will have to adjust to their militancy, just as the sisters will have to work hard to alleviate her suspicion of them.

I keep trying to emphasize from the lecture platform that intellectual equality is what it's all about. There isn't a woman in the audience who won't admit she feels as smart as any man—or, rather, that, had she been given the same education and opportunities, she would feel as smart as any man. The most turned-off older women, who feel uncomfortable about the mere mention of the women's movement, suddenly start to bristle with rage in the audience when I tell some stories of men in business who even today loudly proclaim, to our faces, "You women are not the mental equals of us men. You can't be managers, you can't possibly handle the top executive positions. So forget it!" Very few of my audiences are career women, since those women cannot attend lectures during the day.

Most of my audiences have deliberately chosen the role of staying home to raise their children. They will not accept criticism of this choice, nor should they have to. Each year, more and more of them tell me about their parttime jobs, teaching, selling, working in libraries and hospitals, all occupations that make them feel needed and useful with their children grown and away from the home. To a woman, they want their daughters and granddaughters to attend graduate school in order to become lawyers, doctors, and merchant chiefs *as well as* wives and mothers. This much of the movement has gotten through to most of the most conservative of women. It took the militants to push them ahead into thinking this way. God bless the militants.

There could be many more people on the lecture circuits today. Small groups in towns everywhere are anxious for programs—programs that will entertain them, educate them, break up the lonely hours, or teach them how to live better. The lecture bureaus usually handle the larger towns, where the real fees can be asked. Before someone wants to become a public speaker, however, he or she has to learn what is a marketable subject. Lots of older people would like to start lecturing as something enjoyable to do and income-bolstering in their retirement years. They often have a "marvelous program" all ready to give. It turns out that they have just been to Hong Kong (no one else has), and, of course, they have excellent pictures to show (amateur color snapshots, unsuitable for converting into colored slides that could be projected on a screen).

The same topics that sell books—sex, cooking, dieting, getting rich—are the topics that sell lecturers. If you have something to say in one of these fields, can say it with gusto and humor, can illustrate it well, and have christened your talk with a snappy title, then you are ready to go see a lecture bureau. If you drop your biography on a receptionist's desk at a lecture agency, with an accompanying description of a talk entitled "I Can Teach You How to Turn a Hundred Dollars into a Thousand in Thirty Days," someone at the bureau will surely ask to see you. A title such as "It's Fun to Be Fat, Free, and Forty" is also provocative because so many of the lecture audiences are just that.

One woman I know who had never properly arranged a flower in a vase in her life went on the lecture circuit as an expert on the subject. After her husband left her penniless, she had to support herself. She loved beautiful flowers, but she had always had gardeners who grew them and servants who arranged them. She borrowed a thousand dollars, then spent almost a year researching every picture book of flower arranging and photographs of flowers she could find in print. She had colored slides made, for example, of beautiful flower still lifes from seventeenth-century Flemish flower paintings up through the French Impressionists, having received permission from the publishers to do so. She copied pictures of Japanese Ikebana arrangements and Chinese floral treatments from old prints and screens. Her slides were breathtaking; her lecture was chatty, anecdotal, amusing, educational. Women love flowers, and she soon found she was wanted by women's groups all over the country. She trained her very pleasant, soft voice into one that projected, one that was musical. When she died, she was earning around twenty-five thousand dollars a year, without benefit of a lecture agency.

People who know how to communicate features of gardening, cooking, budgeting, or anything to help us live more pleasantly, efficiently, and economically can make a living on lecture tours. If a lecture bureau won't take you on, you can write your own promotion piece and do your own mailing. Simply look up the names and addresses of all the clubs, associations, and church groups in your area, and send a form letter to the program chairman of each group. Describe your talk and state your fee. If you are just starting out, start out low, charging, say, twenty-five dollars per lecture. But first, tape-record your whole talk; listen back and correct your speech faults until the entire lecture sounds pleasing and your voice sounds full of energy and life. The first discovery of how one's own voice really sounds is usually a disastrous surprise. All words must be clearly enunciated in a speech because a microphone can take a fuzzily pronounced word and make it sound like a new lingo from Ghana. If, after countless bouts with the tape recorder, your voice is still unpleasing, go see a speech teacher. Every large town has its own Dorothy Sarnoff who can work wonders with the voice of anyone who will concentrate. The college or university in one's town usually has a speech teacher, and that person might be in need of extra cash earned by moonlighting. I have seen Dorothy Sarnoff in action with some pretty hopeless New York businessmen; she can turn them into golden-tongued orators if they try hard enough.

The more you practice your lecture before local groups (and a "local group" can consist of your husband, children, your neighbors and their children, your hairdresser while he's setting you, or your dog or cat), the more polished you will become and the more able to withstand disasters. It does indeed feel like a disaster when you are speaking to eighteen hundred people in an auditorium and the public-address system won't function or the slide projector won't work.

I resort to prayer at a time like that. A few Hail Marys never hurt anyone, and if Mary doesn't make things start to work at once, at least she makes the audience properly sympathetic and ready to react affirmatively to anything I might do to save face. I've had my slides put in backward by a professional projectionist who is paid to know better;

they ran back to front and completely killed the organization of my lecture. I have had old ladies mumble out loud
during my speeches. (One was "bounced" in Fort Wayne
by two horrified fellow club members.) I have had people
of all ages snore in my face. (I am sympathetic with this
because I have done it to others since college days, without wanting to, because of the lack of fresh air in the
room.) I have given the wrong speech to a group expecting
a totally different topic. Once, thanks to a hotel-suite
mix-up, I gave ten minutes of a Democratic Party campaign speech to a meeting of Republican women. In Honolulu I spoke to the Fashion Group in a lovely restaurant
by the sea, only to find that the restaurant didn't have a
mike. The crashing of the surf drowned out every word of
my talk; a bullhorn wouldn't have helped. I gave up. Once
I flew into Nassau late at night, went directly to bed in my
room at the Paradise Island Hotel, then addressed a retail
buying group the next morning at nine on the subject
"The Relationship of Body Fashions to Home Fashions."
Since I was not being paid a fee for this exhausting trip, I
was gnashing my teeth every inch of the way. I rushed
from the meeting room at ten to check out of the hotel in
order to catch an eleven-o'clock plane for New York. On
my way to board the airport taxi, I stopped in the casino of
the hotel for the first and only time. I had exactly eight
minutes to spare. I put down a ten-dollar bill on *rouge* on
one of the roulette tables. Eight minutes later, I left for the
airport, five hundred dollars richer. I had earned a fee after
all. They tell me there's also a beach in Nassau, but I had
been there many times before. Along with the beach there
are sandflies, and I was glad to leave the retailers behind
me for three days of all of it.

Life on these speaking trips is certainly a contrast of
worlds. Between business, lecture-agency bookings, and
charity appearances, I do an average of thirty-five a year.
Meeting new people, colliding with new frames of refer-

ence, adjusting to different climates is all part of being on the road. One day I am in sweltering Satellite Beach, Florida, addressing the officers' wives of Patrick Air Force Base (part of Cape Canaveral and the space program); and the next I am in chilly Winterthur, Delaware, taking a group of Sears, Roebuck home-furnishings stylists through that great repository of colonial American treasures. The transition between places can be exciting, both visually and mentally.

I enjoy speaking to a mixed audience of men and women, because it's a challenge. I know I will be a success when I am speaking to the Tuckahoe Club of Richmond or to the Shreveport Women's Department Club or to New York's Colony Club. But when men are involved, the entire audience chemistry changes. I have to sound like less of a feminist, more of a traditionalist. Unlike militant feminists who want to "tell it like it is and rub the men's noses in it," I know it is like it is, but I want men to be my friends. If I am speaking to a male audience, I want them to enjoy me, and not to be turned off. I always tell them exactly where I stand, which is on the feminists' side, but we go on from there. Usually, an audience of men is perfectly easy and delightful if one keeps one's sense of humor—and if they have had a drink or two and a good dinner. When I told R.H. I was going to speak before the Rotary Club of Kansas City on the subject "Handsome Interiors on All Budgets," he practically swallowed his lit cigar.

"Tish, you can't."

"Why not?"

"You *can't* lecture to the Rotary Club on decorating. They'll hoot you right out of the old Muehlebach."

"I'm going to do it."

"I never thought you wouldn't."

He laughed, and added that when the men heard what the subject was, decorating, they wouldn't show up, only their wives.

Just because R.H. couldn't sit through one of my decorating lectures doesn't mean that the Rotarians couldn't. The wives were invited, too, and the big ballroom was jammed. The men were enthusiastic, warm, and delightful. I received a gold Rotary charm as well as the Key to Kansas City to remind me that husbands aren't always right.

When the speaking topic is wrong, of course, there is absolutely nothing one can do to win that audience. I will never forget the day I traveled to another city in a snowstorm to address a professional-women's luncheon. I had been assigned a topic, "Affirmative Attitudes about Middle Age," but my audience had obviously thought I was going to talk about Jackie. I was almost frozen out of the dining room, which was very fitting in view of the snow raging outside. It was apparent that the younger members didn't want to cogitate middle age; it would simply never happen to them. As for the majority, middle-aged women all, they refused to accept the fact that they were. They did not even want to hear the subject mentioned. It was a great afternoon for me; I struck out so badly, I learned a good lesson—never to address myself again to that topic.

One's love of the spotlight and enjoyment of being there are normally reduced when one is in a foreign country and handicapped by the presence of another language. In the late 1960s the Merchandise Mart sent me to nine European countries on a giant import project. I held a press conference in each of the American embassies in those countries. When no one in the room understands your little jokes because of language problems (one must never admit to oneself that the joke could be bad), then any remnants of spontaneity and humor will, of necessity, disappear. I spoke Italian in Italy and French in both France and Spain, and although everyone understood me, I had to stick to the message. All asides seemed superfluous. When I faced a sea of men in Germany and Austria, none of them understanding my English too well, the wait for the interpreter to finish translating my remarks seemed interminable. No one even smiled. I also knew that the men in that room felt something close to hostility because they had been made to come hear a woman talking business to them.

When the Portuguese Trade Mission invited interior designer Ellen McCluskey and me to survey their home-furnishings marketing potential, we found ourselves having to give press conferences and little speeches with no warning whatsoever. The art of bluffing is of paramount importance at a time like this, and I also remember the traditional standard advice for unrehearsed speaking, "If you suddenly don't know what to say, praise something or someone."

When the Finnish Trade and Marketing Association invited me to address their annual Congress in Helsinki, I accepted, knowing full well I couldn't bluff on this one. Several weeks were required to prepare the hour-long demonstration of how public-relations techniques backstop advertising. I showed clients' filmed TV commercials; then I showed colored slides of projects that we, as the public-relations firm, carried through to extend the advertising program objectives even further. The Finns were not that familiar with public relations as a profession and they were an attentive, enthusiastic audience. I spoke in the big Dipoli Congress Hall, attached to the university, the interior of which was designed, desks and chairs included, in stunning, sweeping curves of blond wood. My audience consisted of eight hundred marketing executives and students. A very savvy simultaneous interpreter, a young woman, sat in a glass booth and managed to get across to the audience my jokes, slang, and technical terms. I knew this because the ones with earphones all laughed in the right places. I felt as though I was standing addressing the U.N.; it was a high moment of satisfaction in my professional career and the Finns were the most gracious of hosts. My niece Alice Baldridge, an interior designer, was along, and afterward they took us on a week's grand tour of the design studios and factories producing Finland's greatest home furnishings, art objects, and fashion designs. They fed us banquets of roast elk and wattle berries, and proudly showed us their fine examples of architecture, from the late-nineteenth-century examples of Eliel Saarinen to the 1970s buildings of Alvar Aalto. They also gave me a good-by present—a chinchilla hat—which is the greatest form of Aloha ever known.

If no one listens to what I have to say at home, at least there are a lot of people "out there" who will. I recommend public speaking for anyone who has trouble finding an audience in her own family.

10
Complaints and Successes, Successes and Complaints

If we can reflect on all the examples of nonphysical inequalities between the sexes at this stage in our society, then we can also reflect on all our advances as women since the founding of this country. No matter what our complaints may be, they can't compare to what the griping of our colonial sisters could have been had they been aware of what there was to gripe about. And America is certainly the place to be for a woman. If she has any doubts on that subject, she has only to go live in any other country—even a place like Switzerland, where women were given the vote only a short time ago.

I feel somewhat of a copout not to have been in the front lines with the militants in the women's movement, for I enjoy all the prerogatives of the advances that they have made. I've been riding the crest of the waves of their successes, rather like a gentlewoman riding sidesaddle in the nineteenth century, while my militant sisters have been doing their riding bareback, head-on, straight, and tough. I salute them. So much has happened because of them.

There are so many indirect results of their actions—developments such as young women now being admitted to graduate business schools. This means they will be able to work their way up through Wall Street into positions of power where it counts, which is where the money is. And more women are being elected to public office, which is the second form of power that counts.

Successful, well-adjusted working mothers will soon be so commonplace they will not even be pointed out in conversation. This will happen within just a few years. When the people now in their twenties become experienced parents in their thirties, and when the older, fuddy-duddy corporate male chauvinists have been forced into retirement, then the women's movement will fizzle into nothingness, for good reason. There will be no need for it.

And when that great day comes, women who cannot succeed in a career simply because of their own ineptness and bad attitude will no longer be able to blame "male chauvinism" for their failures, either. The word "chauvinist" will apply to both men and women. "Chauvinist person" will replace the term male chauvinist. Today's youth are handling the problem on their own very well, and because of them each of us will be, in a matter of time, a person, not someone limited in terms of gender.

However, right at this very minute we are still lacking enough role models of successful working mothers to help today's young woman along. Because I travel in so many worlds, I know a great many, working successfully in different fields. They are not known, however, to most young women in high school and college, wrestling with the problem of rejecting their mothers' values and forming their own. The secret of so many successful women I know is that they have maintained what was best of their mothers' values and absorbed new ones of their own, shaped by experience, plus a little wisdom, too. We are not talking here about women who work; we are talking here about women who set high goals for themselves in their work. It takes a lot of stretching.

Two nationally known, very successful women have been longtime friends—and clients, too. One, Erica Wilson, is probably the foremost expert on needlepoint, and she has parlayed that skill into big business. She writes a successful book every other year on the subject, lectures all over the world, runs a school of needlework, and occasionally writes, produces, and stars in her own series for public television. She also manages to design kits for nationwide distribution in stores and runs three retail shops, in New York, Southampton, and Nantucket.

Erica is tall, blond, possessed of a hearty, infectious laugh, and has the typical rosy-cheeked good looks of her English homeland. Her husband, Vladimir Kagan, is shorter and is as darkly handsome and black-olive-eyed as she is fair. He is of Russian blood, with a temperament to match, and is a well known contemporary-furniture designer with his own showrooms. They live with their teen-aged daughter and a younger son and daughter in a Park Avenue apartment filled with Vladdy's furniture, examples of Erica's craft, an oversized bird cage in the living room inhabited by chattering tropical birds, and an ever-growing menagerie of dogs and cats.

Watching Erica in action reminds me of my own life. There are many ongoing lives in her daily routine. It is a world of distraction and interruption, but she keeps her sense of humor, even when the pressures are great. She "orchestrates" at the family breakfast table. I have joined them for business discussions early in the morning, while she instructs the cook about tonight's dinner, takes calls from her Madison Avenue shop, gives orders to the children's nurse, and talks to Nantucket about the three-day needlework seminar being organized for July. In the midst of these activities, she and Vladdy will be discussing the business aspects of her projects, figuring out their guest list for an upcoming cocktail party; she will take a call from the public-television station and afterward have a conference call with the manufacturer of her kits. She will admonish both daughters not to be late for school; and she will hug little Ilya, who has to stay home from school today with a sore throat. She finds a game for him to play with in his room while she is talking to me, drinking her coffee, and absent-mindedly working on a new piece of needlework that lies on a chair next to hers. This is a typical breakfast in the Kagan household.

Erica operates with a kind of delightful vagueness. She is fortunate in having a husband who, although involved in his own affairs, serves as her business manager. It is a three-ring circus, but everything gets done, and all in great good humor. Their household makes me feel somewhat better about the confusion at the Hollensteiners!

Ellen McCluskey has raised three handsome children during her professional life. She started her own interior-design firm in 1946, at a time when women in her social set simply did not do such things as open their own offices. She had already shocked the friends of her mother, the famous beauty Eve Lehman, by training bomber pilots in World War II, instead of rolling bandages and pouring coffee at the USO Canteen.

Ellen's apartment is a short walk from her Madison Avenue office. A sign on the brown door in the quiet hallway of the office building says ELLEN L. MCCLUSKEY ASSOCIATES, A.S.I.D. When one steps inside, that quiet is suddenly very far away. The place looks and sounds like a cramped scene backstage before the curtain goes up. There are bodies and conversation filling up every foot of space. Draftsmen are tucked into cubicles and niches; a slide presentation is being given in the jammed conference room; Ellen McCluskey is seeing a group of hotel planners in her own overcrowded office, sitting around a glass-topped conference table. Young designers are spread out in the other offices and drafting rooms, pouring over sample books of fabrics, wallpapers, and carpeting. Renderings, sketches, molding samples, and swatches are pinned onto bulletin boards jammed between the storage cubicles. Presiding over all this confusion is Edith, Ellen's secretary and right arm. No longer young, Edith, who has worked all her life, is a veritable fountain of energy and efficiency. Her telephone switchboard chimes constantly; she runs the office and supervises the movements of some fifteen people, including keeping her own boss on schedule, no small challenge. Edith is an inspiration to any woman of mature years who might be afraid to accept a demanding job.

During Ellen McCluskey's thirty successful years of designing residences, hotels, clubs, offices, and restaurants all over the world, she has raised her children, become a famous hostess, has been actively involved with several New York charities, particularly for the handicapped, and has been an active member of her professional organization of interior designers, the A.S.I.D. She has also kept herself in shape.

I would give anything to have her discipline. In spite of an arduous schedule, she always makes the time to go figure-skating each day. She attends a weekly ballet class. She is a perfect, trim size eight. The majority of her friends arise around ten in the morning, and feel pressured if they have to work in both the hairdresser and a lunch date in the same day. Because of her great interest in her work and that ability to discipline herself, she outpaces her friends in energy, accomplishment, and looks.

Emily Malino Scheuer, a college classmate of mine, is another successful interior designer. She specializes in hospitals, educational interiors, and other kinds of contract design. She has an office in Washington and lives with her congressman husband and four children in a big old Victorian house. Emily leads three lives—that of a mother who enjoys her children, that of a successful businesswoman, and that of a supportive political wife. Since the elections take place every two years, she always seems to be campaigning in the middle of everything else going on.

Inger McCabe Elliott and her husband Osborn Elliott (Editor-in-Chief of *Newsweek*) together have eight children, including two adopted sons from the Far East. Inger began and runs a highly successful business, China Seas, Inc., which supplies fabric for the fashion and interior design trades. She plays her mother's role enthusiastically, including running a household in the summer for all eight children and their friends in the Elliott weekend home (a converted church) in Connecticut. She is mistress of a large apartment on the East River in New York, plays a necessary role as Os Elliott's wife for magazine matters, manages her own showroom and warehouse factory in New York, and makes several trips a year to the Far East to check up on her Indonesian fabric production in factories there.

My Vassar classmate, Frances "Sissy" Farenthold of Houston, is another expert juggler and master of "putting it all together." I always point to her with pride when young women tell me they are discouraged about being strong enough to handle everything. The Farentholds have four wonderful children, yet Sissy has managed to become a lawyer, to have served two terms in the Texas House of Representatives, to have been nominated for Vice-President of the United States in 1972, and to have run for governor of Texas (winning 46 per cent of the vote). She also did a stint as chairperson of the National Women's Political Caucus, a group that works so hard to get women elected to political office. She not only functions at her full potential, she does it all with style and grace. She, along with Shirley Chisholm and the other women who have been elected to Congress, are people I admire enormously.

I greatly admire some of the members of the long-titled National Commission on the Observance of International Women's Year. These are extraordinary leaders and artful managers of their home lives. The head of the commission is Jill Ruckelshaus, an energetic and attractive mother of five children, a woman exposed at a young age to the glare of public life in Washington. Another commission member, Ella Grasso, governor of Connecticut, is part of a close-knit family that includes a son and daughter. Yet another, Gerridee Wheeler, president of the National Association for Mental Health, and her husband raise eight children in Bismarck, South Dakota, including three adopted Korean orphans. Prominent women like these who combine excellence in professional life and happiness in family are no longer rare. Their working hours are longer than most men's or those of women without families. They fit everything in because they have learned the fundamental secrets of how to pace their schedule and how to utilize every waking minute. They are organized; they never waste time. These are not easy abilities to acquire. They require practice, tenacious repetition, and discipline.

I admire career women who can keep their marriages afloat when one partner lives in one city and the other in another. It requires a great deal of understanding and loyalty; yet it is done more often than most people realize. Two of the more famous couples who work it out successfully are Charlotte Curtis and her husband and Mary Wells and her husband. Charlotte is one of the top editors of *The New York Times*, lives an exceedingly pressured life all week, but flies out on the weekends to Columbus, Ohio, to be with her surgeon husband. He flies into New York on certain weekends, too. Mary Wells has become a legend in our time as the highest-paid woman executive in the world. President of her own powerful advertising agency (a company she started, not one that was left to her by her father or her late husband), she commutes regularly to Dallas to be with her husband, who is head of an airline.

Absences can actually help a marriage—provided the woman is as happily engaged in doing what she wants to do as her husband is. R.H. and I, for example, will never have the time to get a divorce. Whenever we have a rousing good fight, one of us is always leaving for an airport. By the time that person is back, a day or so later, we have both forgotten what the fight was about. Some people are simmer-on-the-fire-until-it-boils types. If I were home all day and had the time to seethe over something R.H. had done wrong (and naturally, of course, whatever goes wrong is always his fault), by the time he returned home in the evening he would be met at the front door by an armored tank with two barrels blasting high-powered explosives at his head. That tank would be me.

Fortunately, as I have already said, when there is so much action in one's day, there is no time to agitate unduly over any of the three sectors of life involving husband, children, or business. This is the plug in the drain of one's sanity. A worry about any one thing is soon crowded out by a worry about one of the others. I keep referring to a juggling act, but that's exactly what it is, because one's mind should always be concentrating on the next ball going up in the air. And since worry never solves anything anyway, not having the time to worry too long about one thing is a great blessing in life. Unconsciously, with the idea of good mental health in mind, I let out all my worry. I let it out on my office associates, family, friends, even Dustin and Pierre if they happen to be around. I do try to keep all my complaints and expressed fears richly varied, so as not to bore my listeners; in fact, I try to give them as much dramatic flare as possible. Since my audience, including the dog and cat, is always wise to my exaggerations anyway, no one is unduly upset.

There are plenty of happy working-mother models all around me in New York. I keep wishing I could fly them all off on magic carpets to campuses all over the country to show the women students what a natural thing it can be to be a success and to maintain a normal home life. And after all, what is "normal," anyway? What suits each family best is what should be normal. If a girl's own mother has not worked, she may have a difficult time sorting it all out in her mind. I have noticed this often on my campus visits: many young women fight the concept of marriage or having children because they are so afraid they cannot manage it all. The proof that it can be done exists in big cities all over America. The bigger the city, the more adjusted working mothers there seem to be. That is why New York's environment makes our lives seem natural; that is why there are more women here who have risen to the top than in any other place.

Joan Glynn (former Bloomingdale's vice-president and president of Simplicity Patterns and now a top Revlon executive) commutes home at night from her offices to four children in a house in Connecticut. Diana Vreeland, former fashion-magazine editor and head of the successful exhibits mounted in the Metropolitan Museum's Costume Institute, has raised two sons, enjoys their families, and can look back on a long and demanding career that was always part of a happy family life. Dr. Judy Densen-Gerber, psychiatrist, lawyer, and head of the Odyssey House drug-rehabilitation programs all over the country, manages to be happily married, to raise four children, to teach law, to write books, and to agitate for aid to abused children and better conditions and legal rights for women in prison. She worked through a normally hectic day before she delivered her last child two years ago.

The women with whom I cross paths in my professional life have no time to think about what would exhaust them and what would not. Rita Reif, hard-working *New York Times* editor, runs a house and has a close-knit family life with her husband and two sons; Dorothy Collins managed to rise up the ladder of the public-relations firm Burson-Marsteller while she and her husband raised their daughter. She has a long commute up the Hudson River every night; yet she is in the office every day before nine. Madelon Talley, one of the few women holding a really important job in the financial world, lives in New York; she and her publisher husband, Mac Talley, raise two girls and a boy. She is one of the major executives of the Dreyfus Fund. Nancy White, former editor of *Harper's Bazaar* and Bergdorf Goodman executive, raised two daughters along with her husband. The exigencies of her high-powered career never interfered with their home life.

There is no doubt but that these working mothers have summoned an extra measure of energy in their lives to get them through their days. We often discuss this magic process; we have come to the conclusion that one maintains good health habits but that the excess energy is self-willed. If one says to oneself, "That would make me tired," then, indeed, that would make one tired.

In this era of women-and-careers emphasis, too little attention is paid to the women who work hard for our society but who do not earn money for it. Without these volunteers, our communities could not function. When they take on a project for their city or their schools, they are professionals. They work at it five days a week, sometimes even seven. They understand fund-raising, investment portfolios, costing out, intelligent cost-cutting, finding the right person for the job. They are executives who work without pay. Some members of the women's movement malign the volunteer, on the basis that it is degrading for women to work without pay. I, on the other hand, admire the dedicated ones wholeheartedly, simply for the fact that the community in which I live would be zero without them.

Elly Elliott, wife of the chairman of Ogilvy and Mather, Jock Elliott, has been so outstanding in her volunteer activities all of her life, such as president of the Board of Trustees of Barnard College, that she has been recognized by industry in a field where few women are recognized. She is the first woman director of the Celanese Corporation. In her various jobs, all volunteer, she has had much more business experience than many of the high-paid men in industry.

Kay Evans, wife of the Washington political columnist Rowland Evans, has kept herself constantly busy working for her community as well as for her husband and children. One of her Vassar Trustee duties is keeping a firm eye on the Vassar *Alumnae Quarterly,* which she has helped a gifted young editor turn from a rather dull publication into a lively one with handsome graphics. Kay could be earning a lot of money for her consulting activities; instead she gives her time. A lot of chief executive officers could well learn how to run their board meetings from her.

All of the female talent in this country is certainly not vested in the executive suite. Women like these are volunteers, in the sense they are unpaid; however, they are professional in every sense of the word. Without them our educational, cultural, and medical facilities would simply cease to exist. If these community "heroines" decide to enter the business field and be paid for their ability, they should not be embarrassed about filling out the "experience" column on the application. They've had plenty of it.

My relationships with men in the office is a subject women often ask me about, particularly on points of view of protocol, but it's something I just don't often think about. I have always treated men in business as people, and strangely enough, that's just the way I've always wanted them to treat me. I write them thank-you notes when they take me to lunch, send them silly birthday cards, and flowers when something like a promotion happens in their lives. My rules of office protocol are simple, whether they concern men or women. When someone calls on me in my office, I stand up behind my desk, greet him with a firm handshake, and offer him a chair (as well as a good cup of coffee, if our discussion is going to be a lengthy one). I see him to the outer door when we are finished and put out my hand again. None of this is anything other than simple manners. I adopted all the handshaking as a student in Europe, in accordance with their customs, just as I still eat with my fork in my left hand and my knife in my right. A handshake establishes body contact. That's important because it immediately breaks down a lot of psychological and physical barriers. (Some men are still embarrassed to be in a woman's office.)

I once had a very elegant pair of contemporary chairs on the other side of my desk. I noticed an old friend of mine, whom I hadn't seen in quite a while, squirming in his seat one day.

"You're not comfortable, Sam," I said, "come on, out with it."

"It's these chairs, Tish," he replied, changing position once again. "They're so damned low, and I'm so short. And there you sit, so very high in that tall red chair. You're—you're overpowering."

We had a big laugh over it, but the minute he left, I exchanged the chairs for two more ordinary-looking ones that sit as high as my own executive chair. I had never even thought about men feeling overpowered in the chairs they used, relative to mine. Since that day, however, I notice what men do with their chairs, and I have concluded that a man who is feeling ill at ease inevitably chooses the chair farthest away. Then he will push it back a bit farther still, almost as if to make a protective barrier. An aggressive person who is trying to sell me something will often pull his chair alongside my desk until it's practically next to mine. He will lean over my papers, and we are face to face, a situation I do not find comfortable with either sex. I've noticed, too, that someone who is perfectly relaxed with me will take any chair, pull it close to my desk, and yet leave the desk between us, granting each of us our privacy. I call all this shifting of seats in my office the art of "chairmanship," but I'm not yet ready to present a paper on my psychological theories.

Women can work in creative fields, such as those of art, music, interior design, fashion, advertising, and be themselves, but in the business world, in the corporate executive suite, this is still not so. It will take a few more years before the old traditions will relax—but perhaps less than a decade.

It may still require an extra touch of charm to respond to a successful male executive colleague in the manner in which he unconsciously wishes to be treated. I do not mean flirtation, which has seduction as its goal, but rather friendship for someone of the opposite sex expressed quite naturally. One has to take a few more pains with one's manners, that's all, with the sole aim of putting the other person at ease. Men often feel awkward with women who are close to them or ahead of them in salary and position. They are especially ill at ease if they feel their female colleagues are brighter; they would much rather compete with another man at any time. Men in the traditional businesses—law, finance, industry—really do feel threatened by women executives, simply because they have had so few around them in their working experience. When a woman enters the scene, there's a whole new chemistry in the air. Many tend first to look at the woman newcomer with suspicion, as if to speculate on whether she is a man-eater or a lesbian, or perhaps a sex kitten waiting to be seduced. This is where a woman's sense of humor is doubly important. She has to work her way through male distrust with her own charm, and with a firm sense of security about her own talents and ability to contribute. Women are certainly at a disadvantage in the executive situation; a woman has to prove herself first. The worth of a well-recommended man coming into a job is taken for granted. He is given the benefit of the doubt.

Too many times I have seen a capable but insecure woman ruining her chances of being accepted in the male sanctum sanctorum (and believe me, big business still is that) because she comes on strong and acts like "one of the boys." Some women think they will be accepted in the in-group if they use rough language. They mistakenly believe that if they treat their cohorts as though they were all about to put up their feet on the bar rail together, the men will all be delighted.

On the contrary. Most men want to know that the person with whom they are dealing and working is really of the sex she's supposed to be. By being true to her sex, I do not mean to imply that when she sits down, she is supposed to stick out her bosoms and put on a leg show. I do mean that when she sits down in the group, she be well mannered, good-humored, businesslike, and polite. A woman is supposed to have good manners. A man is forgiven if he doesn't. A woman, never. No one criticizes a man either if his wardrobe isn't put together exactly right. If he is effective in his job, he is forgiven a rumpled suit, an out-of-style necktie, and shoes that need shining. People laugh good-naturedly and excuse him for being "absent-minded about the way he looks." Let a woman executive of equal rank and ability come into her office badly put together, and suddenly there are secret conferences held. Should the president of the firm tell her? Should his secretary let on casually in the ladies' room that she heard someone say she ought to be neater and more in style, that she should be more chic to better reflect the company's image?

No, women are forgiven relatively little in large corporations. When a man comes into the office, he brags about his terrible hangover, jokes about his "delicate head." Everyone thinks it is funny and joins in teasing him. But let a woman come in complaining similarly about a hangover. Immediately the masculine jaws set coldly. Their smiling reactions to her are forced. This woman is obviously a problem. There is "nothing worse than a woman drinker." She will have to be watched.

When a man is having an emotional problem, he can let it hang out all over for a reasonable amount of time and not be fired. Everyone pours on the sympathy. "Poor Joe. He'll get over it, though. He'll pull through his problem." But when a woman suffers some kind of emotional crisis and lets it show in the office, immediately the word is passed around among the men that she is "hysterical, with those raging hormonal impulses acting up. . . ." There always follows a discussion as to whether she is "losing her marbles," followed by a short Sermon on the Mount given by one of the men on how women are not strong enough emotionally to cope with the office situation. I watched one man in a large corporation miss two or three hours a day from the office for a period of six months, while everyone covered for him to protect his job. His divorce was "troubling him greatly." In the same office a while later, a woman went through her divorce with no absence whatsoever from her office, except for the day of the court proceedings. Then I overheard someone calling in the personnel officer to see if she should be docked a day's vacation for having missed that day.

Often men in the executive suite have an instant therapy solution for their female colleague who is evincing signs of emotional problems. Their idea of instant therapy is a man in her bed—at once. It would never occur to them that perhaps her problem might stem from the fact that she needs fewer men worrying about her bed.

Every normally attractive career woman will have plenty of opportunity in her life to become attracted to men with whom she works. This is an affirmative situation, not a negative one. To go through life never being attracted to anyone other than one's mate is to live seated with one's posterior on an iceberg. However, it is how a woman handles these temporary attractions that matters. This is where self-control, the energizer in one's married life and in one's career alike, is the great leveler. This is where what has been called the "weaker sex" can show itself to be the stronger. As for the women in the office who are truly sexually promiscuous, they represent a tiny minority that can give the large majority a bad name. I feel they are not "liberated women" at all, but are rather making their living from loving for financial gain, which was women's oldest profession.

Perhaps self-willed energy and self-control are the two most important elements that make for success in a woman's career and happiness in her personal life. But it also helps to have a sense of humor. In fact, without one in this particular era, it is difficult to be happy, to cope, or even to survive in a state of good mental health.

There is no question that at this point women still have to work harder, both in their careers and in holding their marriages together. It is not an equal world yet, but all the extra effort is worth it to most of us, to be able to advance in what used to be forbidden territory, and to be judged on our merits and our abilities. Those of us who have already made it have to pave the way for our younger "sisters" coming along, too. It is a responsibility we must assume. We have to show them how to walk softly in the Executive Suite—for now.

And along with all of this consciousness-raising and self-disciplining, it certainly helps to have a good man nearby.

Equality never will change the fact that it's love that makes the world go round.

R.H. will probably never be able to get through this book, but he can certainly take a bow here.